Granger Inde P9-CKX-912

1/2/80

HOMESPUN

HOMESPUN

AN ANTHOLOGY OF POETRY
BY THE
GENERAL FEDERATION OF WOMEN'S CLUBS

COMPILED
AND WITH A FOREWORD BY

ANITA BROWNE

FOUNDER-ORGANIZER
OF POETRY WEEK

Granger Poetry Library

GRANGER BOOK CO., INC.
Great Neck, NY

First Published 1936
Reprinted 1979

INTERNATIONAL STANDARD BOOK NUMBER
0-89609-108-2

LIBRARY OF CONGRESS CATALOG NUMBER
78-73481

PRINTED IN THE UNITED STATES OF AMERICA

FOREWORD

HOMESPUN is an anthology of poems representing the interest in poetry of clubwomen throughout the nation. It brings the thoughts of hundreds who have been inspired at their club gatherings to turn to the pen as a creative force. HOMESPUN is heart-spun, for in it are overtones in the lives of women who have drawn from life itself the patterns which they have woven on the loom of poetry.

This anthology brings to its pages the works of poets whose names are outstanding in their own states; it brings the names of others whose poems are of national significance—state Poet Laureates and the national Poet Laureate of the General Federation of Women's Clubs, Angela Morgan. Besides these, HOMESPUN also introduces the work of the pathfinder, who is seeking the literary trail for the first time. Through the printed word this volume encourages the clubwoman; it gives her strength to proceed on a new way; it does not flaunt her as *arrived*, but rather as seeking and striving toward a poetic goal.

Perhaps the most significant feature of HOMESPUN is the fact that for the first time in history it records in one volume the poetic work of the clubwomen of the nation. Through the federated clubs of each state the poems have been gathered over a period of years, and in the main part represent the response to the National Poetry Contest conducted through the Committee on Poetry of the General Federation of Women's Clubs during the chairmanship of the editor, from 1930 to 1935.

The National Poetry Contest was held with two aims in mind: first, to award prizes to the outstanding poets of the nation in recognition of their work; and second, to raise the standard of poetic appreciation by encouraging women to participate in the craft, not necessarily toward a professional goal, but as a means to a greater interest in poetry through actual personal experience. The book is not presented as the final word in craftsmanship but it *is* presented as an authentic record of the work done by women in the club world, which naturally means women in the home. Therefore it is fittingly entitled, HOMESPUN.

This anthology is presented as a record of the progress of these clubwomen. The poems have not been edited to round out the meters or to perfect the form. That would be to defeat the object of this volume, which is to show the result of the effort made by the General Federation of Women's Clubs to encourage and foster talent, whether new or latent, in the creative hearts of those clubwomen who seek poetic expression.

This introduction would not be complete without the names of those Presidents of the General Federation of Women's Clubs under whom the editor served as Chairman of Poetry from 1930 to 1935, Mrs. John H. Sippel, who endorsed the contest, and Mrs. Grace Morrison Poole, who endorsed the book publication. The current President, Mrs. Roberta Campbell Lawson, is represented in this volume by one of her poems. The winner of the first prize in the National Poetry Contest, Halle W. Warlow, is also of special interest, since she served as the first Chairman of Poetry ever appointed in the General Federation.

Sincere thanks and appreciation are due to those eminent poets and writers who served as judges in the contest: Wilfred J. Funk, poet, and publisher of the *Literary Digest;* Leonora Speyer, former President, Poetry Society of America, and author of *Fiddler's Farewell*, which won the Pulitzer Poetry Prize; Wilson MacDonald, "Poet Laureate of Canada," and author of *The Flagon of Beauty;* Mrs. Edwin Markham, former Chairman of Poetry, New York City Federation; Arthur Guiterman, Honor Poet of Poetry Week for New York State in 1932, and author of *Song and Laughter;* Grace Bronson Purdy, representing the clubwomen; Morris Abel Beer, late Professor of Poetry, College of the City of New York, and author of *Street Lamps;* Alice Hunt Bartlett, American Editor of the Poetry Review, and author of *Road Royal;* Marguerite Janvrin Adams, poet-translator, of the National League of American Pen Women; Ernest H. Peabody, poet, and former Vice-chairman, Literature Committee of the MacDowell Club of New York City; Kathryn White Ryan, author of *Golden Pheasant;* and Violet Alleyn Storey, author of *Tea in an Old House*.

If, through this anthology, a thought that uplifts the spirit, a line that renews hope and faith, or a verse that has pushed aside the veil from the great beauty and reality of life, has been brought to its contributors and readers, then it has not been in vain.

Anita Browne

HOMESPUN

AND AFTER ALL

As, after frost, men rake thc darkening mold
And burn in piles the leaves that lately wore
Green summer's jade and fall's Etruscan gold—
Now whitening ashes on an earthen floor—
So do we burn our letters, sheaves that hold
Dreams of a whole life's visioning, now no more
Than empty shells or vacant rooms all cold,
Their creaking hinges rusting from each door.

What if the spectrum flame of lavish days
Has turned to tender browns and quiet grays,
What if the song of life and love's refrain
Has lost its lilt in struggle with life's pain,
What if both leaves and letters drift in smoke—
Spring knew the lips of April—Love once spoke!

(*First Prize*)
—*Halle W. Warlow*

WHY SHOULD I WAIT?

If, as the oriental mystics say,
This flesh is but a veil we cast aside,
While spirit in its everlasting glide
Flows deathless on between its banks of clay,—
If, as they tell us, death is but a Way
To poppied gardens lapped by Lethe's tide,
Where memories of old errors are denied
That souls may start afresh some kindlier day:

Why should I wait the resurrection gong,
The trumpet from the vast, unhurried sky?
The serpent at the robin's earliest song
Casts off his tarnished scales but does not die.
So I, new-veiled, shall greet tomorrow's morn—
Why should I wait till death to be reborn?

(*Second Prize*)
—*Lilith Lorraine*

TOUCH

I like to go with hands ungloved that I
　　May touch the things of life as I go by;
The softness of a child's bright shining hair,
The petal of a rose that's growing there,
　　The soft folds of a dress I like to wear.

I like to go ungloved that I may feel
　　The touch of everything that's true and real,
A statue with right symmetry and grace,
A tapestry, a jewel, a bit of lace,
　　Some shining silver in its proper place.

I like to go ungloved that I may be
　　Alert to give quick help and sympathy,
To draw into my arms a friend in grief,
To bandage little wounds to give relief,
　　To clasp a hand I love in love's belief.

(*Honorable Mention*)
　　　　　　　　　　　　　　　　　　　　—*Reba Ray*

THEY TELL ME OF A PLACE

They tell me of a place where lovers pine,—
Gaunt cypresses rise darkly—so they say—
Out of the sheltered waters of the bay:
But you loved winds, and a little scarlet vine
That ran among the rocks, the jewel shine
Of harbor lights at dusk. You turned away
From stagnant, dismal things and slow decay,
Pouring your eager beauty out like wine.
And so I will not wall my heart about,
Or mount a pillar like some haggard saint,
Or to a steepled cypress make complaint:
But rather I will turn my spirit out
To wander with its fellows, to pursue
All loveliness made memorable by you.

(*Honorable Mention*)
　　　　　　　　　　　　　　　—*Florence Harris Hooke*

PARTICIPATION[1]

"Let there be light," God said, and spaced
        The sun beyond the hill.
"Let there be light," man thought, and placed
        A candle on the sill.

The glowworm, lowly, lumpish, wet,
        Shared still the wondrous dream;
"Let there be light," he sensed, and set
        His tiny lamp agleam.

(*Honorable Mention*)   —*B. Y. Williams*

THE LINCOLN HOME

One Sunday, on July the twelfth,
Three others and myself
Started early on that morn
To see the home where Lincoln was born.

One hundred and sixty-one miles, they say,
To the old farm where he first saw day,
Now made into a National Park,
Where thousands visit, but not for a lark.

The old spring is still beneath the hill,
Though it has been beautified by modern skill;
The original is still preserved,
And does its duty, always serves.

When we stop and linger here,
It seems he lives, it always will.
His memory the world reveres,
And will through all the many years.

From the flagstaff floats Old Glory,
Proud to tell its part of the story:
Of the millions unchained, their birthright gained,
And her colors just as bright and unstained.

[1]Reprinted from *Apples of Gold*, by permission of A. L. Burt Company, publishers.

His name is reverenced, it has never decayed,
His life was gentle, he was unafraid;
The deeds he did, the thoughts he breathed
Were the best by nature given.

When his life ebbed out, his record was made,
He had done his best, the last word said;
Now to see his humble cabin home upon that hill,
We know his creed lives—others can, who will.

—Zella Ackerman

SURCEASE

When rain is raining wet and gray,
And all the sky is gloomy,
'Tis hard to mind the yesterday
When woods and fields were bloomy;
But when the sun is bending warm
Among the fields and fallows,
How easy to forget the storm
That melted them to shallows!

When racked with pain or bowed with woe,
When all of life is saddened,
'Tis then that mem'ry's tongue is slow
To tell of joys that gladdened;
But when the stars and birds and flowers
Attune their hearts to singing,
Forgotten are the weary hours,
And sorrow, far a-winging.

So doth attending mercy stay
The mind that fain remembers,
And joy and grief go on their way
With Junes and bleak Decembers,
Adown the winding, changing road
From whence to whence we wander,
Beside the Love whose name is God,
Into eternal Yonder.

—Alice Gardner Adams

NOONTIDE

We live . . .
God gave us love
And strength to meet with him
The beautiful and sad . . . and this
Is life.

—Loyce Adams

ANCESTRESS

When I become as history,—long-past history,
And hang within my niche upon the wall,
I shall enjoy the hum of children's voices—
The new young voices, and the clear footfall.
I shall enjoy the merriment and laughter
In the long ages following hereafter.

All the sweet things that we possess and harbor
Must naturally have value of a kind—
But of more transient worth and less regretting
Than the warm rich fulfillment of the mind.
I shall become a proud ancestress when
I see the stalwart grandsons of the men

Whom I have known, whom I have loved in friendship,
Carry the torch beyond the furthest rim
Of far earth's visions. I shall hang resplendent
In my cool niche, and think again of him
Most well-beloved and cherished,—understand
When our great-grandson bends above my hand.

—Marguerite Janvrin Adams

SHIRK OR WORK?

It is easy to sit in the sunshine
And talk to the man in the shade;
It is easy to float in a lovely boat,
And point out the places to wade.

It is easy to tell the toiler
How best he can carry his pack,
But no one can rate a burden's weight
Until it has been on his back.

—Grace Bordelon Agate

EVENTIDE

Hark! what is this I hear?
A village church bell tolls so clear!
Just another soul called from this world of woe,
And added to the heavenly list,
Where all is joy and Peace and bliss.

A vacant chair by the hearth I see,
Where once was joy and mystery;
An aged form is bending low,
With locks of hair as white as snow.
An aching heart, a tear-stained face,
Tells the tale of that vacant place,
But it is not long he'll have to wait,
For he, too, will enter the heavenly gate.

For Silent death comes fluttering in,
An angel whispers and flies away,
Leaving behind a lump of clay.

—Mrs. Mary Agne

MOST ANY BIT OF LANDSCAPE

Most any bit of landscape
    Appeals to me,
If there's just a bush about,
    Or a spreading tree;

Or perchance some broom sedge
    Down a quiet way,
With here and there an aster
    To make it kind of gay.

Some love best the mountains,
    Some best the sea;
But most any bit of landscape
    Appeals to me.

—Jean Cameron Agnew

TOGETHER

He lays his paper by, refills his pipe,
Gropes for a match, and glancing toward me, says;
"How's my old girl?" I straighten up a bit
From patching overalls, and smiling, look
To catch his answering smile. And then we talk
Of all the things that go to make our life,
Neighbors and business, what the boys have done
Of good and bad. Sometimes we search through years
Hunting for names that once were quickly found;
Perhaps we build a castle—plan a trip,
Something we'll buy in that delightful day
When money's plentiful. We know so much
Of things in common, it is hard to choose
Just what to talk of. Always, in my heart
There is a warmth of pride, that he still likes
To visit with me. Married all these years
And such true friends. Oh! these are happy days.
                                              —*Hannah K. Aken*

MY PRAYER FOR TODAY

Keep me, Father, kindly hold me,
    As the shades of night enfold me,
In Thy loving arms so tender;
    Help me always to remember
        Thou art love.

Heart so sad and eyes all teary;
    Day so long and oh so dreary,
House and garden, empty chair
    Speak of one who's "Over there";
        Yet Thou art love.

Help me that I may not falter;
    Bravely as I now must loiter
Here on earth a little longer,
    With Thy precious Word made stronger;
        For Thou art love.

Help my loneliness and heartache;
   Comfort bring—Thou'lt not forsake
Children calling Thee in anguish,
   But wilt grant their fervent wish,
      Oh, God of love.

Give me work—my bread be earning;
   Health—content—peace—while learning
Once again to find life's laughter;
   Oh, never let my faith once falter
      That Thou art love.
            —*Mrs. Maud Akers*

RECOMPENSE

The toils and pains of an honest day
Are redeemed by more than gold can pay.
The toll of time and strength and heart
Is paid by joy and contentment—in part—
The joy of a task that is well done,
The contented heart that asks aught of none.
In part, these pay, but the sum of the whole
Is the love of God and man—all told.
            —*Dorothy Moore Alford*

OUR JUNIORS

They set a light upon the hill
To aid the flier in the night;
'Tis youth who flies across the skies
Guided by this beacon light.

We placed a light upon the hill,
That light is youth with all its beauty;
'Tis courage wins when life is new
And ever filled with sense of duty.

The torch was handed on to one
Who handed on a lantern bright,
And now in place of this there gleams
Upon the hill a beacon light.
            —*Anna M. Allen*

MY LITTLE GARDEN[1]

I love my little garden,
It is a lovely place
Where I can plant and tend my blossoms rare,
And have bouquets each day and some to spare.

I love my little garden,
It is a restful place
Where I can hear the birds send forth their songs of praise,
And watch the setting sun at the end of glorious days.

I love my little garden,
It is a happy place
Where I can go after the refreshing shower of rain
And see the scarlet rambler flash the plea, "Be young again."

I love my little garden,
It is a helpful place
Where I can go when life seems hard and I need aid;
And seeing God's handiwork all around, I no longer feel afraid.
                                                        —*Gwendolen Allen*

NEGRO GIRL

Negro girl,—tall, dusky-skinned Diana,
Molded in gleaming, darksome symmetry,
Full-hipped, full-bosomed, lithe of limb, and straight
As a young tree is straight, why do you seek
To hide, with a white woman's paints and dyes,
Your strange and natural beauty? Who has said
You have not loveliness? Who judged your race
And found it lacking? We who brought you here,
Unsprung as yet from those black, tortured folk,
Who in long, stumbling, sobbing, writhing chains,
Bound one unto the other, whipped and lashed,
Were dragged from out their jungle! What dark fires
Burn yet within you? What strange, thwarted dreams
Have passed, dark mother to dark daughter, till,
Unchanged by years, your own breast hoards them now?

[1] Reprinted from the *Atlantean Poetry Anthology*, by permission of the publishers.

What vast wrong have we done you that, today,
Free, you are yet our slaves? On every hand
We hurt you, tramp you,—choosing not to see
The groping soul of your perverted race
Lying upon our hands. That injury
May never now be righted. . .

Negro girl,
Do flimsy, silken garments light your eyes?
Do paints and powders make you better reach
The realm of your white sister? And, I muse,
Ignorant, are you happy?

                                        —*Irene Cooper Allen*

RECOMPENSE

When sound shall cease, there being none to hear,
When light shall fade, there being none to see,
When time is lost in stark eternity,
And very space itself is void and drear,
Shall beauty end, oblivion draw near,
And all our joy in living cease to be?
Shall God refuse or fail to act? Must He
And all His works, His pride, then disappear?

Or shall the Creator of all things and the sense
To enjoy them, then reveal a new creation?
For all this ghastly loss make recompense?
A realm of light beyond imagination,
Delights beyond our best experience,—
Not failure, not defeat, but consummation!

                                        —*Jessie M. Ball Allen*

THE ROSE I GREW

In pensive mood,
I walked along the garden path one day,
And there beside the wall where shines the sun
I cleared a little place and dug a hole,
And planted there a rosebush, only one.

In careless mood,
I walked along the path again one day,
And on the stem two tiny leaves I found.
My heart leaped up! A miracle I saw,
A growing thing made this a hallowed ground.

In happy mood,
I went to see my rosebush every day,
And dug and sprayed and watered it with care.
My heart rejoiced when each new leaf appeared,
My friends came out to see, my joy to share.

In joyous mood,
I watched each day a tiny bud unfold
And slowly opened leaves of rarest shade,
A velvet pink no artist's brush could tint;
It was my own, its beauty I had made.

(Oh changing mood!)
A full-blown rose I plucked one day with care
And placed it in a vase where I could see.
I think I never saw a rose so rare
As one I grew and watched from day to day!
                                        —*Julia S. Anderson*

O GLORIOUS SNOW

O glorious snow,
I love you so,
You fall so light
From yon great height,
Who could believe
That you could weave
A carpet white
In just a night—
To change our view
To look like new.
I gaze outside,
You've made a bride
Of hills and woods,
All's clothed in hoods;

The bare black earth
Has had rebirth,
So proudly gleams
It almost seems
As if it knew
Its beauty too.
I hope that I
As years flit by
May never stray
So far away
I'd have to miss
A scene like this.
No sunny clime
In winter time
Can lure me on
From winter's fun,
I know full well
I'll always dwell
Where winters come,
To me it's home.
O modest flake,
No blare you make,
Would that we
Like you could be
Unassuming
Yet illuming
Our whole world
In mystery.

                              —*Mrs. Ruth Anderson*

MAY DAY

Oh, world, sometimes I cannot bear the load
Of pain and sorrow laid upon my heart,
My footsteps falter on the lonely road,
And tears well up from hidden springs apart.
I do not know the meaning of the thorn,
The armored bough that bears a tender flower,
Or why the song on fitful breezes borne,
Is fraught with ecstasy for scarce an hour.

I only know, oh world, when all is weighed
Against one radiant, pulsing day in spring,
When trees march up a hill in white arrayed,
And life comes surging back to everything,
I'll gladly walk the lonely road of pain,
If I can see a May day born again.

—Adelaide A. Andrews

MY MOTHER

So gracious, and so sweet,
Such willing hands and feet,
There's nothing quite complete
    Without her.

The love light in her eyes—
Her tender words and wise
Make earth a Paradise
    About her.

We bring all to her side,
New born, and happy bride;
Loved counselor and guide—
    My mother.

—Florence R. Andrews

PIONEER WOMAN[1]

One thought of ivory and precious lace
And lilac blossoms as one looked at her,
So delicately lovely her aged face,
So slim and fine the artist hands that were
Displaying rare pieced coverlets, each one
A miracle of craftsmanship and art,
Designed it seemed from patterns fairy-spun
To ease the ache for beauty in her heart.

They had been pieced in years when she had bowed
To grim Necessity and left a hound
To guard her precious babes the while she plowed
And they sat watching while she made each round.

[1] Reprinted from *The Farmer's Wife Magazine*, by permission of the publishers.

After those long hard days, when tasks were done
And wee ones sleeping, she had wrought with fine
Close stitches, blossom, blazing star, and sun,
Feasting her soul on color and design.

The great world listens as a famed violin
Lifts its clear voice; it watches sunlight flow
From the deft brush of one who watched his slim
Young mother guide the oxen long ago.
And they are sons of her who learned to blend
The rainbow in the watches of the night,
Who fed her spirit's hunger at day's end
And worshiped beauty by a candle's light.

—*Eva K. Anglesburg*

THE DUNES

Out where the sand is mountain high,
The sun rides high in the sky.
Then at eve a crimson ball sinks in the west,
'Mid colors azure and crimson it goes to rest;
And the air is fragrant and sweet,
And the billowy waves lap and meet.
Out there beautiful stars disperse,
Peopling a vast white universe,
Scattering golden dots through the night
Into the radiant loveliness of light.
There, in a silence all serene,
A subtle "something felt" not seen,
'Mid the shadows hushed and wide,
Where wild rose and thistle grow side by side,
And the moon shines down so bright.
There all nature rests in the silent night,
And the days are golden and still,
And you wander and dream at will.
Peopled are the woods with floral splendor
That breathes a fragrance sweet and tender,
And the breezes whisper and sigh
Where long shadows in the moonlight lie.
Out where all nature seems at rest,
This rare place of beauty I love best.

—*Laura B. Annett*

VISION

Again Thou usherest in a verdant spring.
Help me to feel, to see, to hear
Those beauties which are ever near,
The glory of the sunset's glow
When wistful day is waning;
Let me know
Green branches
Heavy with a summer's snow.
I wish ever to realize
The story spoken in another's eyes,
To see the eager yearning written there
For human understanding, and to share
Of life's abundant vintage store;
I would not ask for any more
Or richer heritage, but let me see
Life, beautiful as it was made for me
By the Artist with a lavish hand,
Whose mastery wrought the sea and land,
Whose thought incarnate is the hills,
And whose command
Loosed a mighty water
From the earth;
Ten thousand rippling, singing falls
Followed its birth
In endless wave on wave,
Drink for the growing fields He gave.
Designed and sketched and colored were they
In perfect harmony and plan
Inimitable by finite man.
All this for you—
Let me know gladness
And a little pain
To show me sunshine through the rain,
To prove that violets do not grow in vain,
To teach me beauty that my heart may sing;
O, God, I thank Thee for the spring.

—Rebecca Anthony

PEACE GUARANTEED[1]

Oh, Nations, battle-scarred,
And sin-sick, fear-debarred
From love of mutual gain,
Shall error ever reign?
That peace you now may see,
Have you a guarantee?

Oh, rulers, God-picked men,
War must not come again!
Peace in the land will come
If man is not too dumb.
That peace you now may see
Can God not guarantee?

My Sabbath you shall keep,
What day is not too deep;
God's words distinctly say
The seventh is His day.
That peace you then will see
God's word does guarantee.

Oh, World, disband your arms.
Go home and till your farms.
For rain in season due
And peace, God offers you.
His peace you then will see,
Which God does guarantee.

Oh, peoples of the earth,
Let Truth reveal its worth.
Raise Truth for all to see,
For it will make you free.
Then peace you soon will see
God's Word does guarantee.

—Mary J. Armstrong

[1]Reprinted by permission of Economy Publishers.

HAPPINESS THROUGH THE YEAR

Give me a good book
In a quiet nook,
In July by a bubbling stream;
When Winter is here,
I'll seek for my cheer
With a book by the fire and dream.

But oh, in the Fall,
When the foliage all
Is red, orange, green, brown, and yellow,
I want nothing more
Than just to adore
Old Nature, the jolly fellow.

Then in the Spring,
I just want to sing,
Rejoice with the birds in the sun;
For everything's new,
Earth is lovely to view,
And life seems just only begun.

—*J. Margaret Crute Ashcraft*

MEMORY'S DOOR

Within the sacred portals of my heart,
Where mortal eye can never gaze,—
Is enshrined above all else apart,—
The memory of my Mother's face.

At eventide—that quiet hour,
When sun sinks low and day is o'er,—
I long for her, I feel her power,
'Tis then I open "Memory's Door."
I am carried back to other days,
Down the cycle of the years,
When I could see my Mother's face
Through smiles and not through tears.
Through happy days—through anxious days,
In fancy, then, I wander;

From room to room I fondly roam,
Alone, these scenes to ponder.
I see her dress, her shoes—all worn,—
A token here and there,—
Her kitchen apron, slightly torn,—
Her book—her vacant chair,—
Souvenirs, each one a key
To "Memory's Shrine"—this sacred place,—
They thrill my heart—precious to me—
They bring to me my Mother's face.

So sacred this—her memory—
So infinitely dear,
That only God, Himself, doth see
The memories dwelling here.
And though it be the early dawn,
The noon or midnight hour,
When yearns the heart for her—now gone,
For Mother's soothing power,—
I turn the key, pass through the door
To this "Shrine" known to none other,—
Then, here, in "Memory's Room," once more,—
I see the face of "Mother."

                                        —*Mrs. Mary Otto Asher*

A LEGEND OF MINNESOTA

The stately pines came marching
From out the north one day,
With dignity of motion
Their branches seemed to sway.
They came in strict formation,
A conquering green-robed band
To build a noble empire
Within a promised land.

The fairies had been summoned
From out a sunny clime,
Their dainty rustling mingled
With tinkling bells' sweet chime;

Convening on the border
They counseled with the pines,
On virgin soil great plans were laid
Within four border lines.

The pines built woodland temples
With aisles so dim and cool,
The brownies molded lake beds,
Each bed—a sky-blue pool.
Gay fairies painted flowers,
While their queen in majesty
Shaped a noble river
And sent it to the sea.

They held their dedication
With faces toward the sun,
While Heaven smiled a blessing
On a noble task well done.
Then the pines receded northward,
To stand forever guard,
While kneeling fairies pleaded
Their work would ne'er be marred.

The east wind brought the raindrops,
The west wind flakes of snow,
The north and south wind wrestled
And sought their strength to show.
Then all the hosts united
To blow the victor's horn;
A great state had been founded,
A paradise was born.

—*Lillian Atcherson*

YOUR SMILE

There's a song in my heart, my friend,
There's a song in my heart today;
And it sings, and it sings,
And the glad music rings
All through the live-long day.

And the song that sings in my heart
Has a joyous and sweet melody;
'Tis because your smile makes the day worth while,
And so I am giving to others a smile
Because you gave one to me.

—*Laura L. Atkins*

OLD SAUGATUCK MILL

Who gathers the grist of ghostly grain
    From the hopper of Saugatuck mill,
Where by day the shadows will creep and glide,
    And ever the wheel is still?

But when the storm-king shall ride awrack,
    And the tumult sweeps o'er the lake,
Men say that the ghostly millers come
    And the wheel will creak and shake.

Then round and round in a fashion weird
    Will the mystical grain be ground;
For the souls of men are in peril that night,
    And the wails of woe resound.

But never shall man eat of baken cake
    From meal of the haunted mill;
It will feed in the night the ghostly crew
    Who labor there, somber and still.

—*Grace Jewett Austin*

WHY DID YOU DEPART AT DUSK?

On your last journey, why did you set out at dusk?
    You, who had always loved the dawn,
    Ne'er venturing forth till night was gone,—
Then why, that last, last time, did you depart at dusk?

Or, in his radiant exit, did the King of Day
    Inspire you with courage and gently helm
    You to a fairer dawn beyond the realm
Of earth?—for, unafraid, at dusk you went away.

—*Clarissa M. Bailey*

THE TRIUMPH OF ART

Create! Create!
If it is only the infinitesimal part of a thing,
Create!
Art opens up a new world,
A world fresh from the hands of its maker,
Its lustre undimmed, new as Creation's dawn.
And, ah, what joy is there in the new, the just born,
Unsullied by the things of earth that tarnish.
Life, plain everyday life, it is a pale, unsatisfying thing,
Fit only for the dwellers in caves;
But art lifts us heavenward, and we are borne on celestial wings;
Our imagination takes flight and we leap from worlds to worlds.
Time and space are vanished.
Ah! with art we could live through all eternity.
For each moment a new thing is created.
The artist carries within himself the seeds of immortality.
Forever he creates and recreates himself anew.
Nothing else in life can take the place of art.
It steers us over trackless roads, through mountainous regions.
It smooths the stony paths of life's highway.
It lifts us out of the deep valleys, the abysses of despair.
Ah, Create! Create!
If it is only the infinitesimal part of a thing.
Create!

—Josephine Turck Baker

I AM HERE

Dead? No, not dead, not away!
        I am here!
Though not within your vision, yet always near.
In the very air you breathe—
        I am here.

In the cool of the early morn;
In the warmth of the noonday sun;
In the glory of the sunset glow;
In the peace of the evening dusk;
In the depths of the sky of night—
        I am here.

Blended into the ocean's blue;
Melted into the drifting cloud;
When rain and sun unite together,
And stretch across the misty sky
In the rainbow arch of color—
        I am here.

Though not within your vision, yet always near.
In the very air you breathe—
        I am here.
Dead? No, not dead, not away!
        I am here!

                                    —*Kathrine Baldwin*

FROM AN OFFICE WINDOW

The tulip bed is flaming in the square,
Crimson and lovely against the dim, green trees;
The yellow sunlight over it
Makes a picture like an old Dutch print.

If I could find a little peace
Away from clatter and the click of keys—
Where I could have the cool earth close to me,
I might find Thee also nearer
Than in this high tower where I stand.

                                    —*Frances M. Ballard*

THE BEACHCOMBER

He had not always meant to be
Just a Beachcomber by the sea;
Threadbare trousers rolled to his knees
Exposing legs all coppery;
Judged mad by those who carry keys
For unlocking their properties.

'Twas a shovel, a sieve, and loot
That held him bound by hand and foot
To this sad life so dissolute.
Thus he was destined just to be
An old Beachcomber by the sea
A-digging sand and living free.

When destiny changed his career,
It drove ambition from his heart;
It dulled his soul, bade hope depart;
It gave the world to him to roam,
Always seeking a transient home
And the shore-line loot far and near.

Takes six shovels to fill his sieve,
He lifts them from the cool damp sands
And, as the grains fall through in mounds,
Picks out the loot with his bare hands,
And throws the dregs to leveled grounds,
Seeks again what the sands will give.

Oh Destiny! What means this dole?
Why steal ambition from his soul,
Hand to him a Beachcomber's role,
Letting a shovel, loot, and sieve
Befog the life that he should live,
When better talents you could give?
—*Mildred Dosch Banta*

MAIDEN'S CHOICE

Billy rides in a limousine,
Jack walks in the dusty way;
Billy has hair like a raven's wing
While Jack's is turning gray.

Billy's laughter is glad and free,
Jack's smile is grave and slow;
But Jack, he tells me of wonderful things,
Things Billy will never know.

Jack's brow bears the lines of years ill spent,
And Billy's is smooth and fair;
And Billy he swears that he loves me true,
And Jack, he doesn't care.

So I shall ride in the limousine,
As a sensible girl should do;
For why should I walk in the dust with Jack,
When he hasn't asked me to?
—*Carolyn M. Barber*

A SONG OF THE WESTERN EDEN

Delmarva, the Western Eden,
Between thy sheltering Bays!
Wherever thy children wander,
There do they sing thy praise;
The Saga of roadside orchards,
Of the fields of amber grain,
The murmur of wind in the pines,
The scent of summer rain.

A song to their Western Eden
With its kindly cordial ways,
To the Land of the Tidal Rivers,
To the Land between the Bays.

Fair Land of the Tidal Rivers,
Thy charm endures alway,
The charm that holds thy children
Wherever their feet may stray.
Wherever the Sea Lanes lead them,
Wherever the Land Roads go,
Goes the lure of the misty woodlands,
Of the Rivers that ebb and flow.

Goes the lure of the Western Eden
Where passed their childhood days,
The Land of the Tidal Rivers,
The Land between the Bays.

They feel the spell of the white Sea Fog,
Of the sun on the sandy plain,
And the salty tang of the ocean breeze
To call them home again.
Home to the marsh-edged Rivers
Where the sea tides ebb and flow,
Home to the level woodlands
Where the Holly and Dogwood grow.

Home to their Western Eden
With its glamour of childhood days,
To the Land of the Tidal Rivers,
To the Land between the Bays.

                                        —*Hope S. Barber*

WILD ROSES

Flash of pink by the roadside,
    Framed in lobes of green,
Pink like a sea shell's lining,
    With meadow grasses' sheen.

An old rail fence forms a trellis,
    A heap of rocks, a ledge;
Bits of white cloud make a curtain,
    Butterfly weeds, a hedge.

And flowers of the wild, you're bringing
    Such happy things I knew,
A trudging child, girl dreams—
    O roses, I love you!

                                    —*Rhoda S. Barclay*

OUR CLUB

Our club is just a friendly band
    Of common folk whose aims are high—
To love and serve our native land,
    To greet our Master in the sky.

We long to make the whole world bright,
    Our interests are both far and near;
To shun the wrong, to do the right,
    We try to teach our children dear.

Our days are full of happy things,
    But then sometimes there's sorrow too;
It seems the hours go by with wings,
    We always have so much to do.

We may not always know what's best,
    But if we err our hearts are right;
Each day is just another test
    Of living, striving for the light.

Each kindly deed's a steppingstone
    That leads the way to heights above,
A friendly smile can oft atone,
    E'en more be done with words of love.

We're just a joyous little band
    Of old-time friends, and new ones too;
United, let us take this stand,
    To do our best and carry through.
                                        —*Sylvia Dillavou Barclay*

MEMORY

A stretch of sand,
A turquoise sea,
    A maid,
    A youth,
Ah! joyous memory.

A plighted troth,
A stately church,
    A ring,
    A vow,
A sacred memory.

A cottage home,
A baby's laugh,
    A song,
    A prayer,
Oh! tender memory.

A battlefield,
A cold, white face,
    A mound,
    A cross,
'Tis sorrow's memory.

A country served,
A young life given,
    A star,
    A crown,
A living memory.
                                        —*Amanda Luella Barlow*

PEACE PICTURES

In a dear old-fashioned parlor
Lighted by the firelight glow,
Sitting side by side, a couple,
Both with hair as white as snow.
They have shared both joy and sorrow,
Both, of life have drunk their fill;
Peace is written on their faces
For she is his sweetheart still.

The scene is changed. We see a mother
Bending o'er a little bed.
We can guess that on the pillow
Lies a little curly head.
Angels whisper to her darling;
See, a smile is on his face;
With the proudest Queen the mother
Would not now exchange her place.

Cattle grazing in a meadow,
Near by runs a babbling brook,
Birds are singing in the branches;
Lying in a shady nook,
Rests a man from weary labor,
Soon his day's work will be done
And his wife will come to meet him
At the setting of the sun.

When a great and mighty nation
Has been forced to go to war,
Soon there comes the call for soldiers
And those go we care most for.
Anxiously we watch the papers,
Praying that the strife may cease.
When news comes, the war is ended,
Then—how beautiful is *Peace*.

—Elizabeth I. Barnes

SONG OF AN ATOM

In the golden morn I love to roam
  Over the hills—our hills,
To smell the sweet-scented leafy loam
  And list to the lark-finch trills.

The valley lies so peaceful there,
  Clothed in filmiest green;
The happy river sings an air
  As it gently flows between.
A mockingbird sits on a tall oak tree,
  Up on the swaying top,
While down below, dressed in brown, I see
  A friendly sparrow hop.

On carpets of softest silken grass
  Brown silhouette trees rise tall,
While by a wall of stones I pass,
  Shy ivy tendrils crawl.
Young eager voices of the wind
  Go laughing up the hill.
I seem to see God's face so kind,
  And know He loves me still.

The trees upon the hill are tall,
  Their branches brush the sky,
I wonder God can see at all
  So small a thing as I.

—Josephine Barnett

SUNSET ACROSS THE LAKE

I sit and watch the sun go down
  On the other side of the lake,
As all the colors from the sky
  The waters try to take.

It is such a wonderful picture,
  The Artist, too, is the best,
And as I enjoy its beauty
  The sun sinks low in the west.

And the gates of the New Jerusalem
   Seem left ajar for a bit,
A golden path leads across the lake
   And I catch a glimpse of It.
               —*Augusta M. Barney*

A THOUGHT FOR MOTHER'S DAY

From the pages of earth's history gleam the fairest of the fair,
Flash the helmets of bold conquerors, rise the standards here
    and there
Till we feel the mighty impulse of their influence wide and deep,
Grasping all the powers about us in their universal sweep.
How we read them, know them, love them, kiss the soft and
    queenly hand,
Praise the warrior, statesman, poet, and the good for which they
    stand!
All the forces that surround us telling what our lives shall be,
Each a partial service renders to the master unity.

But there's one whose touch is gentle, one whose influence none
    can frame,
Poet's lore or tender fancy can but echo soft the name—
Mother's love, that rocks the cradle, steers a bark on life's rough
    sea,
Mother's heartthrob for her offspring and her simple piety.

As the bud's exhaling fragrance hides the fullness of the flower
Till a day of revelation, with its sweet unfolding hour;
So they linger in the shadows till the time is opportune
For luxuriant gems of promise to perfect their added bloom.

Mother thought has permeated all the better things of earth,
To the greatest and the strongest mother pulse has given birth.
Mother's hands have left their love prints on life's strange and
    tangled way,
Mother love still guides our footsteps through the long and busy
    day.
               —*Mamie Collins Barry*

OPEN SEASON

The morning wears a misty crown
Of gold, hung in the sky.
In a golden pond black rushes drown,
Tall catkins throw grey shadows down
Across my boat, in a shielding frown,
Where wait my dog and I.

A thrilling cry, though nothing seen,
This is the hunter's fun.
Where blue and gold maze into green,
In a true straight V shape come fifteen
Grey travelers, and their call rings keen.
I do not lift my gun.

I sit and watch them wing away
Into some other land.
A tapestry of gold and grey
Thrown 'cross the sky at break of day,
In mem'ry woven, e'er to stay,
By God's own dext'rous hand.

—Ella Barth

AND THEN?

Why do we enter this queer world of ours,
Since we have such a little while to stay?
Our listening spirits answer to a call—
We come—we linger—gather weeds and flowers—
Then go our way.
Surely, this is not all!

—Helen D. Bassett

ON RETURN FROM THE SHORE

Surely He made His sea for solitude—
    For sun-drenched noons, and for the rapt blue night,
When the long surges rock in tranquil mood,
    And deck their quiet breasts with star dust bright.

Surely He meant no heedless eye to see
  The veiled mist maidens whirl amid the spray,
Or the white horses charging endlessly
  Embattled crags, that hold them still at bay.

How does He bear this idle travesty,
  This clangor as of brazen horns, this flare
Of lights that mock the high stars' majesty,
  This Comus rout, this haste to herd and stare?
How does He bear the crowds that chase and brawl
Like tangled fringe about a silken shawl?

But hold! Is there, in all this multitude,
  One heart that feels, in the wide beaches' sweep,
The wing-soft clasp, the watching eyes that brood—
  Hears, in the diapason of the deep,
The steadfast promise of eternity?
Perhaps it was for this He made His sea.

—*Helen Iffla Bay*

OLD SARUM

Lines on the Conference of the Bishops of the English Church at Salisbury

Old Sarum sleeps,
But one by one or
Two by two, the Deans
And Bishops bold
Creep back into
The sheltering Fold,

Finding within
The ancient time-worn shell
Of ritual,
Morning and evening prayer
And sacerdotal bliss,
An effulgence as of
Ecstasy thrown back
To them more precious
Than efforts new and crude,
Destined to decay
Nourished in too dry a soil.

Amidst the fustiness
Of pomp and power, and tea,
A few keen minds dart
Swift and sure, and listen eagerly
To catch the vast murmuring
Of the many
Minds and hearts,
And guide or follow—
Which or where
It matters not,
For mostly we take tea.

Old Sarum sleeps,
And mostly we take tea.

—*Alice Colburn Beal*

THE WASHINGTON BICENTENNIAL

Dreams are visions of the night;
    Dreams are musings of the day;
By faith, He took those visions bright
    And molded them as potter's clay.

A forest waste, a trackless plain,
    O'errun with beasts and red men bold,
He made a fertile field of grain,
    Where souls grow large and lives unfold.

Th' untutored man, by passions fanned
    In smothered feud and open hate,
Now clasps with joy a brother's hand;—
    He made them masters of the state.

Bold tyranny must yield Him place;
    Oppression feel His power and might;
Fair freedom shows her smiling face
    And gives to man His long-sought right.

He gave His wealth,—a little thing,—
    He gave His life,—'twas all too brief;
We own Him greater than a King,
    And nations join to hail Him Chief.

—*Clara Beck*

THE MAGNOLIA TREE

Just a gorgeous bouquet of blossoms
Was saying, "Spring is here,"
When along came a snow and a freeze
And blasted it this year.

'Twas in truth a large magnolia tree,
Tall and sturdy and strong,
All in bloom in our neighbor's back yard
Heedless of harm or wrong.

Pompous and proud with buds and flowers
Of flaming rare pink hue,
Yes, a Prince in our neighbor's back yard,
Saying, "How do you do?"

But the cruel cold of King Winter
On farewell trip passed by,
And he kissed every bud and blossom,
Waving his last "Good-by."

Next we viewed the gorgeous magnolia—
What did tearful eyes see?
Just a great mass of brown, dead flowers,
Not the beautiful tree.

Was it envy, anger, spite, who knows?
Why old Winter returned
To punish Spring's welcoming angel,
It just could not be learned.

Thus in shame and disgrace it must stand,
'Neath sun and rain of Spring,
But the birds from the South, in its boughs
May take rest, while on wing.

Once a Prince among those of its kind,
Now a pauper poor and old,
It shall again come into its own
When its green leaves unfold.

—Easter Rohrer Becker

WISCONSIN

The Scotsman rightly sings
Of his heather-covered braes,
But the coulees of my native State
Are fairer far than these;
And the little blue-cupped badger,
That braves the frosty Spring,
Is dearer with its word of hope
Than all the flowers you sing;
And there's longing in my heart,
For its beauties I would see,
For there's only one Wisconsin,
And that is home to me.

   Oh, this world is wide and fair,
   With its many lands to see,
   But there's only one Wisconsin,
   And that is home to me.

The Alps may boast of higher peaks,
And mighty banks of snow,
But the beauty of these rolling hills
No other land may know;
I love them when the Autumn
Robes them in brilliant hue;
But when the Spring comes creeping on,
And clothes them fresh and new,
There's not in "green old England"
So fair a sight to see,
For there's only one Wisconsin,
And that is home to me.

   Oh, the world is wide and fair,
   With many lands to see,
   But there's only one Wisconsin,
   And that is home to me.

I love its rushing rivers,
And mighty inland seas,
But, oh, its brown and sparkling brooks

I'm loving more than these;
From southern sun-kissed meadows,
And fertile valleys wide,
To where the forests deep and dark
Stand in their stately pride,
My heart is true and loyal,
And evermore will be—
For there's only one Wisconsin,
And that is home to me.

Oh, the world is wide and fair,
With many lands to see,
But there's only one Wisconsin,
And that is home to me.

—*Cora Blakeslee Beebe*

MY JEWEL CASE

I've the queerest, quaintest Jewel Case
That you'd ever want to see,
And no one can steal my treasures
For I only have the key;
And though I'm very generous,
And let all who care to, peek
And feast their eyes aplenty,
They can't have a one to keep!

Now, this Jewel Case is divided
Into many different parts;
I think I forgot to mention
It is hidden in my heart.
I have Jewels that I like having
And some that are not so fair,
But of those I do not like
I am bound to take good care.

I have Hope and Love and Laughter,
And right next to them lies Gloom;
I have Sympathy and Kindness,
But I'd rather not make room
For all those awfully dark ones,

Sorrow, Pain, and Ghastly Fear,
But they come in every Jewel Case
Just the same as Joy and Tears!

In one corner of the Jewel Case
I have put my greatest treasure.
I am always glad to show it,
And it really gives me pleasure
To share with one less fortunate
This Gem above all others.
I think it has been truly named,
That Wondrous Love of Mother!

—*Besse Burnett Bell*

THE TAJ MAHAL

On Jumna's banks, where wavelets lap the shore,
There stands a tomb in matchless beauty wrought,
Bestud with jewels, stones, and marbles, brought
From every clime to deck the sculptured door
And carven screen and wall and inlaid floor;
A master mind conceived and caged the thought
Which reared this wondrous tomb, forever sought
By those who seek not only art, but more.

For doth it not portray that sacred thing,
The love of man for woman as his mate,
Enduring through the ages and all time,
The endless theme all poets strive to sing?
It raiseth woman to an high estate,
This tribute, of a monument sublime.

—*Laura Bell*

DICKEY

I hear the sound of pattering feet,
I hear the prattling accents sweet;
And so I turn again to greet
The little boy across the street.

I see the faltering little feet,
I see the hand stretched out to meet
The arms I offer, to entreat
The little boy across the street.

Ah! somehow in this still retreat
With all the season's joys replete,
Life surely could not be complete
Without this boy across the street.
                    —*Mrs. Wilbur Bell*

HARVEST

He spoke of harvest, pointed to the field
Where shocks of corn stood boldly in the sun.
The earth was kind to give such lavish yield.
Against the barn were pumpkins piled, each one
A golden promise. Peppers strung and dried
Were red as flame. He took a farmer's pride
In heavy apple trees. He knew the soil.
How well it paid him for a summer's toil!

He spoke of harvest time. She smiled and yet
She hardly heard him. She was gazing where
The children played, a frolicking quartet
Of curls and rompers, and a grateful prayer
Came to her heart. She saw the meaning of
The harvest, felt the strength of boundless love,
Of answered faith. Four children hard at play—
She smiled and brushed a happy tear away.
                    —*Gertrude Ryder Bennett*

CHILD OF MARY'S SOUL

The Star came out to hail Him,
    The angels choired His birth,
The shepherds did not fail Him,
    The Wise Men found His hearth.

The ox and ass bespoke Him,
    The cock crowed loud His praise,
The lamb was fain to stroke Him
    Upon that Day of Days.

Oh, Jesukin Immortal!
   Child of Mary's Soul!
My spirit swings its portal—
   Come in and make me whole!

                —*Susie M. Best*

MY MOTHER

My Mother, dear; Most Beautiful,
The graces which remain
Proclaim you were a dainty belle
And had a regal reign.

Your cheeks were just like apple-bloom—
All soft and luscious pink—
Your eyes were brown as hazel nuts,
Your hair . . . like night . . . I think.

Today, your locks are grey as moss
Festooning live-oak trees.
Though wrinkles line your gentle face,
You store rich memories

Within the Kingdoms of your Heart—
You gave to me its key—
So, there, I wander to and fro
Where Love binds you to me.

                —*Beulah Vick Bickley*

THE DAY

I love the early morning,
At the time of break o' day,
The rose is full of fragrance,
The air is fresh alway.

I love the midday hour,
The time of the noontide heat,
I take a short siesta,
From all weary tasks replete.

I love the evening shadows,
The sun having died away,
A reverie awakens
Of joys of a bygone day.

And when the day is ended,
And when nature's balmy sleep
In gentle arms enfolds me,
And her loving vigil keeps,

To guard me till the morning,
At the time of break o' day;
The rose is full of fragrance,
The air is fresh alway.

—*Margaret Estella Bigham*

THE END OF THE SUNSET TRAIL

Daylight fading,
Softens the sun's bright ray.
Twilight falling,
Tells of the close of day.
Sweet winds blowing
Up from the flow'ry dale,
While I wait for your home-coming
At the end of the Sunset Trail.

Now down the side of the mountain
I can see you coming along,
Down through the pines and the aspens,
And my joy o'erflows with a song.
Here by our own little cabin
While the light is beginning to fail,
I am waiting for you in the gloaming
At the end of the Sunset Trail.

Twilight shadows,
Now in the canyons lie.
Cloud caps painted,
In colors no artist can vie.

Breezes blowing,
Over the sea a sail,
While now to you I am coming
At the end of the Sunset Trail.

Now down the side of the mountain
I am swiftly coming along,
Down through the pines and the aspens,
And my heart responds to your song.
Down by our own little cabin
When the light is beginning to fail,
I am coming to you in the gloaming
At the end of the Sunset Trail.

                                    —*Alma C. Bingham*

GEORGE   WASHINGTON

A nation was born in a vast new domain.
        The travail attending,
        And childhood defending,
        Through trials unending,
Was one who true liberty strove to attain.

This valiant commander, intrepid of soul,
        When armies defied him,
        Calamities tried him,
        And help seemed denied him,
With purpose unwavering pressed on toward the goal.

A leader undaunted in strife or in peace,
        A statesman of vision,
        Who made wise decision
        And sponsored provision
For a unified country in power to increase.

He sought not for self, nor coveted fame.
        He wrought for the nation,
        To lay firm foundation
        For continued duration
Of a self-governed people. May they honor his name!

                                    —*Laura Rew Bixby*

AN INVITATION

I hear my Sunday-school bell ringing,
Soon the choir will be singing,
Calling us to worship thus and so;
The teachers take their places as you know.

Then the lessons we shall heed,
As all so plainly need;
Oh what a happy place to go,
To keep us from the foe.

Yes, it will make our lives better
When we seek no wrong to fetter,
But in a lovely place like this to be;
So come along to my Sunday school with me.
—*Mrs. Ralph Black*

FAITH

I sail my bark on a placid sea—
    A sea of hope and cheer;
I bank my trust in a faith divine—
    A faith in the Father dear.

He guides by day and he guides by night,
    His truth is my steering gear;
Whatever the goal, it is gained if the soul
    Has faith in the Father dear.

I set my sail in the narrow way
    From which I'll never veer;
I press on for aye for the prize of the High,
    For I've faith in the Father dear.

Though clouds of gloom and billows dark
    And devils of doubt and fear
Should tempt me aside, I will yet abide
    By my faith in the Father dear.

He bids, "Sail on! My strength is thine,
    Be sure I am ever near;
Our unity thy shield shall be,
    Still trust in your Father, dear."

O soul serene, O trust sublime
  In the promise His Son gave here!
"Believe and receive" are his words I'll prove
  By my faith in the Father dear.

                                        —*B. M. Blatchley*

AUTUMN LEAVES

Nature turned their somber green
To brilliant orange and red;
Then sent them off tremblingly,
To go where breezes led.

The wind whispered, "Come with me,
Sail away on play-like wings."
They laughed, then sang as off they flew,
With a joy contentment brings.

Fluffy rivals forced them down,
Then wrapped them in woolly snow.
Here they'll sleep till they wake anew
In other things which grow.

                                        —*Pearl B. Bloss*

MARCH'S DAUGHTER

Sunny days, clear skies, and songbirds,
  Wintry blasts and scattered snowflakes—
It's inconstant—March's weather
  Days from every season takes.

Sunny smiles, clear thoughts, and laughter,
  Stormy words, expression grim—
She's inconstant—March's daughter
  Shifts her mood at every whim.

                                        —*Maude Philips Board*

AS LOVELY AS THEY

Let me stand
upright, clean,
like a tall birch
after the rain has drenched
its bark and boughs between.

O'er hill and vale and meadow wide,
   On mountain lone, by ebbing tide
Unfold the buds of promise sweet
   The waiting world again to greet,
And resurrect the flowers fair
   A perfumed incense on the air,
And this, an humble tribute bring,
   Earth's offering to her Easter King.

Let nature's minstrelsy awake!
   The gentle wind love's message take
In music's notes of sweetest strain
   Till flowing brooks catch the refrain,
And murm'ring gently to the sea
   Repeat the song from lea to lea.
Then wakes the ocean's mighty soul
   And o'er its billows anthems roll.
Let woodland carolers be heard,
   And chant again the joyous word,
From cliff to cliff Te Deums ring
   Hosannah to the Saviour King!

Oh lives with these great blessings fraught,
   A gift of love divinely bought,
To Him who hath our ransom paid,
   The hope of joy eternal made,
Let grateful hearts their homage pay
   And give Him praise from day to day
Till round the world we will proclaim
   The glories of the Saviour's name,
And in an endless anthem sing,
   He lives, our resurrected King!
                      —*Nancy S. Boston*

THE ETERNAL TRIANGLE

Two robins on the lawn;
One was singing a lover's song.
The Lady Robin was shy and trim,
And kept a proper distance from him.

He walked toward her, with song so sweet
It would take any damsel off her feet.
She listened demurely, with head on one side
As though the great question she would decide.

Just then, down from the blue
A very dapper robin flew.
He took his place beside the maid
And she never acted a bit afraid.

The first robin kept singing the sweetest song,
And all the time was walking along.
He reached her; she must have had a streak of yellow,
For she flew away with the other fellow.

                                        —*Emma Bowers*

THE SEEKERS

Oh, pity, thou, the seekers,
The unrequited seekers
Whose ships set sail for harbors
Through mist-enshrouded shoals.
They're hounded by dim raptures,
By lost oblivious raptures
As futile and as urgent
And tenuous as their goals.

These know the task unfinished,
These know the mistral chill;
With ardor undiminished
They seek new havens still.

With ineffectual cargoes,
With starry, sorry cargoes
They cleave the far Aegean
With proud and splendid prow.
But the sought-for land of promise,
The fabulous land of promise
Has never been unhidden,
And never will be now.

These seek the realm of wonders,
Whose rims outrun their stride;
Untamed by portent thunders
They march—the Crucified!
—*Hazel McGee Bowman*

THE INDIAN DANCER

O I'm an Indian dancing man;
I dance as only Indians can.
I dance the wild and wicked war dance;
I dance the fierce and furious fire dance;
I dance the sly and subtle snake dance;
I dance the ghastly, gruesome scalp dance.

But when the marching warriors come
A-marching home to beating drum,
I dance the glad and grateful peace dance;
I dance the rich and ripened corn dance;
I dance the pure and precious rain dance;
I dance the solemn, sacred Sun Dance.
Who would not be a dancing man,
And dance as only Indians can!
—*Anna Tillman Boyd*

NEVADA

Where the warm brown sands of the desert lie,
And beauty blooms in the evening sky,
The pungent sage and the whispering pines,
And romantic tales of her silver mines
Put a lilt in the veins that keeps one young
From the time life starts until 'tis done—
In Nevada.

A musician she since her days began,
And she plies her bow on the heartstrings of man;
Love is her bow and her music haunts,
(For wherever one is it's Nevada he wants,)
She is Friday's child, loving and giving
Courage and truth and a heap of living—
Nevada.   —*Helena Grace Bradley*

MOONRISE IN THE ROCKIES

I've seen the moon rise over vast endless plains
Of desert sand and sage,
And over glinting restless waves
As they moaned in sullen rage—
I've seen the magic of its spell
As it glimmered tenderly above
Exotic gardens and fell
Upon my heart's romantic love.
But moonrise in the Rockies is the best—
Where she sheds her lucent light
On those ageless, rugged peaks, pine-crest
Against the glamour of the night.

—Routh Pickett Bradley

OSWEGO LAKE

God's mirror of the mountains,
    God's mirror of the pines,
A bowl of sparkling fountains,
    Earth's font of purest wines.

Lake of the morning's glories,
    Lake of the evening's calms,
Thy mirror films the stories
    Of heaven's holy psalms.

My soul in adoration
    Bows in silent prayers
To Thee, God of creation,
    Whose earth with heaven compares.

—Margaret Bradshaw

SEARCHLIGHTS

When I come back,
All my memories are reborn.
Along familiar streets they form,
As faces, places, come in view—

Searchlights, piercing through
To mad days that live again—
Glad days and
Sad days too.

A voice, a tune,
A faint perfume
Echo down a length of years,
Awake emotions undefined
Groping in a mist of tears,
Searching for the hidden key
To unlock the mystery
Of the voice, the mocking tune,
And the path of faint perfume.

—Mildred Sutton Breneman

RECOMPENSE

Though we are many miles apart,
The ties that bind you to my heart
Grow stronger with each passing day,
And very oft I seem to hear
Your own voice singing sweet and clear
And melodies you used to play.

In fancy I can see your smile,
And though I miss you all the while
And long for you with every day,
I have set for you the highest goal
Of growth in body, mind, and soul;
For this I daily pray.

I wish for you a hand of skill—
Well trained and subject to your will,
The very thought a solace brings.
A gleam of comfort to my mind—
A recompense I truly find
As I help give your spirit wings.

When you have reached my high ideal
And turned my dreams into the real—
Become the man for whom I pray;

This will be recompense to me
For days of absence that I see—
And more I cannot say.

                              —*Hazel Cannon Brinson*

SPRING'S WOOING

February

Spring smiled this morning
    Through a windowpane,
And away went capering.
    I chased her in vain
Some toll to take,
    And found yellow jonquils
        In her wake.

March

Spring woke me from slumber
    With a breathy sigh
That brushed my cheek
    As she frisked by.
I wondered just
    What her gift would be—
        'Twas a blustery gust.

April

Spring kissed my lips today
    And wept in rapture;
While she laughed at her tears
    I made sure her capture.
Upon the warm earth's breast
    The sparkling drops fell greenly.
        Spring was gay dressed.

May

Spring held in warm embrace
    Offers sweet flowers,
Travail of sun and wind
    And gentle showers.
Tender farewell, alas!
    Summer's hot breath comes,
        Spring must pass.

                              —*Nellie Bristow*

THE HILLS WE LOVE

There are hills down near the South Seas,
   Where the sun pours his hottest rays;
There are hills in thrilling China
   Nestling closely near the bays;
There are hills in gay old Europe,
   Where the skies are blue above,
But the hills of our home State
   Are the only hills we love.
                  —Grace Lowe Broadhead

SNOWLESS WINTER

The earth is bleak and bare.
Sharp cold is everywhere.
     The wind is wild.

The stars are shining clear.
The ground is brown and sere.
     The moon's pale glow
Is shining through the night
A cool, clean, crystal light.
     There is no snow.

The rivers roar and leap.
The trees are still asleep.
     They dare not wake.
They stand there on the hill
Though winds call high and shrill
     Above the lake.
                  —Merta M. Brookings

I WOULD I COULD DANCE

I would I could dance
   So lightly and airily,
Toe tripping, feet skipping,
   So gracefully, fairily.

My soul I would pawn
    To be able to twirl,
To make pulses quicken
    As I prance and whirl.

I would I could dance—
    You scoff as I try—
My clown antics prance
    'Fore your laughing eye.
                                    —*Helen M. Brough*

PITY

It would not hurt me quite as much,
    If you one spoken word had said,
Had shunned not, dear, my willing touch,
    When all your own poor love was dead.

If you had shown a little grace,
    Had made me think I might be brave!
If you had dared to see my face,
    In pity for the love I crave.

You broke my heart in more cruel way,
    Although you did not think I knew.
You feared to pick the pieces up,
    Lest they might pierce the joy in you.
                                    —*Flora Warren Brown*

NOVICE

The arms of the elm
Reach out in the storm,
Grotesquely groping,
Reaching for the wind.

Twinkling snow
Spins over the floor
Writing in silver tracery . . .

So gropes my pen
For words the heart does know
But cannot spin
In silver arabesque.

—Julia Field Brown

POTTERY MAKER[1]

Yellow the pueblo, Sun!
Tanoa squats with her clay, kneading,
Coiling rope on rope of rich red earth,
Pinching, molding.
O Sun, dry the tall olla!
Tanoa's eager brown hands are waiting,
Mixing chalk and water, pointing
Her yucca brush.
A good urn like Tanoa's
Must sell for much gold, considering
What Those Above gave for the making
To a woman.

—Margaret Marchand Brown

HOSPITAL FLOWERS

In all the silent halls and rooms
Where pain and sorrows dwell,
Your presence breathes a sweet perfume
    When words their sympathy can't tell.
You are in love and reverence held,
    God fashioned you so fair,—
No matter how your name is spelled,
    Love and friendship placed you there.
The memory of you cannot fade
    Though you were cast aside,
Your leaves, all dried from too much shade,
    Your beauty in my heart abides.

—Mrs. Virgil Browne

---

[1] Reprinted from the *Improvement Era*, by permission of the publishers.

THE THUD OF THE CLODS

It was a most solemn occasion—
We stood on the brink of a newly-made grave,—
Friends had gathered from near and afar—
The children were all there—
With their children's children,—
The preacher was ill—three came in his stead—
The choir sang softly and tenderly—
The touch of the pallbearers was so gentle—
  Their tread so light—their manners so reverent.

The flowers were—oh so beautiful—
The space round about—was filled with their fragrance,—
The white ones attested to her purity—
The green fernery—to her memory *ever* kept—
The number of offerings—to her esteem—
And when all together—a blanket of *love*—
  Akin to that something—
  That is like Heaven above.

The preachers eulogized—
The soul that had gone out to God—
And quoted God's words—one after another—
To lessen the pain, suffering, and sorrow,—
They said that *care* had all passed away—
That *she* would *sleep*, until *He* returned—
He had gone to prepare a place—
For in God's house are many mansions,—
  We all felt comforted.

But when the gaping grave—
Swallowed up that withered form—
And the *clods* fell in with a *thud!*—
The poignancy of that hour—
Could hardly be appeased,—
Though the preacher read and read—
From God's Holy Book—His choicest words,—
The *occasion* was the *saddest* of all—
  For, today, *Mother* was put away.

                                                    —*Julia E. Brumfield*

WINDS ARE THE WATCHMEN

Winds are the watchmen of the broad Sky-way,
They point passing clouds this way and that.
They are gentle when old gray clouds move slowly,
Trailing long faded skirts,
But they are swift to follow, whistling shrilly,
When bold clouds speed from the northern hill.
They give right of way to the serene sun
And let storm clouds grumble when held back.
They brush lightly aside all tattered cloud vagrants
Gathered at the gate of the Moon Mansion,
And the Lady Moon rides undisturbed up the Sky-way,
Radiant leader of the great Star Parade.
No cloud disobeys the winds,
They are wise watchmen.

—Iva Purdum Bruton

VICTORIAN LADIES

"This picture that you see, sir, on the wall
Presents a lady wearing what we call
A costume mid-Victorian. For years
The baited objects of our jibes and jeers
These great puffed sleeves and collars neatly pinned
Beneath the chin! Sartorially they sinned!
'How could they wear such clothes!' my daughter said,
And airily she tossed her saucy head
This way and that as she emerged from chrys-
alis to butterfly—'Now *I* like this!'
And since that speech but scarce a year has passed—
Yes, sir, the lady on the wall? My mother.
And standing near, in big puffed sleeves, that other,
With quaint brooch at the throat? You must know her,
You've seen her often here. My daughter, sir!"

—Mildred Hatton Bryan

TWILIGHT TIME

When the sun has gone behind the hill,
When the dark comes creeping
And the earth is very still;
Then I call my little children
To come home to me—
Back to their fireside again.

The day is made for playing and fun
Under the friendly sky;
But at dusk, when day is done,
I call them home to me.
I close the door on all the world
And gather them round my knee.

We talk of birds and men and flowers,
Of what we've seen and heard;
How we've spent the daytime hours,
How much we love each other!
How glad we are for the twilight time
When we can all be together!

—*Mildred Southworth Bryan*

QUEEN MOUNTAIN

I marvel as you chameleonize
While you go passing by,
Wearing long robes of varying hues,
Your haloed head held high.

I see your charm, when you dress in gray,
And in the clouds and mist
Your head hangs lowered in humble grief,
Whose brow Sunlight has kissed.

And when tears drop from your lashes green
Along your ashen face
And form into little rivulets
Which look like Irish lace.

Again, when you don your regal robes
Of gold and purple light
And march along in triumphant strides,
You are a splendid sight.

With your snow-capped head and dress of white
You seem severe and cold;
For those who know you intimately,
Delightful charms you hold.

But when in your autumnal glory
The sun shines on your breast
And the rouge is on your regal cheeks,
That's when I like you best.

—*Blanche Brown Bryant*

TO THE DAUGHTER OF A NYMPH

Your mother? You would know of her?
I cannot tell, my child,
None understood the heart of her
So passionate and wild!

Your mother was a vivid spark
Of phosphorescent fire,
She was the offspring of a dream,
A creature of desire.

She never took a marriage vow,
Or knew a marriage bed,
She was paramour to all four winds,
(So I have heard it said).

Her eyes were eerie beams of light,
Her breath a poignant breeze,
Her voice an aching, wind-blown flute
Echoing through the trees.

She was a phantom in the woods
When Pan was piping sweet,
Intent among the waving reeds
For flashes of his feet.

Days and nights upon his trail
She sped swift as a fawn,
Then like a tuft of eider down
Came drifting home at dawn.

The last I ever saw of her,
(I seem to see her yet)
She danced before an orange moon—
An ivory silhouette!

Four jealous winds stood on the hill,
Shrilling a fiery tune,
Watched her unwind a silver scarf
And hang it on the moon.

I don't know where she went, my child,
She's been gone ages long,
'Twere best you fetter your young heart,
And hush your lips to song!

                                        —*Agnes Cochran Buamblett*

BEAUTY CRUCIFIED

My neighbor's tree, in sunny field,
Was tall and frail, a graceful thing.
I watched its growth from year to year
And treasured every leafy wing,

It hid from view a wretched sight,
Rough lumber piles, a rambling shed
With patched-up doors and smoky roof,
Old dingy walls, gray, black, and red.

But yesterday my living screen
Was doomed to death, by ruthless pride.
Its fall disclosed the sordid view
Revealed by Beauty crucified!

                                        —*Anna Shaw Buck*

IF I WERE YOU

If you were I, and I were you,
What are the things that we would do?
Perhaps we do not know just what,
And so to tell would rather not!
How can we know what we would do
If you were I, and I were you?

Perhaps the things that now seem strange,
Would not be so at closer range;
They might indeed quite disappear,
And everything might be made clear;
So we would have a different view,
If you were I, and I were you!

So when I do things that seem queer,
And you—well—I'll not interfere—
Let us remember as we go,
That causes are unknown, and so
We cannot tell what we would do
If you were I, and I were you!

—*Carrie Burrington*

YOUTH SPEAKS

I am just turned sixteen
And my hair is red gold;
My lips are like wine,
And my eyes they are bold.

The boys like me lots
But I like just one.
We dance and we ride
And we swim—O, what fun!

Mother looks at me sadly,
And says, "Dear, you should
Sew, read, study Latin, and grow
To be useful and good."

Dear Mother is fifty and useful,
But what does she have for her pains?
She knows Latin, but what does she know
Of the torrent that flows in my veins?

I suppose that I too
Shall be good when I'm old;
But just now I'm sixteen
And my hair is red gold.

—Mabel M. Burton

MY LAD

I know a lad, a sailor free,
Whose good ship drifts right merrily
To seek a vast and distant land,
With every fate at his command.

I know a lad, a warrior bold,
Who conquers every foe foretold;
Like leaves beneath the whirlwind's sway,
The baffled enemy flee away.

I know a lad, a builder grand,
Who shapes fine castles out of sand,
With moats and bridges, turrets high,
And gardens that delight the eye.

All these pursuits and many more
Employ my busy lad of four,
Who lives in realms of make-believe
From happy morn till drowsy eve.

—Fay H. Butler

SYMBOL OF OUR COUNTRY

Cabin stands in clearing, unkempt, deserted;
Leans against the hillside, by highway skirted;
Peers through haloed memories, on scenes perverted,
        Vandaled by progress.

Always, it is muttering some old, old story;
Always, it is whispering some allegory.
Can it be the spirit of former glory
      Dwelling in sadness?

It was friendly shelter against weird presences;
Habitat of settlers who trekked vast distances;
Home of pioneers who endured the silences,
      Born of the stillness.

Morning-glories clambered upon its clapboards;
Maple trees in springtime gave up their sap-hoards,
Forests harmonized the woodpeckers' tap-swords
      Drummed in the wildness.

Lonely hut, neglected by prideful nation;
Empty, it is Rachel, in lamentation;
Should it not be given some consideration
      In its aloneness?

Cabin, born of wildwood, whose arms were far-flung,
Guardian of frontier where the trails were star-hung,
Symbol of our country where always are sung
      Songs of the fearless.
                    —Maud McKinsey Butler

MY MOTHER'S HANDS

Soft and gentle—
Soft and gentle as the petals of the rose
Are my Mother's hands.
In childhood she stooped
And clasped my face
With her dear loving hands,
And smiled away my tears.
Soothing and cool
Upon my fevered brow
Were my Mother's hands;
The hands that seemed
To hold me here when Death
Was entering in.

The tragedies
That come with life,
Sorrows, blighted hopes
Are all vanquished by the touch
Of her dear healing hands.
Age has placed its mark
Upon my Mother's hands,
But only Death can take away
The power to soothe and heal.
No! Death can not take
From these soft and gentle hands
The power to soothe and heal.
Forever I shall feel the touch
Of my dear Mother's hands.

—*Anna Mikesell Byers*

ON HAPPY WOMEN

Somehow Life had passed me by
And left me gazing on,
With envious eyes, the things
That happy women don:

Their rosy cheeks, their sparkling eyes,
Their gleaming, snow-white teeth—
The red of joy in well-kissed lips . . .
Things happy loves bequeath.

And then that day . . . that glorious day . . .
I looked into your eyes,
I felt myself take on these things
That loving women prize.

—*Mary D. Cain*

RAVINE PATH

This is not a path for heedless going—
    A spur of rock, a blackly naked root
    Or crumbling ledge would snare the idle foot—
But lovelier reasons: one would not miss knowing

Where star flowers lean against a shaggy shoulder
   Of old oak stump, or emerald shadows turn,
   Nearer, to feathery fountain-sprays of fern,
Or mosses robe the knees of some gray boulder.

This is not a path for eager seeking—
   Here where wood violets peer from grassy dusk,
   And sweet earth smells taunt every breeze, like musk,
There is no need for search, nor hurried speaking:
Feet stumbling blindly, heavy with new-found sorrow,
   Need only pause, or follow through the winding
   Fragrance and hush, to earn reward in finding
Healing and peace toward the unwished-for tomorrow.
                  —*Maud Ludington Cain*

GOD'S ANSWER TO A GRIEVING MOTHER

Dear lonely mother-heart,—I heard your prayer.
Last night just as the purple shadows fell upon the Earth,
There was the softest sound upon the stair
       That leads to Heaven's door—
And when we flung the golden portals wide,
A host of tiny ones were waiting there
       To come inside.
Such happy laughing eyes and dimples sweet,
Such cuddly baby hands and tiny feet,
       Oh we were glad to welcome back this band
Who left us such a little time before.

And waiting just inside the door
Were all the Mothers who had come that day
And left their little ones so far away
       Upon the Earth.
And arms were opened wide and faces smiled,
And Mother Angels clasped an Angel child,
And Mothers' breasts each couched a sleepy head,
And carried them away to tuck in bed.
       And then I lit the stars outside their door.

Have you not seen the million tiny stars up in the skies
       Lit just before the dark?

They all are lit for frightened baby-eyes.
Have you forgotten, I, like you, have lost a Son?
      I have been lonely too.
                      —Harriet Parker Camden

A SONG OF THE HILLS

When blue mists of fair Aurora
Twine gay rainbow-tinted hills,
Voices call and Echoes answer
Birds and trees by mountain rills.

"Spring is here, with flow'rs adorning;
Leap to greet the gay glad Morning;
Sing afar with lilting voices:
Day is near and Earth rejoices.

Chorus

"Hark! 'Dance in the morning,' gay redbirds sing;
Hark! Bluebirds are singing and bluebells ring;
List! Greet Day with laughter, in rose and gold;
List! Spread well the story Day's whispers told:
Shout! Praise the Great Father whose Will gave birth
  To all the Beauties of Heav'n and Earth.

"Day is here, new gladness bringing;
Love is here with maidens singing;
Buds are bursting, hearts revealing;
Youth is mating—Time is stealing."
                      —May Lackey Campbell

AN AUTUMN DAY

Out of the Infinite Unknown Plan
There is born a wonderful Day.—
The earth is clad in a tawn-gold sheen,
The leaves are casting aside their green,
And the field flowers whispering sway.
Sing, Oh Earth, a carol of bloom,
While the wind lute wafts its wild perfume,

Hush the sounds of sorrow and gloom
With the lilt of your magic lay!
You are breath of the Orient, fragrant, bland,
Beautiful Autumn Day!

Into the haze of the mellow dusk
You are gliding, Wonderful Day—
To be drenched in a sea of dewy bliss,
To be lulled to sleep by the moonbeams' kiss,
While you fade into shadows gray.
A star hangs low in the eastern sky,
There's a cricket's fife and a bird's lone cry,
And the restless night winds sob and sigh
As you silently steal away.
Sleep and dream in your shroud of mist,
Beautiful Autumn Day!

—Daisie le Reu S. Capp

FROM A CAR WINDOW

A glimpse and a glance and a fathomless gaze,
　　As fleeting as sunbeam, or fleck of snow;
Onward I started: he stumbled within
　　The shadowy lengths of the evening's glow;
But out of the stillness a something yet calls
From the heart of that boy in the overalls.

His eyes wore the clear, wistful look of the stars;
　　Did he ask what they held in the boy-realm dim?
His brown feet were bounded by boulders and bars,
　　And this was a glimpse of the world for him.
O Nature, there's nothing my vision enthralls
As the picturesque boy in the overalls.

The print of the mountain embranded his brow,
　　The strength of its strongholds was there;
A hint of the valley's rich regions a-plow
　　Freed the quizzical face of its care;
And O, could I creep through those crude wordless walls,
Clasp hearts with the boy in the overalls!

On the highways and byways such faces I see,
   No face, like to these, found on fame's featured walls;
And the men, counted best, in the years yet to be,
   Shall arise from the ranks of the Overalls.
                          —*Josie Frazee Cappleman*

THE VOICE OF HUMAN LABOR

I am human labor,
Mighty power of the human race.
My shoulders bear the past,
The present, and the future of man.
In my hands I hold the world
And destiny of nations.

I seek truth and knowledge
Of laws of the universe,
And nature has unfolded
Unto me her wondrous secrets.
I put forth my hand,
And earth blooms rich in flower
And in fruitage.

If my hand be withdrawn
From the earth,
The human race shall perish.
If I be debased, the world
Shall be debased.
If I be lifted up, the world
Shall be uplifted.

I have come up out of chaos.
I have conquered slavery
And won the realm of freedom.
I shall win the realm of freedom,
Of creative labor,
Wherein all may put forth hands
And labor be awarded justice.

I am human labor.
Builder of a world of nations,
I shall win fulfillment of ambition.

I shall build the way into
The realm of peace
Wherein the nations of the world shall dwell.
The war gods and the hosts of war fiends
Shall flee from before me,
And the peace of God, Jehovah,
Ruler of the heavens and earth,
Shall be upon all nations.

—Mrs. W. N. Carleton

LOVE'S EVENING

Love cannot always burn at noonday heat,
The wild, sweet thrill that your first kiss awoke
Is mine no more; nor does the quick heartbeat,
The downcast eye, and flushing cheek mark me,
As when the first low words of love you spoke.

But since I know that to you I can turn
And be so sure that you will understand,
So quick to comfort me when grief's tears burn
My eyes, so tender when my heart is sore,
And glad when joy walks with me hand in hand.

I mourn not for the hour of Youth's springtime,
I have its mem'ry, golden-hued and bright,
Nor ask that greater blessing shall be mine
Than by your side to stand when my sun sinks,
And wait, with you, the coming of the night.

—Anna C. Carraher

MOTHER

Mother sits in the old armchair,
Great-grandmother of children fair,
She has seen of life here and there,
Hardships endured we would not dare,
And still, a sweet smile lingers there
On her face—crowned with silver hair;
And she all of our trouble shares
To ease crossing the bridge of cares;
Children and mother, a loyal pair.

—Catharine Carstensen

NEW VISION

When laughter lived at home with me
And joy left not a room for doubt,
I drew a magic circle round
To keep love in, and sorrow out.

But, one day, all was dark and still,
For lads and laughter went away;
And, then, I saw, beyond my door
Were many lads who passed each day.

Some were so eager, some, so frail . . .
Some, troubled . . . some . . . just wondering,
No matter . . . there are ways to spend
My hungry, unused mothering!
                                    —*Pearle R. Casey*

THE METEORITE

A meteoric soul of heavenly birth,
A swift out-runner of all mortal things,
Beating the ether with his shining wings,
Counted all other orbs of little worth,
If, in his frenzy, he might reach the Earth
And hear, at closer range, the song it sings
And breathe the fragrance that around it clings;
Or, but to lay hot fingers on its girth.
In dazzling brilliancy the panting soul
Saw, with proud eyes, his victory achieved.
With outstretched wings he darted to his goal.
But, as he struck the Earth, his joy received
A shock that changed him to a blackened coal:
A dull, dead thing by wanton Earth deceived.
                                    —*Almeda M. Castello*

LONGING

I long for the peace of the desert,
    And the sagebrush in the sun . . .
The rosy sky of the morning,
    And the blue when the day is done . . .

The rustle of hot, dry grasses,
  The lake bed, alkali pale . . .
The crackle of brush in the herder's fire . . .
  The scent of a cattle trail . . .

The loneliness of the desert . . .
  The stillness that needs no *word* . . .
The sound of a sheep bell in the dusk,
  The song in the throat of a bird . . .

The voice of the desert is calling,
  The desert beckons to me . . .
The soft caress of the night wind . . .
  And the lull of a silent sea.

                         —Claire Cave

MOTHERS

Mothers are such lovely things,
  I wonder they do not have wings!
Their tender bodies cradle us,
  For us they sound pain's deepest seas;
We learn of God, we learn to pray
  At Mothers' knees!

Mothers are such lovely things,
  I wonder they do not have wings!
They guard our helpless years with love,
  Their loving arms are childhood's nest,
They dry our tears, and to our wounds
  Their lips are pressed!

Mothers are such lovely things,
  I wonder they do not have wings!
We may forget, slight them, and scorn,
  Their love lives on ever the same.
We may go down, be steeped in sin;
  They hide our shame!

Mothers are such lovely things!
  I wonder they do not have wings!

                   —Catherine Key Cavender

WE'RE HOMEWARD BOUND

When autumn leaves are glowing,
  And purple haze pervades,
I hear a far, high calling
  Above the ridge and glades.

The wild geese there are honking
  Aloft in cloud-fleck'd sky,
Far to the Southland homing,
  Like arrows straight they fly.

Voices so wild, sweet, tender,
  Throbbing exultantly,
They thrill my heart to utter
  Paeons of ecstasy!

Sorrows and cares oppress me,
  Fetters my spirit bind,
But still I hear their glad, free
  Melodies down the wind.

O, wild geese weirdly honking,
  Triumphant, strong, and gay!
"Courage," I hear them chanting,
  "Onward thy course and way."

When gentians blue are gleaming,
  Witch hazel,—pale and sweet,
May life's last autumn, closing,
  Bring far-flung songs to greet.

May Heaven's wings unfurling
  Lift me to upward flight,
While caroling wild geese, calling,
  Chime softly through the night.
                    —*Mary Ingersoll Chamberlain*

A DREAM OF PEACE

I dreamed that Peace had come,—that nevermore
Would man arise to smite his fellow man
In ruthless hate and cruel greed of gain.
I said: "Our human race is now advanced
Too far from savagery, has now approached
Too near the likeness of his God to lapse
Again into the brute that slays his kind.
Henceforth calm Reason, from her lofty throne,
Shall arbitrate the strifes of men, and rule
With justice all the nations of the earth."

My dream was shattered by a blast of war
That shook the world; and four long years of blood
And devastation, pain, and misery
Ensued, that seemed an age of endless woe.
My country called to arms; I gave my sons,—
Three noble sons whom I had reared for Peace.
I sent them forth with cheerful words, with lips
That did not quiver, eyes that did not shed
A tear; and from the bulwark of my home
I fought the fight that is a woman's part
When man goes forth to strive against a foe.
I fought as I would wish my sons to fight
Upon those battlefields beyond the sea;
But all the while my loyal spirit grieved
To feel that only thus could be maintained
The high ideals and the code of right
Evolved through ages since our race began.

Then came the end. And, "From Versailles," I said,
"The reign of Peace, for which we long have yearned,
Will surely now begin its kindly sway."
Alas, I felt again that bitter pang,
The pain of wounded Faith; and once I thought
That Hope within my trustful heart was dead,—
It lay so cold, so silent, and so numb.
But Hope is an immortal gift; and soon
It stirred and breathed, it lived and moved again.

And now that plans for Peace are taking form,
It sings anew, an ever-swelling song
Of final good, triumphant over ill.

I must believe. I nevermore shall doubt
That in the human soul a spark divine
From Heaven glows, and guides us on our path
From age to age, from height to nobler height,
Along the upward way that progress leads;
And coming years will surely bring to pass
That man shall rise above his baser self
To planes of life as never yet attained,
And form a universal brotherhood.

Far distant still that happy time may be;
I shall not see it in my little day.
But it will come; and from some fairer height
Of being, in another sphere than this,
My waiting soul shall know, and leap with joy
To see on earth the golden age begin
Of which the angels to the shepherds sang
That night, above the calm Judean hills,—
The age of Peace on Earth, good will to men.

—Lily Pearl Chamberlin

SUMMER—THE NUN

Summer—
Like a nun has shaved her tresses,
Changed her green and golden dresses
For the dull, dark, sheenless clothes
With which cold, sleek winter robes.

Summer—
By her convent the whole world passes,
She has donned sackcloth and ashes.
As a nun goes to seclusion,
She has gone from out our vision.

—Ann Chambers

A NEW YEAR'S MESSAGE

As I look all around me and wonder
  Just what the New Year holds,
I hear a Voice saying, "Fear Not";
  And I know it's the One who molds
The lives of men, and their destiny.
  I am afraid to travel alone
The rough, rugged pathway I trod;
  Yet I will have sure, safe council,
If I will but listen to God.
  I am so weak and sinful,
And know not the best thing to do;
  But I have a Friend who is loyal,
I have a Friend who is true;
  And when I would fail Him and falter,
When temptations spring up anew;
  I list to the Voice above
As it tells me of Jesus' love;
  And I know I am safe, as I go my way
Living the New Year, day by day.

          —Blanche Edens Chandler

STONES

Stones there be in fences and in the tall gray towers,
Friendly stones in garden walks between the rows of flowers,
Stones in the country byway and in the city street,
Doorway stones smoothed through the years by countless restless
  feet.
But oh the stones with names upon—set quietly apart!
These are the stones that crush upon
A lonely heart!

          —Mabel Munns Charles

TO A SILVER BIRCH

I never knew until I crossed the prairie
  The value of a tree;
Of shade forevermore shall I be chary
  For now at last I see,

With eyes that looked on miles and miles of plain land,
  Dusty and hot and dry,
Acres and acres of lonely golden grain land
  Reaching from sky to sky.

I come to stand beneath your singing branches,
  Of trees the faery queen,
To live within the glen your shade enhances,
  A lover of your sheen.

Your beauty shakes my heart like purple thunder
  Upon a mountain peak,
For leaf and branch and bole an awesome wonder
  Have grown, I cannot speak.

I never knew until I crossed the prairie
  The value of a tree;
Of shade forevermore shall I be chary
  For now at last I see.

                              —*Beulah Charmley*

MORNING

When through the clouds the sun's first ray
Comes darting swift and bright,
The moon slips silently away
  Before the coming light.

The fairies dance away in glee
To sleep beneath the ferns,
From school and lessons they are free
  Until the moon returns.

The birds awake and sing their best,
The flowers lift their heads,
The children waken from their rest
  And tumble from their beds.

                              —*Agnes M. Chatham*

AUTUMN

The Maple, standing long in green,
Decided now to change her gown.
She chose one of a golden sheen
And touched it up with red and brown.
She spread afar her golden arms
O'er Autumn's changing scene,
While sturdy oaks took quick alarm
And wore a sombre mien.

But soon her gown to tatters flew,
Torn by the fitful lust
Of ardent winds that scampered through
And shook her with each gust.
At last she stood in naked shame,
Her finery blown away,
While sturdy oaks grew quick aflame
Before her stark array.

—Daisie Dell Churchward

DEBTS

"I'll never be able to pay
What I owe,"
Somebody said to me.
I've wondered since
If he meant—to man—
Or to Christ,
Who died on the tree.

—Ada Neill Clark

GLAD YOUTH

Glad youth and strength!
Happy spirit and free—
A gold-misty east,
The song in the wood,
The dew on the grass,
A wild rose where I pass,
And love! Ah me,
What must heaven be!

—Calista Barker Clark

HOME

Home is what we make it,
A haven of content,
Or just a place at which to stay
Where with cares we are bent.

So why not have the former?
'Tis as easy as can be,
Just smile and look for happiness
And what a change you'll see.

It's not material things that count
Or that make a home worth while,
It is the occupants within
That live, and love, and smile.

     —Dorothy A. Clark

UNCONQUERED

I did not know if stalwart courage you possessed.
 You gaily danced o'er paths with sun-lit petals strewn.
Love's fingers,—magic—soft—your trusting heart caressed,
 And this world bloomed for you,—a garden bright in June.

Fair fame adorned your brow;—wealth added golden pleasure;
 Kind Fates brought precious gifts to you, in generous mood.
You laughed in tune to sheer frivolity's light measure,—
 Nor dreamed that storm clouds gather,—swift and sombre-
   hued.

Fame died. Wealth fled. Misfortune's grief-edged saber pressed.
 Your weary feet trod, bleeding, down disillusion's road.
And faithless love tore out the heart from your poor breast,—
 To leave a wilderness, where once Romance abode.

Your heart rebounds above disaster's dead débris;
 No cry of cowardly defeat rose from your throat.
With eyes and spirit high,—life's master e'er to be,—
 Your soul, in victory, sounds Faith's triumphant note.

     —Rose Gould Clark

THE FAVORITE FLOWER

Wild Rose! sweet rose, your beauty charms the heart,
Your flowers hail the nation's growing cheer,
The leaves unfold to welcome childhood's part
In blooming peace as signaled over here.
While sunshine gleams with kindness on the way,
Both rose and robin prize their mutual care,
With fitting high lights to adorn the day
Encircling glory sparkles in the air.

Since bird and rose are dear, their joy encores
Our own fair country's progress on the wing,
"All For Good Will" exchanged as knowledge scores,
A happy land of fellowship to ring:—
Ambassador of love, the world-wide rose,
With friendship's call we thrive, our future glows.
                                        —*Marianne Clarke*

NEW YEAR'S GREETING

Across the frozen spaces,
And o'er the rounded hill,
Listen to the echoing
Of all the notes of song combined—
A Happy New Year's here.

Old Father Time goes shuffling on;
Today the infant year is born,
Stands smiling with expectant eyes,
Our year to fashion
And revise.

Conceived within our hearts,
We hold the image
Each has visioned of himself.
Something to live by, grow toward,
Finally achieve.
If then we cannot reach the height
Our spirit is contending,
How happy he who strives.

He adds a virtue here,
And there chips off an edge
Of faulty character.
And each year draws new lines
Of strength and grace
To add unto this pattern
Of his life.

And each of us will know
'Tis well to say,
On New Year's Day,
I do resolve:

To walk with cheerfulness
Where'er I go;
To do whatever task is mine
The best I know;
To write without delay;
Be prompt to pay
All obligations;
With fine courtesy
Invest my way,
And generous judgment give
To all my fellows;
Thus will I strive to live
Each day.

—*Eleanor B. Clausen*

LONGING

I need you dear, you know I do.
  I think of you the whole day through.
I need you, need you so, dear heart,
  And I would always do my part;
My silent longing sends to you
  The hope that you will need me too.
Long since my heart to you was lost.
  Your love I'd win whate'er the cost,
Because the love I give to you,
  My dear, is loyal, firm, and true.

—*Cyrinthia J. Clayton*

ILLUSION

We are but travelers treading o'er a path
Which weary pilgrims oft have trod before
And many yet unborn will tread again.
Yet on we go with joy, as if 'twere new.
Though strewn ofttimes with thorns that pierce our feet,
And roses bloom but rarely on the way,
We still must e'er traverse it and we do,
Remembering not the sharpness of the thorns
One half so much as the roses' sweet perfume,
Their charm and loveliness. And well it is
That memory treasures most and most retains
The things that give us pleasure; for by them
The path is brightened by a roseate glow
That doth illumine all the days of yore.

Sometimes the path's so narrow—steep the way—
We most concentred are upon the new
And fear to retrospect or look beyond
Lest the distractions then should fatal prove.
But not for long; soon the hills divide;
A valley lies between, through which is caught
A vista of the scenes henceforth to come;
And through the haze, though dimly, we discern
The future—bright with a resplendent sun,
Roses without a thorn, and life itself
One grand unending song. Foes are as naught
Compared with our superior strength and skill.
The world is ours, existing, as it seems,
To grant us power, to make us feel that we
Are conquerors, and e'en the world itself
May overcome. Victorious future days!

Such is our view. What though its color fade
And less resplendent prove as we approach,
If in the future it so lovely seem,
And in the past retaineth most its charm
And not its sting when claimed as memory's own.
Well may we thankful be, and e'er remain,
That in Pandora's box when 'scaped the ills

That should afflict the world forevermore,
One solace given was—illusive ray—
That on this path we tread from birth to death,
Forever makes the future charming seem,
And aiding retrospection in her task,
Makes past become to us a source of joy.
Illusion was a gift which ne'er can be surpassed—
It stimulates the rare, enchanting talisman of Hope,
And makes Life more worth living!

—Ethelyn Hardesty Cleaver

FIRST WIFE TO THE SECOND

All's fair! my dear,
All's fair in Love and War!
You have won completely
What I was loath to share.
The spoils take
Unto your charming self.
Drink deep of Life and Love—
All you had dreamed,—
And more.

But this I ask—
In his declining years
Be his gay comrade,
Laugh through tears;
Slow to see a fault,
Quick to sympathize;
Tenderly sweet
But not too wise;
A lithe and winsome staff
To lean upon.

The loneliness of twilight,
The moonlight's ghastly glow,
The hangman's grip upon the throat
That will not give nor go—
'Tis comforting to think, my dear,
These he shall never know;

Brave as he is, 'tis good to think
He shall never know.—
To you I surrender him,
Prisoner bound;
While I go on alone
Bearing a mortal wound.

—Glenna Morris Clevenger

MY CHILDHOOD HOME

I am thinking today of the "Old Home"
That stands at the foot of a hill.
'Twas built to make somebody happy,
Though sorrow came often to fill
The rooms that were big and old-fashioned,
With furniture simple and old,
But someone who lived there was dearer
Than any fine silver or gold.

My Home! in the old apple orchard,
You seemed like a mansion to me
In the days when I was a youngster
And living so happy and free.
'Twas there that our loved ones would gather,
And oh! the dear friends that we met,
The kind that you like to have near you,
The ones you will never forget.

So often I find myself dreaming,
And sometimes my eyes fill with tears;
I see my dear Mother still waiting
To greet me, as in the past years.
Oh! memories dear ever linger,
Stay with me wherever I roam,
For it is so sweet to remember
The scenes of my dear childhood home.

—Oleta Fox Cloos

VAGABOND'S VERSE

Not for me the bright, clean hearth nor a woman's clinging
        hands!
Give me the smell of pungent earth and the sweep of desert sands!
For within me lies a ceaseless yearn to wander, wander ever
Out where gypsy campfires burn; constant I am never!

Every morn when the blazing sun rises over the hill,
Rise I, too, and wander on, feeling my pulses thrill
To the wild delight of a vagrant breeze and a newer, stranger
        road,
Singing a drifter's melodies, carrying never a load
Of trouble or care. I'm fancy-free and wild as the western wave;
I take whatever comes to me, and it's little that I crave.

Alone I search for a Promised Land where chance and change
        may dwell,
But sometimes I think of a tender hand that clasped mine in
        farewell;
And then I curse my wayward heart—but what is the good of
        that?
For I'm a vagabond—set apart—and my home's where I hang
        my hat!

                                        —*Grayce Cole Clymer*

TEXAS

O Texas, my Texas, my native state,
Of thy wonders and glories many poets prate,
Of thy thinking sons and daughters, whose
Thrift and courage determines thy fate,
While across thy broad and fertile land
Soft and gentle southerly breezes fan,
Laden with the fragrance from the products of
        thy land.
O Texas, my Texas, you have no equal
In the minds and hearts of thy people.

                                        —*Alla Coalson*

THE HAPPY VOYAGE

As those who stand upon an unknown shore
To launch a precious vessel, all untried
By shock of storm and impact of the tide,
Nor heed the wreck of vessels launched before,
So we embarked together. Side by side
And hand in hand, upon that unknown sea
Untried adventurers in life were we,
No chart but love our voyaging to guide.

There is so little can be sung or told
Of uneventful journeys. Sun and rain
Are gifts for growth; so ecstasy and pain
Burn out the dross and leave the virgin gold.
I only know that, come what may of fears,
Our love and faith have glorified the years.
                              —*Ethel Gates Coates*

LIFE

I snatched the sparkling cup of life
In feverish haste to drink both long and deep,—
It fell and shivered at my feet.
A broken fragment held a few stray drops
Which mingled with my tears.
With trembling hands I bore it to my lips
And slowly sipped; and lo, the very dregs were sweet.
                    —*Elizabeth Roosa Coddington*

THE OLD PATHWAY

Little path with
              crooked angles
Running like a
              silver thread
Out beyond the
              picket gateway
Out beyond the holly's red.

Friends and loved ones
                    wandered o'er thee
Weaving on the
                    loom of life
Memories golden—dreams
                    so olden,
Reveries of pure delight.

One by one they
                    left the gateway
Down the angles'
                    rugged path,
One by one they left
                    me lonely
Lost in memory's sailing craft.

When I, too, go down
                    the pathway,
Fringed with joys and
                    sorrows too,
May sweet memories
                    sleep eternal
'Neath the shining, morning dew.

May the sunbeams
                    hover o'er thee,
Let the stars like
                    lanterns gleam
On an olden,—golden
                    pathway,
Reveries, redeemed.

                                    —*Nelle J. Colbert*

MARY

O little town of Nazareth
    In the hills of Galilee—
Sweet was the heavenly message borne
    On angel lips to thee.

The choice of all thy maidens
  Of high and low degree,
The message came to Mary,
  Gentle maid of Galilee.

With awe she heard the tidings
  Which soon were understood—
She, the chosen to be crowned,
  The Queen of Motherhood.

Mother of the Saviour—
  Her lips in sweet accord
Sang out in thankful praise,
  "My soul doth magnify the Lord."
                    —*Nelle Collow*

"THE PEACE OF GOD,
WHICH PASSETH ALL UNDERSTANDING"

As through this burdened life,
Struggling with tasks, I plod,
I trust the close of strife
Brings "Peace of God."

Through paths of bitter pain
With tired feet I've trod;
Let the long trial's gain
Be "Peace of God."

When death shall come for me,
In that strange silence shod,
May the sure guerdon be
"The Peace of God."
                    —*Sylvia T. Colony*

BEAUTY OF LIFE

Beauty of life has been given to me
In the patterned leaf of every tree;
In the golden gleam of each ray of light
That comes to me from morn till night;

In the radiant color of every flower,
In fashioned garden or country bower;
In the lilting music of wood bird's call,
In the voice of dear one, best of all.

Beauty for eye and ear and hand,
In voice of sea and voice of land;
Roaring of waves with a rhythmic din,
A low refrain from a violin;
Touch of the hand of a dear old friend,
Words of kindness without end;
Love of man and woman and child,
Of all God's creatures tame and wild.

Love of the life that was given to me,
Love of the life that is to be;
Love of my work and its stern command,
Love of the strength that is in my hand;
O, beauty of life that has come to me,
Let me be grateful enough for thee;
Let me live on and say alway,
"Thank God for the beauty I've found today."

—*Mary Miles Colvin*

FLOWERS

Oh, friend, if you truly love me,
　　Give me my flowers now;
Don't wait until the death-cold damp
　　Has settled on my brow.

I cannot smell their fragrance then,
　　Or hear your loving voice;
So give them to me now, dear friend,
　　And make my heart rejoice.

The path of life is hard to tread,
　　'Tis now I need you most;
When I have passed to that bright shore
　　To greet the Heavenly host,

I will not need you then, my dear,
 So please love me today,
And tell me all the kind, sweet things
 That you some day will say.

Do that little thing today, friend,
 You've waited long to do,
And prove to all the world, my dear,
 That Jesus lives in you.
    —*Nettie McCarver Conover*

GOOD-BY SUMMER

O summer, you have said good-by once more,
And autumn now comes knocking at my door
In rust-gold raiment . . . with lusty throat
Crying the harvest . . . too, murmuring a note

On winter with its glistening rain . . .
The hills will be green again.
The mountains, still and stately, ponder beneath cloaks of white
On spring flowers, gay and colored, and the might

Of rushing streams. O summer, I shall miss you,
Want you so . . . your white moon and the blue
Of dreaming hours . . . surely the zenith is your purpling haze,
And O the splendor of your golden days!
    —*Caroline Converse*

A SUPPLICATION

I could not be
A thing apart—
Aloof from you,
From skies of blue,
From flowers so sweet,
From every leaf
 And twig
 And tree,
I could not be
A thing apart—

So help me
  To be
In unison
  With thee,
And every leaf,
  And twig,
  And tree.

                —Effie Truex Cook

REMEMBRANCE

"Give rosemary for remembrance,"
A saying old yet new,
As through the air—a fragrance rare
Brings thoughts of friendship true.

We wear a poppy once a year
For those who marched away;
They seem so near—yet for their bier
A blood-stained field of clay.

"We take a cup and drink it up"
For friends both far and near;
Then mem'ry strays—to other days
And other scenes so dear.

"I find among my souvenirs"
A letter from a friend;
I read it o'er—then as before
The tears fall to the end.

We often think of those we love
"That we have lost awhile,"
But hearts of gold—are those who hold
The memory of a smile.

                —Elizabeth M. Cooper

PINE WOODS IN WINTER [1]

Oh, little wood, knee-deep in snow
And hemmed in by the old fence row,
With crystal beam and frosted star,
How beautiful and still you are!
I wonder if I might intrude
Upon your lovely solitude.
Instead I only stare and stare,
There's radiant beauty everywhere.
The trees along each columned aisle
Are pyramids of silver, while
A low wind comes to shake them free
And scatter snowflakes carelessly . . .
Each silver flake a parting word
To breathe a prayer my heart has heard.

Oh, little wood, knee-deep in snow,
Just one more look before I go!
—*Inez Culver Corbin*

ON THE PROGRAM [2]

The well-dressed throng of women murmured—stirred;
The singer faced them—bland and calm of mien.
How could he know what miracle occurred
For her who thought she could not dream again—

She was a princess, slender, tall, and fair,
Whose casement opened slowly to the night
That she might lean to throw a red rose where
A troubadour stood singing in the night.

How short are dreams! His magic notes were stilled—
She tucked a white curl close and smoothed her dress.
The promise of her years had been fulfilled—
This youth approached the brink of happiness.

With studied grace she poured and passed his tea—
Spoke graciously, "Your songs enchanted me!"
—*Annette Patton Cornell*

[1] Reprinted from *Blue Moon*, by permission of the publishers.
[2] Reprinted from the *Poets' Forum*, by permission of the publishers.

LIFE'S MORNING, NOON, AND EVENING

Dawn breaks, soft breezes blow, 'tis morning time of life;
The tiny wavelets ebb and flow, there's little now of strife.
A rosy tint adorns the sky, 'tis springtime in the heart;
A burst of song, a lark sweeps by, life plays a joyous part.
A golden radiance over all, love's harp is vibrant, bold!
As out of dreamland comes a call, and the old sweet story's told.

The full-blown rose its beauty sheds in the noontime sun of life;
The tides rise high and roaring ebb against the shoals in strife;
There's warmth and splendor everywhere, and harvest's fruitful
    yield,
And nature's fragrance fills the air, as we roam far afield.
'Tis truth that guides our steps aright, spurred onward to our
    goal—
Our riper years like strong floodlights reveal our wealth of soul.

'Tis eventide, the sun sinks low, yet guides us to our tryst;
Brave helmsmen hold our ships in tow, though skies are amethyst.
The vastness of the deep reveals life's greatest joy and woe,
Strange mysteries that oft conceal the brave heart's overflow.
So rise my soul on life's top crest, and bear the victor's palm,
Submerged in faith, then sink to rest in twilight's holy calm.
                                        —*Audra Powell Cottrille*

THE BROWN BEAVER

Oh, Man, I think I know just why it is you sigh—
It is to be as beautiful and soft and brown as I.

Knowing that when I'm dead, my warm and cuddly skin
Will be tucked tenderly beneath a dimpled chin,

Will be so gently fingered and adored . . .
Death will, to me, much happiness afford.

There be far better things than a smooth, round bosom?
Then you, my doubting friend, are free to choose 'em;

And I'll always have this soothing thought to bless,
That many a brave and daring man has died for less!
                                        —*Flossie Deane Craig*

ON CATOCTIN

Lovely are the distances where peaceful valleys lie,
Blue-walled by mountain ranges, lifting mist-veiled to the sky.

There are cornfields, rich, abundant, and many a white-walled
home,
Green spreading trees and meadows where tranquil cattle roam.

Glowing golden in the picture are the harvest fields of grain,
Nature's bounty richly nurtured by God's gifts of sun and rain.

On the mountain tops, at evening, there are gorgeous tints that
show
In the sun's departing splendor, a rich jeweled afterglow.

There is peace upon the valleys—there is peace upon the hills,
A heaven-sent benediction that my restless spirit stills;

And I know the great Creator through the works of His own hand
Speaks a message in His beauty that my soul may understand.
                                              —*Maria Briscoe Croker*

THE OLD BRASS CLOCK

Within the cracked and scarred mahogany frame,
Black figures on the metal face
Stare out of a faded rose wreath;
In the dim, crude gilt on the glass door
One scarcely sees the peasant women gathering faggots.

The tarnished brass wheels keep turning;
The lead weights sinking;
The pendulum swinging—
After almost a century,
   "Tick tock, tick tock, tick tock.—"
The yellowed mark says,
   "Brass clock,
   Warranted good."

At night,
A little old woman,
Bent, wrinkled, white-haired;
Blue eyes strained and dim;
Cheeks still soft and pink,—
Stands on a chair to wind the clock.—
  "Tick tock, tick tock, tick tock—"
It strikes;
Loudly the harsh, business-like tone
Clangs through the house.

—Mary Cromer

WHEN WINTER COMES

When winter comes with its chilly blast,
  And all the world seems dreary;
We dream of memories of the past,
  All of which makes us cheery.

We see the fields with their blanket of snow,
  As o'er the country we gaze;
And smile to ourselves, as we all know
  It's merely taking the place of the maize.

We miss the green grass all over the lawns,
  And the birds that would come after crumbs.
For unto us a new world dawns,
  Unfolding itself about us, when winter comes.

—Pearl Crooks

TO ONE WHO NEVER KNEW I CARED

I wonder what it was that made me say
"Good-by," and leave you, dear, that fateful day.
How could I stay away, nor even write,
Loving you all the while the way I did?
Instinct, perhaps. I was too young to know
That only if I left you so, I'd keep
The you that I had known, beside me, dear,
Glorious and beautiful, through all these lengthening years.
Instinct, my husband says, guides womenfolk,
Where sense and reason, masculine 'tributes, fail.

I couldn't bear to know you fat and bald,
And hear you chafe about my woman's club!
—*Elsie Thomas Culver*

CHRIST WRITES IN THE SAND

Crafty words and questions at Jesus Christ were flung,
Cruel, and only half hiding the fury of those Pharisees,
As they sought to entangle Him, Who, standing there among
That throng of men, did but use a truth that leapt and stung
The very fibres of their being, and robbed them of their ease.

A stir! the Pharisees draw their holy robes aside,
As thrusting forward into their midst, they drag a woman of sin,
And now—yes, now—what can He say to make her justified,
While her sin and degredation are being loudly cried,
And eager hands reach out for stones, her punishment to begin?

But He, heeding not their vile mouthings and cruelty of word,
Stoops down, and tracing with His right hand
Some unknown letters,—as though He had not heard—
Until a silence fell and a moment passed e'er one had stirred,
And as He rose up, a message lay written in the sand.

"Let him cast the first stone who is without sin,"
He said, and knelt down and began again to write.
And they who had with pride and boasting entered in,
Now slunk out one by one—leaving only the thin
Sound of the woman's sobs, filled with shame and fright.

His writing ended, He turned to her saying, "Woman, where
Are thine accusers now?" and with new wonder she
Answered, "Master, none," sensing in the midst of her despair
The forgiving heart of Him; she heard Him then declare,
"Go thou and sin no more, for neither do I condemn thee."

What wrote Jesus in the sand so long ago?
Not trivial nor idle words with no meaning to impart;
But though no man ever read them, this we know,
He lived that day a message that should grow
In flaming letters of forgiveness in our heart.

—*Lucy Cutright*

A DREAM

I fain would build a little house
　　Up at the end of the street,
In sight of waving fields of corn,
　　Where pavement and meadows meet.

I would not ask for many rooms
　　Just so they'd sunny be,
With flowers and grasses growing round
　　And space to plant a tree.

And oh! I'd want a garden,
　　Where I might hoe and dig
And bring in greens and salsify
　　And cabbages so big!

And in this little dreamed-of house,
　　May there be a little den
With books and blocks and dolls about
　　For children when they come.

And for the grownups always be
　　Good fare and cheer in store;
Where friends might talk, read, sleep, or walk
　　And find a welcome there.

—Irene T. Dague

MOMENTS

I saw a seagull,
Clinging hard against the wind,
Climb a ladder of rain
Up to a low sky.
I saw the silver-bodied drops
Fall gleaming on his wings,—
Saw him, as he cut the rain,
Turn his head sharply
And gulp the cool fresh drops,
Greedy with thirst and pain.

I have shining thoughts
That escape the dusk of my mind
And go soaring
Through the shallows of the sky,
Following wonder
And a broken word,—
Thoughts that return
Refreshed,
And waken me
Breathless in the dawn.

—Martha Brindley Darbyshire

SHADOWS

Bent, vagabondlike,
Tired, worn, humiliated
Because of disappointments left in his bag,
Knowing sweet memories only were taken
And treasured as valuable—
Is dimly visible a silhouette.

Erect, gleeful, buoyant—
Even just born;
Radiant, hopeful, promising
The greatest treasure
Humanity seeks—
But the twain have never met.

—Bert Davis

LIFE'S SECRETS

The dreams of youth to ripe fruition never came;
   No vain regrets for what I sought are mine;
The wine of life, to very dregs, I drain;
   And all its richness in my heart I find.

I have a friend or two, some loved ones dear,
   Who smile with me their love and friendship true,
And drop with mine a sympathizing tear
   When sorrows come, and strengthen me anew.

I have the dawns and sunsets of the years;
  Mine are the seasons, with their changing hue:
For me the massive mountain peak uprears;
  Before me spreads the ocean, deep and blue.

The lilt of bird song from the waving trees;
  The voice of childhood, with its laughter sweet;
The strains of music on the evening breeze;
  All are rich trophies at my feet.

I hold them close, these treasures of my soul,
  Let others have the fame, and pomp of pride,
Vast mansions, jeweled crowns, and heaps of gold;
  The secrets of life's day with me abide.
                                        —*Eliza Timberlake Davis*

ASHES TO ASHES

Ashes to ashes, and one by one
  The names drop out of our prayers;
And one hardly smiles at the face in the glass,
  For who is there left that cares?

There's never a night but the longing comes,
  (For only the wise forget)
And the hour when the clock ticks loudest seems
  The time for a fool's regret.

What does it profit to lie awake,
  Worn with the day's care and cark?
What does it profit to sob and sigh
  And wring one's hands in the dark?

Is there never a chance to set things right,
  Or forget them in all the years?
Can we find no place of repentance if
  We search for it long, with tears?
                                        —*Harriet Winton Davis*

UNRECOMPENSED

They say for every loss there is a gain,
And for each joy our hearts are wrung with woe;
They tell me if a cup of sorrow I must drain,
Then radiant heights I too shall know.

And so I set my feet the tangled way to go;
I strive with whatsoever skill be mine
A rich mosaic of my life below
To weave with balance true and texture fine.

But oh, when in the lonely dark of night
I wakeful lie and scan my feeble art,
I know there is no earthly gain so bright
To recompense for empty arms and aching heart

Because no sunny head within my arms e'er rests
Nor baby hands lie soft upon my fallow breasts.

—Helen H. Davis

ABIGAIL

With great delight I watch
   Sweet Abigail,
When sewing on her quilt
   Of gay percale.

The double wedding ring
   Is the design,
In which two rings are made
   To intertwine.

How fortunate to be
   The one to share
The rings with Abigail
   Who sews with care.

—Sarah Field Davison

THE FOREST

I walked in the forest at morning,
The grass all wet with dew,
And the Sun in majestic splendor
From the East came smiling through.
The birds were twittering love songs
Awakened by Nature's call,
And stepping softly in reverence
I paused to admire it all.

I walked in the forest at noontime
Away from the heat and the strife,
Its cool and refreshing shelter
Brought peace and calm to my life.
The trees stood like giant sentinels
That seemed to challenge my right
To walk in this lovely forest
At morning, at noon, or night.

I walked in the forest at evening
As the Sun sank low in the West,
And high in the leafy bowers
The birds were returning to rest.
Soon night with its inky curtain
Would cover all land and sea
And blot out this lovely forest
That God gave to you and to me.

—Ann Hawley DeLong

RECOMPENSE

Fate hath decreed our lives be lived apart,
But oh, my dear, you're safe within my heart,
And oft in lonely watches of the night
To you my spirit takes its wingèd flight.
What matter, though your face I seldom see,
Doth not the Soul of you belong to me?
And will not God at last with love Divine
Give unto me the Jewel that is mine?
Of small moment the wretched years will be;
For love like ours, there's glad Eternity.

—Edith Curtis De Long

REGRET

If you had been Demeter, Doso named
In that fragrant country where she, grieving, cast
Her lot with mortals, a little while the vast
Wild anger of her heart entrapped and tamed
By earth-made tasks; and I, Demophoon, famed
That even for an hour she held him fast—
You could not more have striven to the last
To give me life unsullied and unlamed.

But when you held me in the potent fire,
I felt it scorch and could not bear the smart;
And not contented with ambrosial mead,
Hungering for food, I satisfied desire.
Now I must walk the low road through the mart
And only glimpse, far up, the road I need.

       —Juanita DeLong

PIONEER WOMAN

I want my own to come to me
When dusk begins to fall;
Strange shadows flit across the floor,
I hear a coyote's call;
And specters grim stalk through the sage,
There shines no friendly light;
My being shrinks with haunting fear,—
Come back, My Own, with night!

Against the fading saffron sky
Strained eyes pursue their quest,
Till they behold a dim grey form,
When lo, my heart's at rest.

       —Elizabeth De Mary

THE RETURN

Now you are gone
 Where lovelier flowers bloom,
Will you forget
 This garden,—yours and mine,

Gay with the patterns
   Woven on Spring's swift loom
In tulips, daffodils,
   And columbine?

Nay, when the first
   Bright star shines in the sky,
And winds are sweet
   With perfume and with dew
Along our path,—
   I hear a night bird cry,—
Oh, not in vain
   My hushed heart waits for you.
                                    —*Lucia Stevens DeMotte*

ANOTHER TOMORROW

Was it only last night in half darkness that I met him midway on
   the stair,
That he gave me a friend's greeting only as I held longing arms
   to him there?
His lips just brushed mine as I waited, not once did he toy with
   my hair—
               Does it come with surprise
               That the Stars have his eyes?
Shivering, I am thrust from our dream world to a plain by the
   wind swept bare.

What is it I have been expecting? I'm no longer a simpering
   bride;
I still have my books and my writing, green fields, blue hills,
   surging tide.
I shall mold my own life to my liking. Where is all that strong
   woman pride?—
               Is the wind sighing so
               Or a dove moaning low?
Dead love cannot be heartbreaking. Tomorrow I'll feel satisfied.

A year has been long in the passing, Oh God of my contrite heart!
Could I thrill once again to his footstep, I would play a wife's
   humblest part.

Life froze when I tried to live without love, so empty are honor
    and art—
              Gentle patters of rain!
              To revive the dead grain?
Pray grant me another tomorrow! Love stirs like new life at its
    start.
                                  —Pauline Lewelling Devitt

YOUTH

Youth is a fragile sweet blossom
    That fades in the noon's burning ray,
Exchanging its delicate petals
    For fruit at the close of the day.

So with the fruit rich in wisdom,
    And mellowed by patience with pain,
The fragile sweet blossom of morning
    Shall know all its beauty again.

Then when the long night has fallen,
    The fruit being garnered in store,
The fragile sweet blossom of morning
    Shall bloom on Eternity's shore.
                              —Julia Hadley Dill

HOME ON THE COLUMBIA

Stands a white old house on the crest of a hill,
    Looking out on a sunrise sky,
Where snow mountains vigil a western stream,
    While the ships of the world go by.

Forest firs shadow this old-time house
    And forest flowers grow in the shade;
An orchard and garden are standing by
    And steppingstone pathways are laid.

In the old-time house are sturdy chairs
    And tables and beds and things;
And toys and games and a trundle bed;—
    Treasures to which memory clings.

Rugs and counterpanes wrought by hand;
   Clocks and pictures and candlesticks,
Books and tea things and linens quaint,
   Fireplaces builded of old red bricks.

There is one who dwells in the white old house
   To keep its altar fires burning,
To welcome and cheer the sons of men
   From the battles of life returning.

From courts of justice and marts of trade
   Wherever they may roam,
Men come in gladness or in grief,
   For the old-time house is "Home."
                     —*Susie B. Dillard*

MY MOUNTAIN NEIGHBORS

The hem of her skirt makes a path to my gate,
   Her hat bears the plume of a cloud.
Her waist is encircled with spruce and with pine,
   My neighbor—so strong and so proud.

Her face is deep-furrowed by storms that have blown;
   She's wrinkled and wind-swept and brown.
Though countless the ages that pass o'er her head,
   She stands there serene, looking down.

A mother she is to the birds and the deer,
   And all the shy life of the wild;
Then why does she seem so forbidding to me,
   An exile, a lost prairie child?

I climb to her shoulder, to glimpse once again
   Horizons she shuts from my sight,
But I see only mountains, range upon range—
   More mountains, to left and to right.

And so when my spirit feels prisoned and sad,
   And I long for my prairies so dear,
I frown at my neighbors, so close and so tall,
   And wish they did not live so near.

But tonight they are outlined, protective and strong,
 Against the blue, star-sprinkled sky;
I think we shall some day be good friends and true,
 My tall mountain neighbors and I.

         —Mildred Gavitt Dodge

"THIS CONTRACT STUFF"

Things round our house have changed, by gum,
The beds are never made and the dishes never done,
My socks are full of holes and the clothes are in a stack
Since Maw's learned how to play this fool game *"contract."*

We used to have hot biscuits that would melt right in your mouth
Now Maw gets home in time to see that the cat's well let out,
And she woke me up the other night when I was dead as a board
And yelled at me to the top of her voice, "I've adequate trump
 support."

The only time I've ever heard Maw not say so very much
Is when she's in a huddle over this fool contract stuff.
Then all she says is words which I don't call as nice
Like "you're vulgarable" and "I've a bust"—but maybe at that
 she's right.

Some ladies came in the other night for just a friendly stop
Which ended in a grand old fight over a card-table top.
And I see why men beat up their wives and this "Reno or Bust"
Those husbands feel the way I do—It's this fool contract stuff.

We used to hear of some real great men like Washington and
 Gandhi
And Maw and I got an awful kick out of old Amos and Andy,
But the real great guy that has done more harm
Than a cyclone has, by heck—
Is this Culbertson guy and whoever he is
I'd like to wring his neck.

         —Mrs. L. M. Donelson

MEMORIAL DAY

The dead immortal! They are the ones whom we honor today,
Over their graves a wreath and tears we lay;
Yet we cannot honor enough those brave, courageous youths
Who fought for our country, for freedom, love, and truth.

Ay! They have won, but have sacrificed their lives,
Have left, to see no more their mothers and their wives;
Out on the turbulent field they had one sacred thought,
It was to save their country, and so they bravely fought.

Yes! It is Memorial Day, a noble day indeed,
Back to our memories come those soldiers' valiant deeds;
A love so deep fills our hearts as we salute and pay tribute
To the ashes of our mourned and lost immortal youths!

—Floria Doria

REALISM

Why do we gaze at the mud and the slime,
When there are clouds and the stars,
And the myriad beautiful sights to be seen
On this wonderful planet of ours?
We know there is mud and we know there is slime,
But we know there is blue sky and fair;
Why do we gaze at the scum and the filth
Instead of this loveliness rare?

Why unceasingly prate of his faults and his sins,
When the goodness of man is so great;
When there's love and compassion and tenderness deep,
More potent than envy and hate?
We know there is always the sin and the wrong,
But we know there is honor and right;
Why do we mention the evil and crime
Instead of nobility's might?

—Vera Wardner Dougan

WEALTH

Flowers by my door;
A babbling brook;
In friends not poor;
Favorite books;
Inglenook.

Bird matins at dusk;
A child at my knee;
Orient musk
On every breeze;
Leafy trees.

Night candles lit
Sounding day's knell;
Drowsy insects that flit
Whispering—All's well;
Carillon bell.

—Nettie A. Downey

A TRIBUTE TO MOTHER

Today we wear the white carnation
In praise of you, Mother dear,
We sons and daughters of all the nation
Return our love to you so near.
In anxious pain you bore us
And in patience you reared us with care,
All through childhood you have watched o'er us,
Our happiness and sorrows did share.

Yours as no other human passion
In all the world doth so endure,
Your Mother love and patience
And all so infinitely pure.
The light of heaven by beauty
Shines in your tender face,
And has pointed us the path of duty,
The way from sin to grace.

Today, to you, my loving Mother,
In cabin, mansion, palace, or hall,
Where'er you are, I send my praises
To let you know you are all in all.
God grant that I, your loving child,
May heed your call of love,
And prove to you there is no other
Like you in all the world, my loving Mother.
                                        —*Innice M. Draper*

"THE CLUB WOMAN"

I'm just a little magazine
So humble and demure,
But if you have not seen me,
You're missing much, I'm sure.

I'm published by the women
From clubs o'er all the state;
And all the news and happenings
I do to you relate.

I'm a friend of all clubwomen,
Cost just fifty cents a year;
If you once subscribe for me,
You'll renew again each year.

I'd like to offer a suggestion
For your Christmas gift, that's new,
Give a subscription to "The Club Woman."
I'd enjoy it, wouldn't you?

If you should have a party,
I'd like to be a prize;
I'm sure that my new owner
Would think you were quite wise.

I've been talked of at conventions
By your own club president,
Won't you try this year to be
A club that's hundred percent?
                                        —*Helen Ritterskamp Dunkerly*

A GOLDEN DREAM

The sun came out of the East
　　And went to the West—
Fourscore years have drifted by
　　Since caravans struggling, steeds perspiring,
Lusty babes suckling, mothers soothing,
　　The Forty-Niners toiled and pushed to the West.

Through mountain crevice and rocky-peak summit,
　　O'er S-Path bridges that wended west
The ox carts jolted; the house goods rattled,
　　Women fainted, but the men pushed west;
The Indians painted and whooped on the summit,
　　The bluebirds startled, fluttered in distance.

The steeds pranced slower, but the men went west
　　O'er rocky summits, bathed violet in sunset;
The sun rose warmer as the throng pushed west.
　　The sun rose warmer and lasted longer,
Its rays grew mellow—the ocean bounded,
　　Faint heart cheered when they found the West.

Orange-blossom fragrance, heavy on misty air,
　　A land o'erburdened with nature's treasure;
The skies more mellow with clouds o'erlaid;
　　A woman's heart and humanity's courage—
A golden dream came out of the East
　　And found a place in the West.
　　　　　　　　　　　　—Kathryn Roeser Dunlap

HOME IS WHERE THE HEART IS

Home is where the heart is,
And friendship is a guest;
A book, a fire, a handclasp,
A place where souls can rest.

Home is where the heart is,
Where children's voices ring;
A blossom at the window,
A tiny bird to sing.

Home is where the heart is,
Be it mansion on the hill,
Or cabin in the valley,
Or cottage by the rill.

Home is where the heart is,
Where friendship is a guest,
Where love and faith and gentleness
Can soothe a heart to rest.

—*Bessie Cary Dunn*

KINDO' DIFFERENT

There is something kindo' different
    In the early Autumn days,
You can feel it in the breezes,
    You can see it in the haze;
Sorto' lazy-like and peaceful
    As if Earth had done her best—
Barrin' lack of rain or sunshine,
    And had settled back to rest.

Nature grows, just like a picture,
    Kindo' faded, worn, and old,
When along comes Autumn trailin'
    Skirts of purple, red, and gold,
And she brushes off the cobwebs,
    Adds some touches here and there
Till the spots that seemed so dingy
    Glow with colors, rich and rare.

Birds, forgettin' wooin' sonnets,
    Fuss and wrangle all tha day,
Callin' jamborees to settle
    When they'd better fly away,
And they congregate together,
    Holdin' tournaments to try
Out the wings of every fledglin'
    For the comin' southward fly.

Mornin's, when the frost is sparklin'
  And the corn a-turnin' brown,
Make you feel it's purtnigh Heaven
  Just to be a-hangin' round,
For the atmosphere, as pungent
  As a wine that's old and rare,
Seems to drive away your worries
  And to banish every care.

There is something kindo' different
  In the early Autumn days,
You can feel it in the breezes,
  You can see it in the haze.
Spring and Summer may be pleasant
  And the Winter weather fine,
But the Autumn, as a season,
  Is the favorite of mine.

—Maude Huston Dunn

SHADOWS

A strange and pensive stillness fills my heart,
While memory recalls a vanished day,
Whose glorious dawn was fated to depart
In clouds that left life's aftermath so gray.

We did not know when we beheld that day
The shadows on the amethystine hills,
We would regret, so soon, deep shades that lay
Between our lives, unsponsored by our wills.

Love's fragrant blossoms turned to golden fruit
Of high esteem, and yet our little tree
Began to wilt and shrivel branch and root,
While we beheld, amazed that this could be.

I hold it true, that vast and boundless love
Fills all the cosmic realm of time and space.
Else, unsustained by succor from above,
Bewildered souls would find no resting place.

—Minnie C. Dunn

REMEMBRANCE

To you, dear heart, who came when skies were darkened
And sorrow's heavy cloud hung drear and low;
Who brought life's sunshine to my heart's lone garden
And caused the fragrant flowers of hope to grow.

To you, whose tender love so pure and glowing
Hath lifted me from darkness and despair
New heights to gain; to you all joy is owing,
And life is rich, so rich, because you care.

To you, beloved, though we are far asunder,
My soul your image fair will ever keep.
Dreaming, I walk with you through autumn sunshine
Finding the peace that made your life complete.

—*Ethel Pechin Dupuis*

COURAGE

Metallic sky, dull coppered slate;
A straggling cornfield, parched and dead;
Unpainted shack, bleak, desolate;
A woman with a drooping head.
But bravely, where the sun is shining still,
Six red tomatoes on a window sill.

Sagging barn; bare, rocky ground;
Hot wind that blasts and chokes and sears;
A crop in ruins all around;
A man bent low with fruitless years.
But bravely, as he plods home after while,
A whistle on the lips that cannot smile.

—*Caroline Cain Durkee*

AUTUMN LEAVES

A roll
A tumble
One by one
They're coming down
With Autumn winds
In Western town.

Jumping
Sliding
Gliding on
All aflutter
Chasing each other
In the gutter.

Bumping
Tumbling
They're coming
Down the hill
Like children playing
Then suddenly still.

Two runs
A leap
Breeze dancing
Frost, rain, snow,
Sunshine vanishing,
North winds blow
Autumn leaves
Aheap
Asleep.

—*Pige Early*

WHAT GOLD CANNOT BUY

A miser old,
A chest of gold,
With trembling hands
The gold he holds.
The time draws nigh
To say good-by—
His eyes are dim,
And dark, the sky.
What does it hold
This chest of gold?
A miser's dreams
Are there all told,
A passport now
It cannot buy
To heaven's port beyond the sky.

A passport now
He cannot buy
To heaven's port beyond the sky.
                    —*Katheryn Sweet Easterday*

A PASSING THOUGHT

There came a thought into my mind,
    A thought of beauty rare;
I loved it and I nurtured it,
    And tried to keep it there.

The month was June,—a perfect day,
    The place a garden sweet,
Where souls of men and flowers dare
    Their God of Life to greet.

My soul was open to the sight
    Of angels hovering near:
A thought of love and peace came in
    To find a lodging there.

In vain, I hoped to keep my guest.
    Though bound with chains of will,
He stole so silently away
    That I am lonely still.
                    —*Maude Brannen Edge*

POSSESSIONS

No one can take away from me:
The shimmering silk of blue-green sea;

The lure
Of tinted sky that softly glows
Through plume-like eucalyptus rows;
Or tall young sycamores gray-white
Against a purple hill at night.

For me
White peak above a scarf of mist
And foothills veiled in amethyst
No dearer are
Than rainbow carpets where flower faces
Enchantment spread in desert places.

And *You*——
No other eyes than mine can see
The stars your clear eyes held for me;
Your symphony of gracious years
Is living music to my ears;
And though you may be worlds away,
Your winging thoughts are mine today.

Rare canvases—my Father's art
Forever burnt upon my heart—
Are mine at will; they paint for me
Possessions—no one else can see.

—*Lillian M. Edmison*

AMERICANIZATION

She sits with tired, work-worn hands at rest,
    Folded and idle in her aproned lap,
The while the teacher spells each word in turn,
    "R-a-p, rap; c-a-p, cap."

What does she think as with her greedy eyes
    She scans each line and tries to take it in?
Will she be happier as she grows more wise?
    "T-i-n, tin; p-i-n, pin."

When now the hour is up and work is done,
    And quietly the books are put away,
She pins her shawl about and takes her leave;
    "B-a-y, bay; d-a-y, day."

Now in her home the children come from school,
    Romping and laughing, telling tales of fun;
With pride she gathers them about her knee;
    "R-u-n, run; s-u-n, sun."

With pride she tells them what she too has learned,
    "Americano" soon she too will speak!
It is for them she labors with those nouns and verbs,
            For them!
For *Tony, Mario,* and *Angélique!*

—*Clara Edwards*

WHAT MAKES A WOMAN'S CLUB

It takes a heap o' plannin' to make a woman's club,
A heap o' thought and notions, and sometimes there's a rub
The wrong way, so that somehow things don't seem to go just
    right;
But rubbin' is the polisher of the mind to keep it bright.
It don't make any difference how good a club has been,
There's always some improvin' if you'll only buckle in
And do your best to fill the part that's been assigned to you;
Now when you're through with plannin',—well—the job is just
    half through.

It takes a heap o' strivin' at the plans that you've outlined,
To make 'em workable and please the folk, but you will find
That for all your earnest strivin' and your days of toil and strain,
You've become a bigger woman and the work was not in vain.
And when at length the year has gone and you reflect a bit,
You're glad that you have made the test and measured up to it.

It takes a heap o' lovin' and some forgivin' too;
You've got to give and take a lot the way yer used to do
When you were playin' at the games of yesteryear, I ken
The rules don't change in club life, any more than they did then.
You've got to bury everything of strife, and if you do—
With plannin', strivin', lovin', you'll come a-smilin' through.
                        —*Zoe Brainerd Edwards*

LEST WE FORGET

When death shall curtain them about,
And all is dark within, without;
When lonely hearts no more can feel,
And trembling lips Death's hand doth seal,
Forget them then, they shall not care,
For naught you say shall enter there.
They shall not see the tears that flow;—
Give them your love before they go.

E'en though you strew their bier with flowers
That blossom midst the summer showers;
And though their fragrance fill the air,
Shedding their perfume everywhere;
'Twill matter not, they ne'er shall know
Aught of their fragrance or their glow;—
Now is the time that you should give
The lovely blossoms, while they live.

If they have caused one tear to flow
As on life's journey they did go;
Forgive them now, too late 'twill be
When still in death their form you see.
Some unkind word maybe you've said,
And made them bitter tears to shed;—
Then right the wrong while they have breath;
There's no forgiveness after death.

—Lois M. Eish

GEORGE WASHINGTON

"First in war" was he,
A soldier and a friend.
A people's freedom was his field,
Which loyally he did defend.

"First in peace" was he,
A leader tested and tried.
A new-born nation was his realm
Which wisely he did guide.

"First in their hearts" was he—
Brave hearts of his countrymen,
Who happy now, from bondage free,
Most gratefully did adore him.

"Father of his country," *is* he,
Honored and revered by all,
Whose name down through the ages
His valiant deeds will ever recall.

—Maryann Weeks Ellis

FROM DAWNING TILL DAWNING

I wish that I could see once more
And see with childish vision keen
The country road that lay between
The schoolhouse and my old home door.

But when in truth I pass that way
Where once abode perennial May,
The dull gray dust lies thick alway
On grass and flower and leafy spray.

The old house too has lost its lure,
For mother isn't in the door
And father plows the fields no more,
Only the old time loves endure.

But love is first and love is last
And love shall greet us on yon shore
And guide us to the friends of yore,
All earthly duties done at last.
                                        —*Mrs. Jennie Emery*

THE WILD CANARIES

They came as always at this time of year;
A thread-like twitter, finer than the talk
Of year-round sparrows, told me they were here.
They swept about upon a golden gale,
They stoned the lawn in gusts of gorgeous hail,
And formed bright drifts beside the garden walk.
They sped more active bombs of bolder bloom
Where dandelion hosts had cast sharp doom.
They rose on wings of sunshine to the crest
Of the persimmon—and the budding haw;
Made yellow outcry I both heard and saw—
In famed magnificence these pilgrims dressed.
—And so, a few hours in the springs and falls
They flash about my yard like gilded balls,
Their coming proving earth's unbroken law.
                                        —*Clara P. Entrekin*

WHEN GOD SPEAKS

God does not speak in crowded rooms,
   But in quiet, empty places
     He speaks to you,
Your heart with courage to imbue.

A crowded room and crowded mind
     He cannot reach;
On mountain tops—in open spaces
     He can best teach,
      And your heart find.
                   —Clara Cox Epperson

NOSTALGIA

O my heart is longing, longing
For my children far away,
And the wind is sighing, sighing,
'Tis a bleak November day.
Leaves are falling on the grass
Whispering hope for those long gone,
While my heart is calling, calling,
Come, my children, come, come home.
                   —Myrtle Hill Erdmann

FROSTY SHADOWS

When peeping o'er the East's gray brink,
Old Sun once caught young Frost's gay wink,
     He laughingly arose
     And lumberingly chose
To chase the merry sprite;

And save where giggling Frost had slid
Between fat trees and safely hid,
     O'er hill and dale
     The sun's bright trail
Splashed green on Winter's white.
                   —Pearl Potter Etz

EVEN WEEDS

The one that sins, judge not.
You cannot know the way
He grew, nor whence he came.
He could not choose the clay
That fashioned him. Perhaps he sprung
From loins old in sin that blindly flung
This soul upon the earth.
Perhaps he dimly seeks
The good you know
By right of better birth.

Through darkened heritage
Groping toward the sun
He falls. Your hand should lead,
You, the enlightened one.
Love's miracle still heals the blind,
And humble helping hands new mercies find.
Know, in the quest of right,
Though some were born but weeds,
Yet even weeds
Reach upward toward the light.

—*Estella Shields Fahringer*

THE FABLE OF THE FINCHES[1]

Little friendly, golden Finches
Singing in my linden tree!
I can measure you by inches,
Fragile bits of living glee.

Once, a sunbeam—dropped and broken
All to smithereens, and more!—
Sprouted wings on each wee token,
Grew to Finches, by the score.

All my plans may break and shatter,
Spoiling all that I would do,
But I courage take (no matter),
Finches out of fragments grew!

—*Ruth Scofield Fargo*

[1]Reprinted from *Byways of Beauty*, by permission of the publishers.

LIFE WAS ALL ABOUT HIM

I heard a boy, a high-school boy,
complain and fret, the
town was small, and cramped
his style, and hindered his stride;
he must get out into the world where things
happen, where Life abounds,
Life and Things—
Ah me.

When just around the corner
towards the setting sun,
a baby lay dead, a puny little
weakling, made so through lack
of bread; the father shiftless,
dull of mind, and slow;
the poor mother watched the
child weaker, weaker grow;
and in the big house
on the hill, a wee bit
of femininity
has arrived, "out of the
nowhere into here."
Ah me—

If I could only make
that boy, that bright-
eyed high-school boy, to
know and understand that
Life was all about him, for
some day he'll know there are
no bigger things on this old
earth than being trained to meet
both Death and Birth.

—Maude Arney Farnsworth

LIEBESTRAUM

A melody so haunting
Has woven a fairy spell,
Its charming theme of romance
Within our hearts to dwell.

It seems to tell a story
Of something rare and fine,
Love in all its mystery
Between your life and mine.

The miles that lie between us
Are nothing if we hear
The magic strains of *Liebestraum*—
Our dream of love, my dear.

                              —*Hilda Butler Farr*

MISPLACED SYMPATHY

Poor city man! I pity you,
   Deep in my heart, I really do.
Hearing you say as you did today,
   "How tiresome to make small towns this way;
A man might as well in prison stay,
   As to travel the country roads, *I* say."

Would you like better the city street,
   The hurrying throng with no thought at all
For the men and women who toil and rush
   Hither and yon at the time-clock's call?

Why, man! I woke at break of day,
   Hearing a lovely cardinal say,
"Pretty—pretty—pretty, the day is fine,
   Wake up! Wake up! Oh, friend of mine,
Thanks for the meal your hands have spread;
   Sunflower seeds are my daily bread."

Trees are budding, tulips are up
   Out of snow-covered garden bed—
In a very short time their gorgeous bloom
   Will be a riot of color red.

So let me travel the country way,
   Friendly trees lining the paths I stray,
Leading to joys that are always new,
   Lovely green meadows and skies so blue;
Poor city man, don't pity *me*,
   Your unseeing eyes need *my* sympathy!
                —*Zoe H. Feldwisch*

JANUARY

A pale moon was watching "Jack Frost" paint the trees
With a magical brush,
While the leaves that had fallen were blown by the breeze
In a terrible rush.
A wee drop of dew turned to diamonds and jade,
That a monarch might wear;
A breath of south wind through the valley and glade
Lent a song to the air.

Old "Mother Earth" with a smile to the Fall
Had said, "Can't you see—
The blossoms and trees, the flowers and all
Will come back to me?"
Even you, as life's pleasures drop off by degrees,
Will hail a new birth,
And will pillow your head—like any of these,
On the bosom of Earth.
                —*Margaret Cotter Ferguson*

JUST WORDS

Words, just little things are they,
   Lightly spoken every day.
Roses, thorns, or thistledown
   Are immured in every sound.

Words, just little things, you know,
　Ofttimes into mountains grow.
Just one tiny little word
　Someone spoke or overheard.

Words, just one can mar a day,
　Cause the sun to fade away,
Break the heart of someone gay,
　Or a soul to go astray.

Words, ah words of love and cheer!
　Echo them afar and near,
Let our lives be one glad song
　Of the words that do no wrong.
　　　　　　　　　—Tilla Ferguson

'TIS SPRING

Let's see, I hardly know
Where to begin, which way to go.

The dishes to wash, the bed to make,
A picture to paint, a cake to bake.

There's a poem I'd like to write,
My! This house is a fright!

Oh, well, for today the house can go,
There's just no time to mend or sew.

The out-of-doors is calling me,
The call of bird and bumblebee.

The wistaria is heavy with perfume,
So why stay here and fret and fume.

I'll take time to paint the flowers,
Outside enjoy the golden hours.
　　　　　　　　—Helen Wilson Fernandez

AN ILLUSION

If I could have seen you depart
And known the touch of your hand,
While wraiths of grief surged at my heart,
Could I have waited the angel band?

If I knew the celestial glen to search,
The way to follow that leads to you,
I'd come when the night birds from leafy perch
Call through the twilight the way we knew.

If my longing soul could understand
Why dreams of life's visioning are no more
Than an empty shell from the strand
As it wails from its long-lost shore;

If I tremble with love's suppressed yearning,
Waiting in wonderment for the day
When to my beloved's arm I will cling,
While on memories' harp a faith note we play;

If when the yesterdays are today,
And our song of life, love's refrain;
Oh! then how joyous shall be our lay,
Its lilt ne'er again lost in life's pain.

If it be true, death is but a Way,
Then I have looked in shadowy eyes so sweet;
And trembling, enrapt in a strange ray,
Our souls thrilled as they smiled to meet.

—Margherita Gardner Fetter

EVENING

Dreamy, poising dragonflies
With purple-dusted wings
Hover over waters
Where endless evening sings . . .

This fading, lovely evening
Runs through me like a stream
Of straying moments
Known once, in a dream.

—Iduna Bertel Field

SUNSET CLOUDS

The sunset clouds are gathering over yonder in the west,
While the sun is sinking slowly as all nature goes to rest;
The gold and silver lining shows the clouds in bright array,
As the evening shadows linger at the closing of the day.
Oh! Sunset Clouds, we love thee.

No one can paint the beauty of the sunset clouds so fair;
Their rainbow tints are glittering like jewels rich and rare,
A flame of light and glory as they're rolling o'er and o'er
In perfect gleams of splendor that will last forevermore.
Oh! Sunset Clouds, we adore thee.

The twilight shadows lengthen scattering dewdrops on the flowers,
The sunset clouds are hovering o'er all the leafy bowers.
Be quick, my soul, to grasp the hand that paints them in the sky,
The Lord of all the Universe, no mortal can deny.
Oh! Sunset Clouds, good-by.

—Maud Brockett Finch

TO NATURE

When I look into your eyes,
I feel the mystic, dreamy, subtle charm
Of a wonder world.
I sense the muse of the woodland nymphs,
The moods and ecstasies of angel realms,
And the delight of busy fairy hands.
I see love clothed in radiant forms,
Myriad-colored cloaks of celestial splendor—
Shining garbs of true realities
Untouched by man's much thinking;
While the softer tones of your winged lyre
Border in pastel shades a path you've made
To the ever-flowing fount of truth,
Of wisdom, and of life abundant, free—
Beckoning me on to quaff
Of the naked bliss of eternity,
Where in His fullness
God dwells.

—Emma O. Finney

EARTH-BOUND

I am a miser, for I hoard my treasures,
Selfish through loving them o'ermuch,
Hearts given me for safekeeping;
Fragile they are beneath an alien touch.

I am a spendthrift, for I waste my substance.
Love to the least of His I try to give;
All the inanimate creation
Takes of the strength I have to live.

I am a pauper, for I go through life a-begging,
Begging for virtues that I need each day—
Simeon Stylites on his pillar seeking
For help to know the righteous way.

I am a prince, because gifts have been given
Never deserved, except that I have tried,
Failed, and tried again undaunted.
I am a prince without a bit of pride.

—Lisbeth Fish

SPRING AND MOTHER

Far away in wooded fields,
Neath the grass and mosses
Sleeping,
Nestling so still, so low,
Little heads are shyly peeping,
Waiting for the snows to go;
Violets, May-apple blossoms,
Forget-me-nots that you loved so.

They bring back childhood days to me,
School hours over, oft I
Gathered,
Mother, these sweet flowers for thee.
O'er hill and bank of stream I wandered;
To part from thee I never thought;
Dear to me are first Spring blossoms,
Dear the precepts that you taught.

—Caroline Darr Fitzsimmons

AMERICA'S FLOWER SONG

Wild wayside flowers are we,
Sweet buds of liberty,
In joy we sing.
In land of wanderer's pride,
Often his way we guide,
From every mountainside
True joy we bring.

Aroma in the breeze,
Floating from all the trees—
In odors sweet.
Let mortal hearts awake;
Let all that breathe partake;
And for their joyous sake
Our fragrance meet.

Our folk, we beg of thee,
People of liberty,
To leave us free.
Long may the land be bright
With our glorious sight;
Protect us with thy right—
Our country thee.

—*Margaret Paxson Flack*

MOTHERHOOD

How still the house is!
Yesterday noisy little trucks dashed down the hall,
And sturdy heels left marks upon my polished floors.
Today the steps are free of mud,
There are no toys to put away.
My little boy is sick.
Lord Jesus, heal my little boy!

He is burning hot,
And there is nothing I can do. I dread the night.
O Jesus, you were once a little boy.

I wonder were you ever sick,
And did the gentle Mary pray for you?
O hear me now.
Lord Jesus, heal my little boy!

—Elizabeth Poate Fleming

ODE TO WASHINGTON

Out of the pages of history, beyond our memories' ken,
A figure stands colossal, high o'er the heads of men.
Time has burnished the luster of his brilliant and clear-seeing
    mind,
He only built the foundation and left a dream behind.

Now it would seem that the powers above had sent a man such
    as him
To shape the path for a nation to tread, then so obscure and dim.
Ways of the Old World, just shaken free, new guides, new laws
    yet untried,
A future he saw, without shackles or shame, the old order defied.

Two hundred years of struggle and strife, joy and achievement,
    too,
A nation as stanch as the foundation rock, to his ideal we hew.
Washington, this day we need your faith, your courage, and
    vision to see afar
Beyond the dim horizon, light of tomorrow's star.

—Lillian R. Fletcher

CHRISTMAS MORN—THEN AND NOW

Gray dawn, pale candlelight, and bubbling glee
Of childish ecstasy. Oh, see, ahoy!
Beneath the gayly glitt'ring Christmas tree,
A life-sized doll. What paroxysms of joy!
Gray dawn, dimm'd chapel lights, and vested choir
That chants of Christ's Nativity. A tear
Of joy, a soul enthralled in radiant fire
Of awe—a mutual dream with Mary, clear!
The snows of thirty years—of happy years—
Have brought their worries, cares, and painful woes;

But, too, their wisdom, wealth of joys and cheers
Enrich the worth of life, whence Love's spring flows.
Dear Child, fondling that selfsame doll! I see
With Mother—heart and soul, what joys have we!
                              —*Rhoda Hartman Fogle*

LOVE SPEAKS

If I could stand, dear child of mine,
Between the world and you,
And keep your life untouched by sin,
The sordid from your view;

If I could make the world come close,
Yet yield but precious truths,
And keeping back the pain of life,
Give only that which soothes;

If I could keep your trust in men,
Your faith in God and right,
And all the things that bring unrest
Put far beyond your sight;

I wonder, child, if through the years—
'Twould show my love, I know—
And yet I wonder from my heart,
If you'd be happier so.

There is a pain that purifies;
Loss may be gain, I know;
Each life must bear its own proud load,
And reap what it shall sow.

But standing by each hour, my child,
My heart shall bleed anew,
For every pain that comes to you
Shall be to me as two!
                              —*Ida M. Folsom*

YOUTH

Youth is not a time of life
  Measured by the years,
The young are often aged
  By sorrow and tears.

Youth is but a state of mind,
  Measured by ideals;
Those old in years are often young,
  The game of life reveals.

Wrinkles in the face appear,
  Painted by the years,
But wrinkles etched upon the soul
  Are put there by our fears.

Faith and hope will keep us young,
  Courage kills despair,
Time cannot take the toll of years
  If enthusiasm's there.

So hold fast to your ideals,
  Fill your life with worth-while things,
So that in the end we marvel
  At the joy such living brings.

—Ida M. Forrest

RAINY NIGHTS

By day my lawn is stark and bare,
(What strength have I to make it fair!)
The Sun's fierce glare in noonday's heat
Reveals its scars, weed-grown and deep.
I turn my eyes and will not trace
The ugly lines across the place;
They think I do not care, but oh!
The jagged ruts tear at me so!

But rainy nights! why then I creep
To sit in darkness still and deep,
And from my window gaze upon
My much transfigured, radiant lawn,
And dream it is a lovely lake
O'er which the quivering moonbeams shake.
(The moonbeams though are naught at all
But rays from street lights straight and tall.)
Yet still I sit, while the kind rain
Taps gently on my windowpane;
While now and then a fitful breeze
Sets leaves to dancing on the trees.

When morning nears, all wet and gray,
I draw my shades and turn away,
For well I know, the prying dawn
Will turn my lake to barren lawn.

                                              —*Nannie Laura Fortson*

SUNSET

I saw an aeroplane
    Against the setting sun,
There in the waning light
    Just as my task was done.

Like some great bird outstretched,
    Silhouetted in the sky,
Straight to its course it held,
    Gallantly did it fly.

Upward and ever on
    Into the limitless blue;
Gazing in body below,
    My spirit aloft with it flew.

When I come to the end,
    And life's long race is run,
Would that I too might fly
    Straight into the setting sun!

                                       —*Mrs. Dorothy Talbott Foster*

WE KNOW

During this life that we have to live,
If we receive, we must surely give.

That others' rights we have to respect;
Many duties we must not neglect.

God has a plan for each day and year,
If we follow it, we need not fear.

This world is filled with sorrow and care,
Heartaches, loneliness, poverty, despair.

That would have always been our sad plight,
If Christ had not come to earth that night.

How much does He mean to us today,
The Babe that came to earth that glad day?

He brought joy, peace, happiness, and mirth
Down from high heaven to save the earth.

We can all have this peace in our heart,
If we live for Him and do our part.

Let us live for others, make them glad;
Help the needy, and comfort the sad.

Christ will look down from his home above
And bless our lives with His divine love.

We can make this year the best of all,
And know with His help we will not fall.

We haven't long on this earth to roam
Until He will say, "Well done, come home."

We must not sin and fall by the way,
But stand firm and true until that day.
—*Mrs. Ovie Fralick*

A PRAYER

More than lure of mystic lands beyond the sea,
Do the beauties of my Homeland call to me.
Great and wondrous are the scenes of ancient Rome;
Dearer to me are the tender ties of home.

Wealth and power a gay existence oft portray;
Make me happy in the blessings of the day.
In the journey o'er life's highway as I go,
Lasting peace and true perspective may I know.

Not in vain and futile search for the rainbow,
Give content and peace in simple joys I know.
Banish longing for the things that cannot be,
Grant me, Lord, a calm felicity.

—Martha Jeannette Francis

ALONE

Over the trackless sea, from dawn to dawn,
    Ever the ships sail on,—
    Vessels of many sorts,—
Bearing on sturdy keel, to distant ports,
Peasants and belted earls,—kings and their courts.
    Buffeted sore, and blown,
Yet must each gallant vessel make its destined way—alone.

Freighter and liner vast, and yacht and yawl,—
    Ocean-craft great and small
    Follow a guiding star.
Often they sight each other from afar,
Or heed the wireless call, where dangers are.
    Yet, though its path be known,
Onward through storm and sunshine each must find its way—
    alone.

Out on the restless, changing Sea of Life,
    Breasting its waves of strife,
    Myriad human souls
Speed over far-flung ways to fated goals.

Many a barque, too frail for deeps and shoals,
　Dreading the years' unknown,
Flies a courageous banner as it struggles on—alone.

Fleets of immortal souls may stem the tide,
　Voyaging side by side.
　Love is the shining ray,
Lighting the path of duty day by day.
Yet, in a secret chamber, hid away,
　Agonies all its own,
Doubts and misunderstandings, every soul must bear—alone.

Master of Human Ships, who launched them all,
　List to our wireless call:—
　Send us a beacon light,
So that we be not frightened in the night,
Nor change our course to one that seems more bright.
　Then, when the day is done,
Fearlessly toward the sunset we shall sail away—alone.
　　　　　　　　　　　　　　　—Elizabeth Frear

TO HER

Your life was lyric. When the woods were dumb,
And April's heralds failed to come,
Lilting and jocund your prophetic ear
Caught the first wistful notes of spring,
And heard in ecstasy the whirring wing
Of the awakening year.

In breathless days of August yours the thrill
Of silvery ripples on the hill;
You spread your joyous wings and blithely danced.
In answer to the south wind's moan
You called the trade wind in a clarion tone;
You laughed; you were entranced.

Always an oasis the desert held
For you where cooling waters welled,
Purling through meadow grasses of your mind.
Far inland you would hear the roar
Of breakers, and exulting in that shore
You leaped to meet your kind.

O Lyric Love, tell me how do you fare
Beyond our sea, beyond our air,
But not beyond my fountain of desire!
A sister to the Pleiades,
Upon the hills of heaven, by starry seas,
You dance and strike the lyre?
                              —*Mary Dillingham Frear*

DO YOU KNOW?

About ten or fifteen years ago,
  Or thereabouts, more or less or so,
It was surprising how much I knew
  About the way other folks should do.

I knew just how Mrs. Z. could make
  Fancywork that would take the cake;
Though Mrs. Z's swollen hands
  Were held in rheumatism's bands.

I could, also, almost tell
  Where my neighbor should have his well;
Why, anyone with half a brain
  Would put it between the barn and drain.

When Mr. Skinner's dog was dead,
  Hit by a car and lost his head,
I could have told him what to do;
  Yes, indeed, sue, man, sue.

Now I surely know much more
  Than I ever did before,
Yet when someone wants to know
  About this or that, and shall they do it so;

In which bank they'll put their dough;
  Whether they'll draw it out or no?
I can't even guess, much less know,
  Then honestly and frankly tell them so.
                              —*Grace Brown Frink*

LONELINESS

Was e'er a pen so fine and strong
That it could trace the lonely song,
A song that could but half express
The bitter pain of loneliness?

Though ores be forged with skill and care,
And point be set with diamond rare,
Though be the metal steel or gold,
The heart's lone pain is still untold.

Nor can it ever be expressed,
This pain that haunts the lonely breast,
Too subtle far for mortal mind
To pen its depths in verse refined.

—Susie Whitmarsh Fry

HERITAGE

Our birdman loved his ship.
The spirit of the pioneers was in
        his veins.
Adventuring was the acme of his dreams.
And so we feel
That as his spirit winged its way into
        the Great Unknown
That bright Autumnal morn,
It was with hope and courage that he
        ventured forth
To take his place with friends and
        kin e'en as he did on earth.

—May Bryant Fullam

THE RUIN

About this place there drifts a sense of peace,
Of fulsome days and rosy twilights when,
On cool-cropped lawn, young children found release,
And shouted with the wind against their brows.

Out of the past a fragrant incense darts
Of wood smoke, and a high thin note is set
To merge with dreams. The broken things and hearts
The world forgets, turn silently to dust;
While round about, men pound and build in steel
Their monuments, to crumble and reveal.

—Merle Fullmer

A MOTHER'S LOVE

Who knows what depths it reaches,
To what heights it goes?
Only a gleam of sun upon life's ocean rests,
As the sands in the hourglass run.
Has it but touched the restless waves
It sought with such intensity to warm?
The mighty deep flows on and on with unconcern.
There is no path to tell whence came the sun,
There is no way to judge this force of Mother love.
Sometimes it seems a vain and useless memory,
Yet down the ages, long as time and tide themselves,
We've held this legend sacred.
Shall I have faith then to go on
Believing that the sun still shines,
That warmth still lingers on at Sundown?

—Mary Wanzer Furnish

A LITTLE BIT OF HEAVEN

A little bit of heaven
Comes earthward every day,
And you will sense its presence
When it comes along your way,
If your thoughts are pure and wholesome
And your heart is full of love,
And you're glad that you are living,
And that there's a God above.

A little bit of heaven
Can be seen the whole day through
From early dawn till nightfall
In the kind acts that we do.

Just an impulse put in action
To do something for man's good,
Adds another stone so noble
To the shrine of brotherhood.

A little bit of heaven
Comes to us in song of bird,
In the babbling brook's sweet music,
Or a kindly, spoken word,
In a friendly smile or handclasp;
Oh, how wonderful to know
That a little bit of heaven
Is sent to earth below!

—Katharine Gordon Gabell

MY GARDEN GUESTS

A bluebird found a hole in my old china tree,
"Chir-rip, chir-ree,"
He said to me.
"Go on in,"
I said to him,
"And I shall gladly your hostess be."

Another one joined him from not far away,
"Chir-rip, chir-ray,"
She was so gay!
"Yes, I know
He's your beau.
I, too, was married the month of May."

Three more in the little hole now there be,
"Chee-chee, chee-chee,"
So say all three.
House or nest,
Which is best?
God fits the need for them as for me.

—Roberta Gage

DESIRE MINTER

"Mr. Carver and his wife dyed the first year; he in ye spring, she in ye somer; also, his man Roger and ye little boy Jasper dyed before either of them, of ye commone infection. Desire Minter returned to her friends, & proved not very well, and dyed in England."

Bradford's History of Plimouth Plantation

She sees the white mist rise to blot the land . . .
The homeland of her childhood! . . . England's shore!
Now only trails the winding path of foam
To kiss the keel and write a brief farewell.
So like the moon that drifts across the day,
The light that dreams within her land-locked eyes;
So like cool lilies clouds have wept upon,
The silky pallor of her tear-washed cheeks.

She draws a small child closer from the wind
That whips her gray frock to a dancing sail
More fair to look upon than those that fill
With power of progress high above her head,
And flap an answer to the gulls' bleak cry
As ever circling they descend and rise
In broken rhythm. *All the world for her*
In this still moment is the visioning
Of distant hopes and dear remembrances.

The day grows dark, and darker grows the wave,—
The wind drives fury with a cruel hand
Against the shivering frame of this brave ship,
The Mayflower! . . . the hope of troubled souls
Who seek a quiet place to reach their God.
Desire reads her prayers, and talks and sings
To keep the child from fear, and ease the look
Of terror on the mother's face.
There is no fear in her . . . she walks as one
Compelled by powers not her own to move—
A flower budding in a desert place
With perfect patience.

At last the day!
A fir-masked shore beneath November skies;
Her voice ascending in the common prayer;

New soil at last beneath her eager feet;
The song unburdened in a flood of tears!

The days of cruel hardship come too near.
She lays a flower in the child's cold hands
And dares not look upon the mother's face.
All is so still, so still, beneath this sky,
And God's way further from the mind's belief.
Oh, bitter, bitter days of praise and grief!

She sees the dry sod turned to take the dead
Three times within the sun's swift flight.
Too great the price this stern New World demands.
She kneels upon the sandy beach and knows
More than a sadness . . . in each frowning cloud
She sights an enemy, and in the sea
A stubborn ally daring her to leave
This place and find her youth once more!

She sees the white mist rise to blot the land . . .
Now only trails the winding path of foam
To kiss the keel and write a brief farewell.
"Farewell, ye Pilgrims, let the axe take toll . . .
England . . . England is calling to my soul!"
—*Marion Perham Gale*

HEAVENLY FACES

Thy faces before me now I see,
A radiance filled with joy and glee,
As though from heaven looking down
To speed us dear ones left below
To great works of love and cheer,
To make the old world brighter.

Sometimes our path is hard here below,
But when we think of all we love,
Our task seems brighter as to God
We grow nearer every day and
The ones gone before.
—*Mrs. Cora Young Ganner*

IMMACULATE

I have always admired women
Who kept immaculate houses,
The restfulness of everything in place,
No littered papers or books awry.

My house has always had schoolbooks
On chairs and unexpected places,
Skates in the hall, and
Tennis rackets on the tables.

It is in order now.
My boy has gone away to school.
The papers are neatly folded,
His baseball bat is in the closet.

I do not like an immaculate house—
It shelters a hungry heart.
                              —*Uarda Rosamond Garrett*

ECHOES

Snapped!—is the string of the Harp,
    And ended is the singing.
The Storyteller's tale is told;
    And the Bell's stopped ringing.

Yet is there silence? No, ah no!
    The Echoes will not have it so.
And all the Dead are dumb, you say?
    But who so eloquent as they!
                              —*Margaret Root Garvin*

FULFILLMENT

Happy is he who in life's field shall gain
One fair, tall flower, strong-rooted, fully blown,
From all the dreams his youth had fondly sown;
One flower, to recompense his toil and pain,
And triumph breathe above the stress and strain
Of long endeavor. Shall the tree bemoan
That all its eager blossoms have not grown
To leafy heights, and sigh that life is vain?

Rather rejoice, old tree, that many a bud
Gladdened a little child's soft clasp, and died
Contented there; that yet another part
Lived but to give the downy nestlings food;
And others, early fallen, crushed, yet bide
Close round thy roots, enriching thine own heart.
                              —*Frances Moore Geiger*

A MOTHER'S PRAYER

The sun is brightly shining,
Not a cloud is overhead,
Yet the heart is repining,
And a tear or two is shed.
   For babyhood is past,
   The day has come at last
When our Bobby starts to school.

Father, lend Thy watchful care,
Wilt Thou ever present be?
Mothers can't be everywhere,
They may only trust in Thee.
   E'er keep him in Thy sight,
   From morning till the night,
When our Bobby goes to school.

Bless his little hands that they
May away from mischief keep,
Round about him in his play,
Let no evil shadows creep.
   May he know, in Thy love,
   Thou'rt watching from above,
When our Bobby is at school.

Bless his feet—lead where is best,
Only good for Thee to do,
And thus may his life be blessed
By the lovely, pure, and true.
   May his soul give Thee praise,
   For Thy care through the days,
When our Bobby goes to school.
                              —*Edith M. Gemmer*

ARCTURUS LENDS HIS LIGHT

Arcturus! shepherd of the crimson beams,
Thou lovely radiance of summer night,
Whose constant benediction gently streams
From out the heavens, forty years of light
Away, what vagrant dream directed thee
To fan thy living spark into a flame
Blazing a trail across infinity,
Giving to science an enduring name?

"Or canst thou guide Arcturus with his sons?"
Yea, over highways of celestial sod,
Where only silver heel of star mist runs,
Where only wing the cosmic rays of God.
Man's vision leaps another earthly bar,
To light an exposition with a star.

—*Marie D'Autremont Gerry*

HOUSE OF CARDS

I builded carelessly, nor gave much thought
To workmanship; my structure towered high,
Its splendor dazzling to the casual eye.—
So ornate was this edifice I wrought,
The world acclaimed me as each wing and tower
Took shape, as if by subtle genius planned.
None guessed the narrow distance that it spanned;
A few there were who envied me my power.
And then,—almost without a warning sound,
The entire structure toppled to the ground.

The plaudits ceased; the world, in hurrying by,
Too soon forgot my meteoric part.
I lacked an understanding of my art;
How could I hope my tower would reach the sky
When no foundation held it firm and sure?
No architect can carry out his dreams
With crooked columns, worn and crumbling beams,
Rich, painted glass with shutters insecure.—
I since have learned no structure stands alone,
Unless Love helps to build the cornerstone.

—*Sara Roberta Getty*

MY PRAYER

Dear Lord, I pray for simple things;
　　A song, a smile,
The joy of friendship true,
Friendship that warms my very soul
　　And thrills me through and through.

A sparkling stream where sunlight's caught
And flashed at me again like rippling laughter.

A bird on high in the clear blue sky,
A violet hid 'neath a stone.

My baby's little pattering feet
And his precious smile it is mine to greet.

A kitchen bright with dishes blue,
Someone's eyes that shine like the morning dew,
I pray for these simple things—
　　Don't you?

　　　　　　　　　　　　—Mrs. Louise Gewin

THE THOROUGHBRED

'Way out in front just a-breezin' along—
Like nobody's business—listen for the gong,
A thoroughbred is racin', his hoofs beat a song—
You'll find him in front just breezin' along.

Steppin' out in front, his head held so high,
You'd think he was seein' stars in the sky—
A thoroughbred is racin'—see the sparks fly—
'Way out in front he's tellin' 'em good-by.

Bet your bottom dollar, you'll not go wrong,
See the lordly air he's castin' o'er the throng—
A thoroughbred is racin', he's goin' strong
'Way out in front just a-breezin' along.

A lesson he is teachin'—Are you goin' strong—
Are you steppin' lively, on your lips a song—
A thoroughbred in breedin'?—Then you belong
'Way out in front just a-breezin' along.

—*Kate Downing Ghent*

EMPTY AIR CASTLES

I have closed the doors of my castle
   After I looked inside;
It was empty, lone, and dreary,
   And I cared not there to abide.

For no more do my airy fancies come
   To dance through my castle halls,
And no more do my fancied heroes now
   Hang on my castle walls.

Ah, many a time I came with joy
   To open my castle gate;
From a tired day I came to play
   And there for my love to wait.

But now I have no more illusions,
   No dreams do I dream as of old,
And out of my dear dead fancies
   A story might be told.

Ah, many a story might be told
   Of our dreams and our loves now dead,
Of the eyes that were bright with love's true light
   And the things that were left unsaid.

Of the thoughts that our hearts were filled with,
   Of our loves left unexpressed,
Of the hearts once so warm and tender
   Now gone to eternal rest.

I have closed the last door of my castle,
   As nothing was left inside,
And I could not bear to stay long there
   When love was no more by my side.

—*Marguerite Gianella*

PRAYERS I SAW ASCEND

I never saw a prayer ascend to God
Until I went to Ireland.

Incense breathing from a censer
Simulates a prayer,
But it is colorless,
Its swinging mechanism apparent
To eye and ear.

In Ireland,
From every humble roof of thatch,
From the one peat fire through the one chimney,
Household prayers arise,
Pale blue, transparent,
Natural and unlabored as a placid breath,
So nearly matching the calm of heaven's blue
As scarcely to be discerned
Till seen against a tree's green foliage.
Fresh and ever young,
They seem the essence made visible
Of that spirit which keeps forever young
The blue eyes, smiling from weathered faces,
Of the mothers of Ireland.

In Ireland I did not see
The little people of the glen,
But many a prayer I saw ascend to God.
                                        —*Bertha L. Gibbons*

MY GARDEN

Come where the columbine and roses too
Are fragrant with the evening dew,
And the stars deck the sky like a queen,
Where foamy white clouds are seen,
Out where the soft breezes blow,
To a place of peace that I know—
Where the leaves whisper and sigh,
And soft shadows in the moonlight lie—

Where all nature breathes of love,
And the moon smiles down from above—
Where tall poplars gleam and nod,
There in the golden silence with God.

—Ethel Annette Gifford

MY PINE TREE

Vandal-scarred—still dost thou keep
     vigil o'er lesser, tenderer things,
Jasmine, azalea, and dainty violet.
And toward thy rugged base a near-by
     shadowed pool
Sends, singing happily, a rivulet.

—Demmon Gilbert

WINGS

The earth is now full of such wonderful things
My feet are too slow, I want strong rushing wings
To ride through the night on the lightning's bright path,
And sink to the earth with the storm's aftermath;
Alone to stand poised on a high mountain peak,
Then deep in a mine, rich treasures to seek;
To cling with both hands to a glittering star
And rush through the ether to glories afar.
No forces could stay me, on earth, sea, or sky,
My arms are outstretched—Oh God! let me fly!

—Elise Brice Gillespie

HEART BALM

Oh! heart, wellspring of the Soul,
Pour your gentle balm of tears
O'er the aching scars of yesterday,
Healing the pain of sweet Memory
As she rushes through the corridors of Time,
Bruising her tenderness
On the great, stone pillars of the Years.

—Mary White Gillespie

THE WHIPPOORWILL'S SONG

Whippoorwill is calling,
Calling, calling me,
All the night enthralling
With his melody.

Something magic in his voice
Makes the tired soul rejoice,
Brings again the carefree years,
Drives away unbidden tears.

Came this weird bird of the night,
Warily hidden out of sight,
To sing to me his "whippoorwill."
How I love his joyous trill!

Though I wander o'er the main,
Though I suffer anguish, pain,
If again at twilight hour,
Hidden in his leafy bower,
Whippoorwill is calling, calling,
'Twill be home to me.

—*Elizabeth Cox Gilliland*

A MEMORY

So clearly stands out in memory's vision
A lane that led to childhood's Elysium.

Through the wood lot we scampered, 'neath tall shady trees,
Where bird calls mingled with the drone of the bees;

Then following the trail still onward we stole,
Till finally we came to the "ole swimmin' hole."

That "ole swimmin' hole"! What a place of delight!
Where the boys knew for sure they were clear out of sight.

Luscious berries hung heavy on vines near by,
The blue of sweet William outrivaled the sky.

Yet onward this path lured our too willing feet—
Such a path! All lined with violets sweet,

While dogwood and redbud grew along each side,
Like sentinels stationed our feet to guide.

Through a cool, dim aisle of o'erlapping boughs,
Where lovers might linger to make rash vows,

The sunlight filtered through a foliage screen,
And made lacy patterns on a carpet of green.

The tinkle of cowbells came faint from afar
To complete this scene that nothing might mar.

But *why* all this urge through a place so fair,
Free from goblins and ghosts and bugaboo's lair?

A place indeed where fairies might throng,
And dance to the tune of the mockingbird's song.

But fairies forsooth! Our aim, our goal
Was a sweet gum tree, with wealth untold.

This grand old tree! A victim of greed.
From its sides all scarred to fill our need,

The clear gum oozed so fragrant and white—
Filled our souls with joy, our hearts with delight.

We swarmed round the tree till shadows grew long—
Then scurried back home with a gleeful song.

Our hands all sticky, but what cared we?
Just kids on a lark from the Sweet Gum Tree.
                                        —*Irene R. Gilmore*

A SONNET

I sometimes wonder what my life would be
If I had never loved you, what the cost
Of loving you has been, will be to me
When sight of you and sound of you is lost.

For not again will there be quiet content,
Knowing whatever comes, the best is gone;
Always there will be memories that dent
The peace of night before the break of dawn.
Each day will be a husk of what could be
If you were there—a feast with only crumbs,
Each dawn reveal a drear eternity,
For without love tomorrow never comes.

Would peace, contentment be a boon to me
Whose heart has known one day of ecstasy?
—*Gladys F. Goodfellow*

THIS HOUSE OF MINE

I live within a house of clay
Which soon must crumble and decay;
But O, my house is passing fair,
And how I do love living there!
No structure e'er conceived by man,
Built since this grand old world began,
Can with my house compare!

Mine? 'Tis just a loan, this house o'er which I yearn!
From dust it came and to dust it must return.
Just as a shell, emptied of its hidden heart
Falls worthless, having done its part;
So this house of mine must crumble and decay
When I—the real I—shall take my way
To my eternal home.
—*Minnie Rowan Goodrich*

ULYSSES GRANT

A village lad
Who walked the village way.
Work, play, and school
Followed day after day,
And in obeying thus he learned to rule.

A quiet man,
A soldier tried and true
Who would not yield
Till our red, white, and blue
Floated o'er northern hill and southern field.

A man of war
Whose great desire was peace,
And yet life brought
Battles that did not cease
Until the last long fight with death was fought.

Ulysses Grant!
A man who sought no fame,
Nor dreamed that he
Should leave a deathless name
Carved on the keystone of our unity.
                                        —*Ruth Winslow Gordon*

NOSTALGIA

I am homesick for the ocean,
For the breakers' mighty roar,
For the waves that chase each other
Toward the sand dunes on the shore.

I would watch the seagulls flying,
I would mark the porpoise leap,
I would see the changing colors
On the ever-changing deep.

I would watch the great ships coming
From strange seas and lands afar,
And pretend, as each reached harbor,
That *my* ship had crossed the bar.

I would watch the sunshine sparkle
On the wave crests' snowy foam—
Oh, I'm homesick for the ocean
And my humble, seaside home!
                                        —*Laura M. Gradick*

SUBLIMITY

Oft in my dreams I wander
To a beautiful land of bliss—
Where the sun is always shining,
And nothing seems amiss.

I seem to walk midst roses;
My feet soft velvet caress,
And the birds so sweetly chanting—
As though my heart to bless.

I wake—serenely happy,
Prepared for life's dullest care;
For I've glimpsed a bit of Heaven,
And talked with God up there.

—Ida Myrtle Granniss

TREES

There is so much beauty in a tree.
Each trembling leaf is a joy
And comfort to mankind.
With a sigh of consolation we seek its shade
And inhale its balmy fragrance.
It reaches out, and reaches up
To the sun, the rain,
To the twinkling stars and heaven above.
With ever a kindly shelter in its regal majesty,
It throws outward and upward its boughs,
As though with hands outstretched in thankfulness
For the many blessings given to it,
And the joy they are enabled to give
To the flowers, the birds, and humankind.
Each tiny leaf and branch
Is perpetually waving us a welcome,
And to the glories of the earth and sky.
Oh, how grandly beautiful is a Tree.

—Ada Graves

THE SONG AMERICAN

Cosmopolitan the American is;
Heritage of the race is his;
Bred in the melting pot of civilization,
His the superadaptation
To changing demands of advancing ages.

Hear ye the song American:
(Hear ye the saga of a nation!)
A majestic song of the *Race of Man!*
'Tis a saga of *All Creation.*
                                        —*Marjory Titus Greene*

NIGHTFALL

When twilight shadows softly fall,
    And peaceful rest is nigh,
I hear again the night call,
    As it goes soaring by.

The rabbits find a sheltered place,
    The cricket chirps near.
I hear the coyote's howl far off,
    Its voice so plaintive clear.

The barnyard family is asleep,
    Or in a quiet rest;
The sun has slipped beyond the deep,
    But left its glory in the west.

A breeze stirs faintly through the trees,
    Reigning kingdom over all;
The vesper of the departed day
    Rests on God's world.
                Nightfall.
                                        —*Gaileen Greenlee*

GLORY

Glorious sunset,
Emblem of Life.

Lord, clear our vision
Of fear—and of strife.

Knowing God's sunlight
Follows the night.

Our sun declineth,
Show us God's light.

Earth's race—victorious!
Heaven—is glorious!

—Helen D. Greenwood

CATHEDRAL OF ST. JOHN THE DIVINE

Majestic City of the Western World,
Enthroned beside the everlasting sea,
Holding the destiny of men from every land,
Guarding vast wealth, born of their industry;
With thy great offices and marts of trade,
Palaces of Light for Youth so unafraid,
Pavilions of Splendor, Galleries of Art,
Is there, for God, no place set apart?

Where is thy Soul, proud city of splendor?
Ah! there on the Heights, in the morning light tender,
There is thy soul!—
Lifted up on Heights sublime,
Fairest dream for all mankind;
Cathedral of St. John Divine.

On the Heights—above the tumult
Of the city's throb and strife,
On the Heights—forever watching,
Guarding, loving every life.
Lifted up on Heights sublime,
Fairest dream for all mankind;
Cathedral of St. John Divine.

Crowning the Heights with the glory of Jesus,
Calling to men of all color and creed,
Offering to all the cup of salvation,
Wiping out slavery, hatred, and greed.
Lifted up on Heights sublime,
Gospel in Stone for all mankind;
Cathedral of St. John Divine.

High on the skyline, His cross is uplifted,
Facing the sunrise of thousands of years;
Flashing the message—"Here is a nation,
Trusting in God, her hopes and her fears."
Lifted up on Heights sublime,
Gospel in Stone for all mankind;
Cathedral of St. John Divine.

—Mrs. Flora D. Grierson

THE PASSING OF A FRIEND

We loved her so!
Each time she came and went
She shed a gentle radiance all about,
            So glad and sweet:—
Her every smile—her speech,
That never uttered harshness,
            Showed no doubt
That in her lovely manner and her grace,
Her Lord looked through
The shining of her face!

We loved her so!
So willing and so dear,
She ever worked, nor shirked a duty clear—
But gave herself, her time, her prayers, her aid,
Her loyalty, her love so unafraid!

We loved her so!
How can we live each day
Without her lovely presence and her smile,
Her dear companionship—her sense of right,
Her brave, blithe spirit with us all the while!

We loved her so!
Dear God in Heaven above,
O lead her softly, gently by the hand,
And let her rest within the Better Land
Where heavenly flowers bloom—
            And Thou Art Love!

—Jessie Stearns Griffiths

THERMOPYLAE

Behold how Greece, the Ancient, stood
  Confronted by the Persian host!
Unnumbered was the robber brood
  That sought to desecrate her coast!
    But with her art, philosophy,
    And learning, were her people free;
    For, through the Pass Thermopylae,
    The armies of the enemy
    Could come but one by one!

Beyond that tortuous mountain pass
  The hordes of Xerxes thronged in vain!
Kept by the brave Leonidas
  And his unyielding Spartan train,
    Safe was the city of the light,
    Confounded the barbarian's might,
    The powers of darkness put to flight;
    For, through the pass, the sons of night
    Must enter one by one!

Could that vast, whelming, human flood
  Have swept her shores in one fell wave,
No mortal arm could have withstood
  To rescue from Oblivion's grave
    The wisdom of old Socrates,
    The fervor of Demosthenes!
    In yon strait gate beside the seas
    Greece conquered all her enemies,
    And slew them one by one!

So stands the hunted human soul
  Confronted by unnumbered days!
But we can win life's hard-fought goal
  And lift to Him our songs of praise,
    Who heaven and earth did so create
    That at our morning sunrise-gate
    Our days in single file must wait;
    And we are masters of our fate,
    When time's fleet course is run!

—Emma E. Grimes

A PIONEER WOMAN

A statue stands in a city block—
   It is called "The Pioneer"—
Of a rugged man with an old flintlock,
   And a cap from the skin of a deer.
His eyes look out to the misty sweep
   Of solitudes, vast and grand;
He sees great plains and forests deep,
   A wide ocean's shifting sand.
His gaze is bold and erect his form,
   Plain-molded his features and strong,
A man to breast the raging storm,
   Well worthy of honor and song.
Then—musing long—I seem to see
   The firm lips move, and live!
I hear these words come full and free:
   "I have a message to give.

"A statue should stand here by my side,
   A woman staunch and brave;
The wife who bore me children, and died,
   To lie in an unmarked grave.

"She toiled with willing and faithful hands
   In cabin, in forest, and field,
And helped to wrest from the savage lands
   A home, that must be our shield
From fierce things prowling when night shut down,
   From storms that swept black and wild.
Her face was free from a sullen frown,
   For she cherished each wee new child
As a soul from God, sent here on earth
   To have a share in the toil
Of giving an empire honored birth.
   She dreamed that the fertile soil
Would teem with homes, and the millions dwell
   Where only wild creatures ran.
The woman gives, as the ages tell,
   In an equal share with man.

"Then place my mate close by my side,
    That woman staunch and brave;
The wife who bore me children, and died,
    To lie in an unmarked grave."

—*Irene Welch Grissom*

ALICE WINTER

Alice Ames wuz never so skeered o' mistakes
    That she couldn't do nothin' at all;
She criticized Congrus fer makin' small brakes
    'Cause it hadn't done nothin' at all.

She'd talk of a vision she had in her heart
    'Bout peace of nations through cinematic art;
As pres'dent, she wuz most uncommonly smart—
    But she hadn't got started at all.

Fer she is the pride of all clubdom today
    Though she's gone to workin', and's now drawin' pay—
Gittin' *World Peace* writ down in the new code—someway—
    An' us wimmin approve uv it all.

—*Garnet Davy Grosse*

TO MY CHICKADEE

From out in the pines under my window
A dear little voice is calling to me.
A fluffy ball of black and gray feathers
And eyes that shine, is all that I can see.
The wind blows cold. The snow is falling.
The summer birds have all gone away.
"I am chick-a-dee-dee; I am out in this tree,"
I think this is what he is meaning to say.

Chick-a-dee-dee, Chick-a-dee-dee.
No matter how hard the wind may blow,
I will be near, just out in this tree,
Here under your window you may know.
Chick-a-dee-dee, I will stay with thee;
Hungry and cold I will not despair,
For my Heavenly Father watches o'er me,
And I am safe when under His care.

Stay with me always, dear little fellow,
Remind me again of that story of old—
How a sparrow falls not without His notice,
Although five birds for two farthings are sold—
How the ravens have no barn nor storehouse—
The lilies are clothed with gorgeous array—
He feedeth the birds and cares for the lilies—
Of how much more value are ye than they?
                                        —*Eva T. Guild*

IF WE COULD SEE

If we could see a beckoning gleam ahead—
On this strange, winding road that we call life—
Revealing heights that we might climb—instead
Of groping here and there through places rife
With danger . . . fighting every day for standing room,
And staking all we have on circumstance;
Oh, then, what splendor unreleased might loom
On paths which often seem controlled by chance.

And yet—no seed can choose where it will grow,
And where sweet perfume of the rose shall greet
The traveler, the rose cannot foreknow,—
But nature never yet has met defeat.
Our steps, perhaps, are firmer in the dark—
Our eyes grow keener searching for a spark?
                                    —*Gertrude B. Gunderson*

SOME MOTHERS AND SOME OTHERS

Within her home a woman dwelled
That not a care or trouble held,
Sheltered and shielded from the gale
By loving thought that could not fail;
And in her turn a shield and shelter
For wee ones playing helter-skelter,
Without a thought, without a care,
For tender love was everywhere.
Those wee ones that such happiness brought,
Brought likewise forward-looking thought:

"Some day wee ones will be less wee;
They cannot always bide with me.
Those tiny feet strange paths must roam;
They cannot ever bide at home.
The school doors now are standing wide,
Leading to halls unknown, untried.
There, too, the mother love must rule;
I'll take the home into the school.
We'll choose their school with watchful care,
That their surroundings may be fair—
An atmosphere of love and light,
To train my precious ones aright.
My bonny babes have every chance,
That in this world they may advance;
But all this must those others lose,
Whose parents cannot pick and choose.
By all alike is all deserved,
And all alike they must be served.
Shall I watch o'er my babes alone,
Simply because they are my own,
And other women's babes resign
To what's not good enough for mine?
Ah, no; it is the common good
That's the true care of motherhood."
And so she formed a plan at length;
She knew in union there is strength—
Strength that herself she did not need,
But many women lacked indeed.
And so she bound within one band
The greatest force within the land,
The force that not a man can cross—
Or if he could, 'twould be his loss.
They came in answer to her call—
Mothers, mothers, mothers all—
Mothers of few, mothers of many,
Those truest mothers without any
Children to look on them as mothers,
Who longed to mother the babes of others.
Many true mothers I have known
Have had no children of their own;

For mother love that's worth its name
Has learned in selfishness there's shame.
"Flesh of my flesh, bone of my bone—
What, shall I cherish this alone?
My neighbor, me to love they tell;
My neighbor's child I'll love as well."
Mothers, mothers, mothers all,
They came in answer to the call.
They formed a *league* which should extend
To wondrous length without an end.
They formed a *club* which truly should
Be a mighty weapon for the good.
You all have heard how foolish men
Have idly said, again, again,
That "women's clubs would take in truth
The women from the home" forsooth.
Ah, no—this club would take the home
Where'er the children chanced to roam.
This is a club, children to guard,
Whose lot is easy, whose lot is hard.
This is a league of perfect unity,
To serve the children of the community:
Children at work, children at play—
To care for them in every way—
Their health, their morals, and their minds,—
And give them pleasure of all kinds.
This is a league where all are mothers
Of all their babes, and all the others.
This is a mighty federation,
To bless the city, state, and nation.

                                        —*Eleonore F. Hahn*

NATURE

A tiny bud I hold in my hand
All fashioned with loving care;
The Master Artist each tint had planned—
Each leaf had placed softly there.

The blue of the sky and the sunbeam's gold
He mixed for the green, I know—
Each pointed leaf He shaped like a star,
A star of the long ago.

Life-giving strength came up from the earth
And coursed through the tiny veins—
The breath of life was caught from the winds—
The wine of life from the rains.

And when June brings the flowers and bees,
The buds will be fully blown;
And nestling close in their cosy depths,
The birds will make their home.

The pot of gold at the Rainbow's end
Is the gift of the Golden Rod—
Man feels the pulsings of Nature
In the Unseen Hand of God.

—Minna D. Haines

MY MOTHER'S HANDS

Dear, sweet, tired hands that were my mother's—

Once they were soft as drifting snow, and fair
As lilies nodding in the summer air;
They twinkled lightly o'er the ivory keys
And flashed among their trite embroideries.

Then they were swift and eager for their work,
No task so burdensome that they would shirk;
Dear hands! Strong hands to smooth a fevered brow!
Oh! would that they were here to lead me now!

See! They are battle-scarred and old; the veins
Stand out like straggling anthills on the plains;
The final garment's smoothed and laid away,
For those dear hands have had their little day.

Dear, sweet, tired hands that were my mother's.

—Albertine O. Hall

FANCIES

I wish I were a mountain breeze—
  I'd play among the aspen leaves;
I'd toss the downy cottonwood,
  And lift the stately lily's hood.

Or, if a bubble in the spray,
  I'd catch the sunshine in my play;
I'd dance and sing and then, at last,
  I'd run to Ocean's mighty clasp.

Or, if a sunbeam I could be,
  I'd cheer the hearts of men at sea;
I'd kiss the lids of children fair,
  And coin gold in ladies' hair.

Upon the garden flowers I'd shine,
  And lift all drooping hearts that pine.
A sunbeam I would rather be,
  Than breeze, or bubble in the sea.

—Corinne S. Hall

THE STORY RETOLD

"Little boat, I made you, you're mine;
  With bit of wood and nail and screw
And saw and hammer I have fashioned you."
  Thus spoke this little boy of mine.

Down to the lake his craft he bore
  And launched it carefully, sails ahoy;
It floats, it moves, it glides, such joy
  Is felt in the heart of the lad on the shore.

A puff of wind, a stronger wave,
  The little boat is his no more;
'Tis out of reach, away from the shore,
  No one in sight, his boat to save.

Midst drift and foam, borne by the tide,
    A merchant chanced his boat to see,
And washed and cleaned it carefully,
    Then placed for sale in his window wide.

Weeks passed. The little lad one day
    Passed by; and to his glad surprise
Saw the craft he had made before his eyes,
    Paid the price that it might be his alway.

In his arms he gently bore it home.
    "You're mine, Little Boat, yes, twice.
I made you and I paid the price;
    None can claim you save me alone."

So the Maker speaks to his children dear,
    "I love you, you're mine, yes, twice.
I made you and I paid the price
    With love divine on Calvary."
                      —*Mrs. R. B. Halstead*

CALVIN COOLIDGE

The stern hills of New England did give thee birth,
    With their calm and silence thou wert endowed,
    Like their towering peaks thou rosest above the crowd—
Today we place thee with the great of earth.

With thy unswerving faith and spirit brave,
    To guide her back thy country needed thee,
    To paths of justice and integrity,
The sacred heritage our fathers gave.

But in the secret chamber of thy heart,
    The weariness and pain thou kept'st concealed,
    For fear lest thy soul hunger be revealed—
Preferring to dwell from the world apart.

Life's glory passed for thee that summer night
    When thy son passed—and with parting's pain
    Thy great heart broke. And never again
Did stars or sunlight shine so bright.

And now, brave heart, thou hast found release.
  Unswerving from thy faith thou hast held thy way
  On to the radiance of a better day—
The pain of living ended in God's peace.
                 —Nancy Winifred Hambly

ELEGY

Never again in your arms shall I lie,
  Never have your breast for my weary head,
Never see the love light gleam in your eye,
  Because—you are dead.

I know a green hill where the trees are tall;
  With the drip, drip, drip of autumn rain
Chanting a requiem over your pall,
  Sharpening my pain.

Earth, let your breast be my pillow now;
  Wind me in leaves for the final sleep;
Wind me in leaves from the willow bough,
  Bury me deep.
                 —Florence Hamilton

LADIES, WE GREET THEE

Ladies, O Ladies, we greet thee in song,
  For we are singing all the day long;
Come then and join us the music today,
  Singing the hours away.

Ladies, O Ladies, we know that you're true,
  And we are with you whatever you do;
With colors and motto and friendship anew,
  Ladies, we welcome you.

Then welcome, O Ladies, we greet thee in song,
  For we are singing all the day long.
Come then and join us the music today,
  Singing the hours away.
              —Maude Slinkard Hamilton

A NEW DAY

I thank Thee, Lord, for this new day;
For help and strength I now do pray;
Each day's a gift from One above,
In which to tell of His great love.

In this new day I'll take some time
For prayer and worship to the Divine;
The moments spent at Thy dear feet
Give strength and courage and not defeat.

Of all the days, today's the day
To drive the gloom and care away;
So help me speak some words of cheer
And brighten the life of someone near.

Souls will perish in this wide land
Without Thy great protecting hand.
We thank Thee, Lord, for tender care;
It's broad enough for everywhere.

And yet, we find many a heart
Where the Word of God is not a part;
So help me now Thy word to send
To my brother, sister, and friend.

Of all the things I undertake,
I'll work this day for Jesus' sake,
The One who died on Calvary
To save the world and set it free.

—Mabel Hammer

ORIGINS

Who sees
fire in a tree

who hears
symphony in
a waterfall

who plucks
Titan from a
thunderbolt—

is a god.

Who is the
fire in a tree;
who is the spirit
of the waterfall—
who is the Titan
unsheathed of lightning—

the poet.

—Hala Jean Hammond

WILD CRAB-APPLE TREE

It grew near the alley by an old fence,
Just sprouted out humbly without any pretense
Of beauty or grandeur—'twas plain to see,
Like an avenger from the wildwood—a tree.
Neither elf nor wood sprite would care to live here,
'Twas covered with thorns which could pierce like a spear.
Man, on this wild thing was prone to frown.
"'Tis a menace," he said, "I shall cut it down."
Independent it grew, wide but not tall,
Spreading out claw-like branches,
But that was not all.
This wild thing was covered with foliage rare—
Thorns seemingly smothered as though never there.
In springtime a sweet perfume
From something unseen;
The foliage that covered this wild thing was green.
A beautiful pink beginning to show,
A bud now full-blown and all aglow
Waved and nodded in beauty supreme.
Man gazed on its beauty as one in a dream.
Summer came, blossoms flew away,
Clusters of apples now held full sway.
Autumn came, leaves turning to brown—

All colors and shades, and some falling down.
Winter with ice and snow;
The poor thing shuddered and seemed to know.
Even now majestic and grand
It holds up its head and thorns to command;
And when the cold winds began to blow—
Caught the first flakes of the beautiful snow.
Happy children from far and near
As they passed by, paused to cheer
The beautiful tree all covered with snow.
A garment of purity, not a thorn did it show.
Beautiful birds happy and free
Sang their sweetest songs
While perched in this tree.
Everlasting friendship, eternal love,
Springtime, Summertime, Autumn—God's love.
No more on this wild thing
Does man ever frown,
Though it grows near the alley
'Twill ne'er be cut down.

—Adelia Fraser Hardy

A LEAN LAMENT

I'm sorry that I waited such a long time to be born,
Then came when sylph-like figures took the whole world by the
    horn.
I envy those "away back when" who dared to dine and drink,
Who could lean back from a four-course lunch, and laugh and
    talk and think.
Perhaps philosophize, and eulogize, and dream.
Easy. Contented. Life deep-drenched in cream.

While now I must perforce be glad and happy when my food
Is bordered on the north by toast, sans butter—not so good!
On the south, black coffee—Bah! Just take the stuff away!
The east is flanked by spinach—green and soggy with decay—
On the west a glass of milk—thin and blue and pale—
For dessert, undressed leaf lettuce—I consume it bale on bale!

I rush my twenty blocks to work and as through the crowd I
    swing,
I hear talk of diet, poundage, reducing—same old thing!
Hard times. Economy. No money.
Hectic. Troubling. Life drained dry of honey.
I sway, and pray my toast and spinach inner
Will give me strength to last until my dinner.

                                —*Fern M. Harlan*

OCTOBER'S HEART OF GOLD

It was autumn, I remember,
   And the leaves were red and brown,
Myriad birds were winging southward
   Ere brown nuts came tumbling down.
Stood we together, eyes downward,
   To the sunshine-mottled ground,
Where the leaves came rustling—rustling
   'Neath our feet there on the mound.

It was autumn-blue October,
   And the north wind whispered low
Of a coming bleak December,
   When a frigid fury'd blow.
Watched we leaf-boats floating seaward
   On the river's current slow—
Saw bright leaves falling—falling,
   As we parted long ago.

In our hearts it was December,
   With a farewell pierced with woe,
Ere we promised to remember,
   Though time in passing be slow.
Each year in memory stand I there
   Where the singing breezes blow,
And leaf-boats on the blue Seschanna—
   Pass in vibrant, golden glow.

Again 'tis autumn—yes—October,
   And the winds bird-laden blow,
Faint smile I at youthful fervor,
   And a parting long ago.

The house of memory is much richer
  For that day on Life's threshold,
Where you whispered low, "Forever,"
  Giving October's heart pure gold.
                    —*Joy Williams Harmon*

A SONG OF STRATFORD

Where Avon's slow and silver stream
  Through lovely Warwick flows,
There blooms the golden English gorse,
  The gallant Tudor rose!
And Stratford town is garlanded
  With wreaths of poetry,
Entwined of sweet forget-me-nots
  And fragrant rosemary.

An old bridge spans the gentle shore
  Where sways the columbine,
And foxgloves grow, and violets,
  And graceful eglantine;
The pansy lifts its thoughtful face,
  Tall lilies scent the air,
All clustered fadeless through the years
  For pilgrims ling'ring there.

O'er gardens gay the rainbow bends,
  Like arching arbors where
The flowering lime and lilac fling
  Their petaled perfume rare.
Broad fields are bright with daffodils,
  And daisies shining white
Repeat the far celestial stars
  That glorify the night!

In every copse and hawthorn hedge
  The thrush divinely sings,
In azure flight the lark ascends
  On music's soaring wings;

Though shower and shadow briefly dim
   The smiling summer day,
The blackbird and the mavis pipe
   A lyric roundelay.

A fig tree flaunts its purple fruit
   Against a trellised wall;
From ruddy eaves the noisy rooks
   Continuously call;
Quaint houses, timbered and demure,
   The sylvan lanes define,
And cherished through time-mellowed years,
   The Birthplace is a shrine!

The hills are periwinkle-blue
   When dusk its incense spills,
And silence, muted as a dream,
   The twilight hour distills.
A vesper bell from ivied tower
   Intones its cadenced chime,
A sundial, lichened-gray, records
   The measured tread of time.

The deathless quill of Stratford's son
   A great Queen paused to praise
Ere riding on to Kenilworth
   In royal Tudor days!
When candles glow at eventide
   Through mullioned bottle glass,
Mysteriously through dark streets
   Remembered footsteps pass!
               —*Dorothy Goldsmith Hartt*

ODE FOR WOMEN'S CLUBS

The women haste to the clubroom
   At the hour that the meeting is called,
They have finished their various house chores
   And are ready to be enthralled.

They hear the reports of committees,
   Of moneys collected and spent,
They listen to plans for the future,
   Till they almost regret that they went.

Sometimes the music is splendid,
   But sometimes it's only a wail,
"But this is one of our civic jobs,
   And as women we must not fail."

They must help to acquire new members,
   Others their joys to share,—
To carry their ideals onward,—
   Their troubles and sorrows to bear.

The lectures are often inspiring,
   Through some are prosy and dull,
Yet with ears that are open for learning,
   There is always some thought they may cull.

At last the business is over,
   Refreshments are served if you'll wait,—
One day should be saved for this meeting,
   In spite of a surfeit of date.

And now they must hie to their husbands,
   To their children who wait at their door,
"Charity begins at home" it is true,
   Though aliens come to their shore.

After the dinner is over,
   And the children are all in bed,
They tell to the ears of their husbands
   All that the speakers have said.

Sometimes the husbands don't listen,
   Sometimes they're inspired too!
Leastways the wives must unburden
   And show what they can do.

And so they keep up their interest
   And further the aims they have had,
May they ever go onward and forward,
   Making this world still more glad!
                 —*Ethel Meers Harvey*

CONTEMPLATION

A mountain
Reaching to the sky,
Contemplating
Him on high—

Gray clouds
Passing swiftly on,
Behold Him
In the sun.

We mortals
Living here below,
Feel His presence
Faith bestow.

Day by day
In the seething crowd,
He calls to us
Out loud.

Would we know Him,
Fall humbly at His feet,
If He pass'd us
In the street?

Then hearken
To the hungry child;
It may be
The Saviour mild.

—*Lina Harvey*

TO A DEAD BABE

Farewell, sweet precious babe, my only one!
Alas, to know thy pain but not thy bliss!
A wanton e'en may find an infant's kiss,
While I, creation's plan revered, feel none.
Broken, hope's thread from age-old longing spun!
Lord, why should I love's joyous crowning miss?

Was it thy plan my crowning should be this—
Anguish? I feebly pray thy will be done.
O grant that on Hereafter's golden sands,
Which lonely years of human tears have laved,
I may once more pick up the severed strands
Of mortal love and there receive unscathed
Motherhood's diadem from baby hands,
For all eternity through sorrow saved!
                              —*Vera Andrew Harvey*

ORANGE

I've thrilled when I've read of purple and gold
Worn by princes and kings;
Crimson hurts my tortured heart . . .
But orange gives my spirit wings.

(The altar candles flamed orange the day
I heard the might Rheims organ play.)

Red throbs with life; yellow is merry;
Mauve tells of mysterious things;
Lavender brings me perfumed peace . . .
But orange . . . orange *sings!*

(I've seen the throat of an oriole
Quiver as he sang his soul.)

I love the green and the gray of the sea,
The laughing blue of the prairie sky,
And the silver in the sea-gull's wing . . .
But orange . . . orange makes me cry.

(My mother died when I was three;
She had made a little orange frock for me.)
                              —*Victoria Adelaide Harvey*

THE REDBIRD IN WINTER

The redbird's singing to himself,
He's humming soft and low;
He hardly knows he's singing,
For thoughts that come and go.

He doesn't see the ice and snow
That covers all the trees;
He's seeing apple blossoms
A-swaying in the breeze,
And purple violets in the grass,
And crocus bright and gay,
A row of golden daffodils
Like butterflies at play.

So he keeps singing to himself
And humming soft and low
The many songs that he had sung
In Spring—a year ago.
And when he finds a favorite tune,
There bursts upon the air
Such a song of joy and rapture,
Melody beyond compare.

While we, who sit around the fire
And think the winter's long,
Just thank Him for the redbird
And for his cheerful song.

—*Ethel M. Hasson*

MORNING

Hark! the birds are singing;
Another day is born.
The flowerets are 'wakening
To welcome glorious morn.
Arise! the sun is shining
To make a joyful day.
Come, laugh and let's be happy,
Help someone else be gay.

—*Mildred Hastings*

TRAVELED

I've seen the blue of Italian skies,
And golden about imperial Rome,
The light that softly fades and softer dies,
Though I've remained at home.

"There, Marie, you may sit just there
And make your map and do your sums,
While I mend this frock for you to wear.
Ah, how blue your eyes, how blue!
Move a bit, Marie,—just so. The light that comes
Through the windowpane, making gold your hair,
Falls soft and softer over you.

"Your map is done? And your sums are too?
So is the frock with its jagged tear—
All mended neat and ready for you.
You would like to know as I sat sewing here
Why I spoke of gold in the light on your hair,
And said that your eyes are Italian blue?
Ah, home-biding mothers will chatter, my dear."

I've seen the blue of Italian skies,
And golden about imperial Rome,
The light that softly fades and softer dies,
Though I've remained at home.

—*Lucy Louise Hatcher*

AUTHORS, WE GREET THEE

Authors, today as a Nation we bring
    Long-delayed tribute—gladly we sing
Praises to all who have shared with mankind
    Treasures of heart and mind.
Voices long hushed still inspire and allure—
    Through preserved pages of literature—
Offering courage to spirits aflame,
    Greater than passing fame.
Lift up the torch, light the way, time is speeding;
Nations in peril, for leaders are pleading.

Chorus

Spirit of Peace, make our every refrain
True to the ideals of sons that were slain.
Grant inspiration to women and men
Till sword obeys the command of the pen.
Crucify selfishness, vain pride restrain,
    Let only love remain.

Writers who've made one heart glad on life's way
    We would remember, this Authors' Day,
Those who defend home and Country in peace,
    Honor and strength increase.
Thus we express and all due honors give
    Those who turn thoughts into words that can live;
Ready to cheer us each day in the year,
    Like friends we hold most dear.
To God and home there can be no retreating;
Enlist for service and work while repeating:

Chorus

Spirit of Peace, make our every refrain
True to the ideals of sons that were slain.
Grant inspiration to women and men
Till sword obeys the command of the pen.
Crucify selfishness, vain pride restrain,
    Let only love remain.

—*Lula Ensley Hatton*

TOO LATE

I never told you of my love.
It was so shy,
It scarcely dared to lift its head
As you passed by.

The friendship true that you bestowed,
I let suffice;
The warmer passion in my breast
Was steeled to ice.

I wed a youth who urged me long,
His children bore;
But still, sealed close within my heart,
Your image wore.

So strong you were, unmoved by men
Of lesser mold;
You walked, unswerving, your own path,
Till you were old.

Heaped high with honors, flower-bespread,
You lie today;
All that was mortal, dust to dust,
Is laid away.

You have not needed love of mine
In all the years;
And so I sit and mourn alone,
With unshed tears.

I loved you well, but all unknown,
So long ago;
Now you are dead, I wish that I
Had told you so.

—*Clarissa Hill Hawkins*

A MISSION FULFILLED

Looking with pity at an old dead tree,
How I longed to know its history
And whether its life had been beautiful or not!
For a tree is somewhat like a friend
Whom we cherish and love until the end,
And when departed is not forgot.

Some day the birds must have loved to nest
Deep in the heart of its bright green breast
And called it home, where their little ones dear
Came to love and grow until the day
When they needed no shield and could fly away;
Now the tree stands silent and useless here.

Don't you suppose when in its prime,
And boys climbed into it many a time,
It must have chuckled and shaken with pride—
To see how sturdy and strong was its arm,
To hold all who came there safe from harm,
And then grew old and withered and died?

If you should pass into the gray of life,
Having borne—like the tree—with storm and strife,
Perhaps one who knew you would this recall:
That your arm held someone back from sin,
And helped one in doubt his battle to win,
Then what else I say could matter at all?

—*Catharine R. Healy*

DIALOGUE

"If I drink all my milk and eat my mush,
I'll be a big boy in the morning."
  "Ah littlest one, hush!
  Don't leave me so, without warning!"
"When I am big I will carry a gun
And shoot at the trees!"
  "Stay in my arms, little son.
  Keep your soft cheek on mine.
  Please!"
"No! I will walk with big feet
Further and further down the street,
Around the corner and out of sight.
But I will come back when it is night."

—*Elsa F. Helfrich*

LILAC

The fragrance of the lilac covers me
As perfumed vapor from a hallowed sea,
Breathing your presence in every vein
With the warmth and freshness of summer rain.

Subdued by years, with misty eyes
I seek alone our paradise.
The blossoms answer for your face;
My longing, aching arms embrace
Consoling clusters—hoping still
For your returning that would fill
My vacant heart, whose glowing fire
Wastes in a hollow of sad desire.

Oh, the scent of lilac bloom—
Incense from a sacred tomb!

—*Nina Hembling*

GOLD FOR GOLD

Gold coin—to repay
For tasks of love!—As well give
Barter for a rose,
Or silver for narcissus,
For their poignant, rare sweetness.

But take, now, my gift
And trade it for spun sunshine.
Hung from your casements
It will bring you cheer and joy,—
This gold of mine that you scorned.

—Bessie S. Henley

GROWING OLD

One by one the years have fled
With their joys and sorrows;
Loving memories for the past,
Hopes for the tomorrows.

Years roll on, we older grow,
Ripening like the grain,
Needing all life's discipline
Through pleasure and through pain.

May we grow lovely, growing old,
Grow mellow with the years.
We, like the flowers, need sun and showers—
Our smiles and our tears.

—Lucy Hall Henley

A PRAYER FOR GREAT MEN OF THE NATIONS

Carve not, Oh Lord, the cypress at this hour
By lightning stroke or winded power;
Dear God, the need is great for these—
These sturdy, stalwart, upright trees;
Then when the ship is firmly tied,
And seas calm, nations unified,
Then, and then only be it safe to say,
"A great man died."

—Mae Baker Henline

MAMMY SUE

In the dim days of the Long Ago,
Mammy Sue,
Your kind old black face seems aglow,
Mammy Sue.
Ah! Would I could climb in your lap,
And hear you croon of Uncle Nap
To the rhythm of the chair's "tap, tap,"
Dear old Mammy Sue!
"Shet yo' eyes, my honey chile,
Uncle Nap's a-comin',
En take you wid him fer a while
To de lan' wid bees a-hummin',
Hummin', hummin', low en low,
Hummin', hummin', hummin'."

You softly sang the sleepy song,
Mammy Sue.
The drowsy sandman stole along,
Mammy Sue.
All cuddled in your arms I lay,
My baby cares quite soothed away,
While round us slipped the shadows grey,
Dear old Mammy Sue!
"Shet yo' eyes, my honey chile,
Uncle Nap's a-comin',
En take you wid him fer a while
To de lan' wid bees a-hummin'.
Hummin', hummin', low en low,
Hummin', hummin', hummin'."

The Master called you to His fold,
Mammy Sue.
Your faithful heart grew still and cold,
Mammy Sue.
In dreamland you come back to me,
The night-gowned child kneels at your knee,
While Memory sings this melody,
Dear black Mammy Sue!

"Shet yo' eyes, my honey chile,
Uncle Nap's a-comin',
En take you wid him fer a while,
To de lan' wid bees a-hummin'.
Hummin', hummin', low en low,
Hummin', hummin', hummin'."

—Mary C. Herget

MIDWAY

Midway on Life's course I pause,
Startled by the dying year.
Time seems to have broken all laws
And Death lurks eternally near.

What if, instead of taking my friend,
The Reaper had called for me?
What ultimate good at the end
Could be counted off for me?

My heart is ablaze with flaming desire
To do some glorious deeds.
But the flame dies down to a smoldering fire
On the altar of life's daily needs.

Shall I, when the curtain shall fall for me
And the fires of life burn low,
Still be midway in uncertainty,
Or shall I Life's mystery know?

—Benita Adams Herrick

GEORGE WASHINGTON

'Twas in seventeen hundred and thirty-two
That the stork decided, on flying through,
To rap at Augustine Washington's door
And leave a boy— There were some more;
We're not sure just when the others came,
Nor can we call each one by name,
But this we know, from our histories true,
That George came February twenty-and-two.

The baby soon became quite a lad,
And like most boys he wasn't all bad;
In fact we're quite sure he was better than most,
And of his honor we make quite a boast.
When the brand new hatchet he espied
And to the cherry tree quickly hied,
The blade, it seems, was very sharp,
And soon went through the tree's thin bark.

Now when George realized what he'd done,
He knew the result wouldn't be much fun,
That when Dad came home and saw the tree,
He'd be just as cross as cross could be.
Which of course is just what happened, we're told;
But George bravely said, though the chills ran cold,
"Now Father, put all the blame on me,
My hatchet just had to try out that tree."

His word was dependable always, 'tis said;
His judgment the best, though he was but a lad.
Thus he was reliable, equally keen,
And a good surveyor when only sixteen.
His books of maxims and regulations,
Called "Behavior in Company and Conversations,"
He compiled when only a boy in school,
And he carefully aimed to live up to each rule.

At the outbreak of the French and Indian War,
When only of age and a trifle more,
He was commander-in-chief of Virginia's forces,
And made the most of all his resources.
And then in seventeen seventy-five
England found the Colonies much alive
When she tried to impose unjust taxes—a few—
(O, that Boston Tea Party sure was some brew!)

And may it be said 'twas an unlucky gun
That fired that shot into Lexington.
But with Washington placed our Commander-in-chief,
England's army eventually all came to grief.

'Twas no easy task to be in command,
With difficulties on every hand,
With foes from within and without to contend,
And that Valley Forge winter, which seemed without end.

But he weathered them all and proved his own worth
As soldier, as statesman, (a hero by birth);
And when to the Federal Convention was sent,
They unanimously made him our first President.
For two terms he served and was offered a third,
But this he declined and would not break his word.
He retired to Mount Vernon on Chesapeake Bay,
And two years later he passed away.

Washington's life is a well-known story.
We know that he even planned Old Glory.
First in war and peace and a nation's heart,
His birthday will always be set apart.
And this year, especially, we'll celebrate
The birth of our hero, so good and so great;
And though at his shrine we all cannot tarry,
Yet each may have part in this bicentenary.

—*Rose L. Herzog*

RAIN POOL

I glimpsed a lovely apparition
That followed in the Summer shower's wake;
'Twas a diminutive, bare-foot maiden
'Neath a glistening, dripping maple tree,
Wading in a sky-reflecting pool
Which mirrored a green and leafy background,
With a bit of Heaven peeping and creeping through.

When from the wet and swaying branches,
Close above her auburn, curly head,
Sprinkled belated, roseate raindrops
Dimpling up the placid, finite pool,
The wee maid cried, "See what you have done:
Shattered my clear, blue, rain-pool mirror
In countless circlets, meeting and sweeping into one."

—*Daisy Faulkner Hickerson*

THE CENSOR

Who is it, I should like to know,
  (It does no harm to ask it)
Who says what's good enough to print,
  And what goes in the basket?
Of course I know there's lots of folk,
  Just plugs, no doubt, like me,
Who try to chauffeur pen and ink
  And meet catastrophe.

But after all what makes good stuff,
  Some highfalootin' phrase,
Or is it diction, clever style
  That editors all praise?
Or is it food for master minds
  That sets a thing apart,
Or just plain, human sympathy,
  That grips the humble heart?

Who feels the need of comfort most,
  The scholar in his den,
Or scores and scores of common folk—
  The lowliest of men?
Is it for praise of cultured minds
  We think and plan and write,
Or is it for some downcast soul,
  To make his burden light?

We all enjoy fine rhetoric,
  Smooth rhythm, too, that sings,
But I like best the happy thought,
  Which to a sad heart brings
Sweet peace and comfort—words of cheer
  By plain folk understood.
If they can brighten just one life,
  Then, surely, they are good.
                              —*Maude Hicks Hickman*

RING ON, LOVE BELLS

Ring on, love bells, with notes so true,
Airy peals, soul-touching and of rosy hue,
With harmony sent from heaven above
Chiming the chord of the golden chain of love.
Deep-souled, echoed on earth around
With its sacred silver-sweet sound,
While its tolls of love are heard between,
Knells of love, pure as spring in green—
Love with its golden keys
Opens happy thoughts as these.

Peal forth, Wedding bells!
Your sacred rites it tells
In its echoing triumphant chord,
Notes over which love is lord.
Sound the solemn nuptial blast!
On the wide world in symphony cast.
Love is hopeful—Love is young,
With fond memories around us hung,
That will now and ever be sung
In every land and every tongue.

Sweet bells, your tolls of love have words
As tuneful as the notes of birds,—
Tuneful as the morning lark's melody rings
When dawning day spreads its wings,
Thoughts sweetened with dreamful ease,
Hopeful memories that dawn and please.
From the joyful peals skyward hung
Heralding forth the message sweetly rung—
Vibrant with joy, ring meadow and field,
Spotless, lily-white, the sacred vow to be sealed.
                                        —*Mrs. Lillian Hiebert*

TO WOMAN

O Woman, whither goest thou?
The four walls of thine ancient stronghold have crumbled,
And from the ruins thou steppest forth as from a chrysalis.

The transformation has been slow, but sure—
Thou knowest how to work, to think, and to endure.
Where man has trod, there canst thou walk alone.
Pick up thy burden and press on
To the ultimate good of thy Sisterhood!

—*Charlotte T. Hill*

A HEART'S PROTEST

Long years to raise my little brood I strove,
Gave up all thought of self—or sex—or love.
Since God took from me, in their tender youth,
The father of my bairns, in very truth
I lived for them alone. What toil! What strife!
What ceaseless care—to make carefree their life.

Now they are grown and think me through with life—and old—
Needing but food—clothes—shelter from the cold.

They cannot know that mutely, fierce and wild,
My heart cries out for love. Not that of friend or child,
But every woman's right—a true kind mate—
One who would walk with me to Heaven's gate
Or to Perdition's door, and would not care
That gone are youth's light charms, and grey my hair—
One who would look within, as on a scroll,
And read the love and beauty of my soul,
And understand that 'spite of years of strife,
I am not old—nor am I through with Life.

—*Ethel Osborn Hill*

UNIVERSAL PEACE

The Angels sang of peace, to men good will,
And ancient seers foretold the time when love should cast out fears,
And plowshares out of swords be turned, and pruning hooks of
    spears.
But when shall peace on earth these words fulfill?

Dawns hope—but three-and-thirty years have gone,
Dark, bitter years they were,—since first the Russian Czar
Assembled all the nations to take council against war.
Instead came death, from sky, from sea—Armageddon.

Again springs hope in hearts of all mankind.
Columbia first a woman sends unto the Conference board.
Geneva holds in thrall the expectations of the world
To break war's chains that still our world do bind.

—Margaret Frater Hill

I LOVE IT, DON'T YOU?

On a stem that is slender and tall there grows
A flower that bends to the breeze as it blows.
Its fleecy white face is turned toward the sky,
And the gold of the sun reflects in its eye.

In the glen of the fairies pray search—if you will—
By mountain, in woodland, near soft singing rill,
But nothing that grows can ever compare
To the simple wild daisy so stately and fair.

A blossom so perfect, a blossom so fair,
It blooms in the meadow with never a care,
It welcomes the sunbeams, the raindrops and dew,
And nods in the starlight—
I love it, don't you?

—Fannie Hoffman Hiner

MEMORIES

There are no friends like the old friends,
    No matter where you roam;
No home like the old home,
    Be it palace, hovel, or none
But the rented shack on the prairie,
    Where the latchstring hangs outside,
And the old-fashioned motto, "Welcome,"
    Greets you from the entrance wide.

If time could only turn backward,
    And the table of friendship be spread
With the dear ones of old gathered round it
    And the ripple of laughter be heard,
How happy would be the reunion—
    How the gathering shadows would fade—
How the sunshine of love would brighten
    The inroads that sorrow has made.

If time could only turn backward,
    Turn backward just once in its flight,
And bring back the dear ones who left us
    If only just for tonight.
But the wheels of time ever roll onward,
    Of our dear ones we still are bereft;
The old home still stands on the prairie,
    There is nothing but memories left.
                                    —*Hattie Josephine Hodgson*

REASON AND SONG

Translated from the French of Anna de Noailles

Priestess ordained of the high God of Speech,
I have served him long;
As the rose has its perfume and petaled corolla
Mixed in the making,
So my words have again and again
Remated reason and song.
The cries of others are sweeter, mayhap,
But not more heartbreaking.
                                    —*May Folwell Hoisington*

TIME

In the black sky tonight, down by the dune,
A silver cradle hangs, a slim young moon;
And young once more am I, and softly croon
My babe to sleep. Years slip away too soon!

Close to my heart I hold him, as I plan
All the brave things he'll do when grown a man;
That time seems far away, as I the future scan.
But how the days sped by, they fairly ran.

Now I am old and withered, brown and sere
Like last year's leaf, that somehow lingers here
After the tree's been stripped—I do not fear
To go my way as leaf and grass, and shed no tear.
                                    —*Lillie Edson Holland*

REDBIRD

Cardinal! cardinal!
A flash of living flame,
Through crisp, clear air
To my cottage you came;
Chewed at a pumpkin seed,
Watchful eyes stirred,
Flew to the cedar hedge
Whistling, "Redbird, redbird."

—*Edna M. Holy*

FAITH

Against the somber sunset, as the day went down,
I saw a wedge-shaped arrow above the darkening town.
I saw another at midnight, and heard their far-flung cry,
Always, always southward toward sheltering hills they fly.
Toward sun and warmth and shelter, with faith and sure intent,
No fear of storms tomorrow, no fear of strength far spent.
To the Captain of trackless journeys I breathed a little prayer:
"Bring them to safe harbor, these wildings of the air.
Give man in his lesser wisdom, as he gropes an uncharted way,
The sureness of destination of those brave free birds today."

—*Olive Honn*

MRS. FRICK'S ANECDOTE

It was the middle of the morning,
    Anne and I walked into the garden.
Halfway up in the sky the sun was shining.
    The air so warm and clear
Touched our faces like a gentle caress.
    Little seedlings had long peeped through.
Their leaves so fresh and green
    Spread a blanket o'er the earth.
The birds high up in the trees
    Had not ceased their morning song.
A little pond so cool and gentle,
    With its mill wheel standing still,
Seemed to beckon us.

Bob's little sailboat
Was being propelled in "girks."
    A Granddad frog was using it
For a resting place.
    Every time his throat burst forth
Its deep sonorous call,
        Bob's little boat moved on.

                                        —*Elsie K. Hopwood*

GOD'S OWN

There's wondrous living beauty in all things loved by God:
In the gentle wind that ripples where the yellow daisies nod,
In the peace of quiet valleys and the slopes of wooded hills,
In the sunshine and the moonlight, everything His glory fills.
God's fingers touch with beauty and weave with wondrous charm,
And His masterpiece, I know, is my Mississippi farm.

There's fragrance and a sweetness in the things beloved by God:
In the freshness and the cleanness of the smell of turning sod,
The rustling leaves of cotton mark the passing of His feet,
And His voice is in the robins' song where lacy treetops meet.
God's presence is about us like a strong encircling arm,
And His 'biding place, I'm certain, is my Mississippi farm.

                                        —*Mrs. L. J. Howard, Jr.*

HANDS

Weak and useless, like pale ghosts
You lie wearily upon my lap.
For your hard long years of service,
I shall reward you justly.
Before the world, reverently you will
Be crossed, above my heart.
The heart you cheated of its roses.
Flung them far from me. So few I'd had.
Faintly their dying perfume reached
My longing senses.
You, too, are withered now, life's past,
Almost gone,—are you forgiven?

                                        —*Marion Howard*

THE JAZZ GIRL

Like a butterfly that flits from flower to flower,
She lends herself to man, from hour to hour.

She gives her caresses and her kisses,
But nature her beauty soon dismisses.

She's like a "four-o'clock" with face to the sun—
Soon to be replaced by another one.

Faded, wilted, who cares about her lost beauty,
In her jazz—she forgot all maidenly duty.
                        —*Myrtle Hickey McCormack Howard*

UNANSWERED

I am not sad
    Because my love was unreturned,
But I shall mourn
    Because you did not understand
That love can be
    Beyond all human frailties,
That love endures
    Beyond the pressure of our lips.
I walked alone
    Amid the maze of human years,
But yet I know
    That love will be the only gift
That I may take
    Down all the centuries to come.
                        —*Inez Baker Howell*

SONG TO AVIATORS

You are the Spirits who show the way
    To gold-wrought gates where the star hosts play;
You are the wings on which we fly,
    Strong white wings—lift up to the sky.

Lift up to Faith—lift up to Life—
    Carry us high—above all Strife;
For what is Death but a dancing wave
    To croon a song to the fair and brave!
                        —*Hannah Cushman Howes*

VERBUM INDICTUM

Words are hid in the depths of me,
Clamoring ever, wild to be free;
Words that would cost the tongue too dear,
Words that would bring the tragic tear
To piteous eyes in an ashen face;
Words, slink back to your hiding place!
Unspoken word, I am master of thee,—
But the spoken word is master of me!
                    —*Edith Folwell Hudson*

MOUNTAINS

Somber . . . Mysterious . . . I love them,
Who have never longed for the sea—
The symbol of eternal silence,
Yet they speak through my heart to me.

The sea has its moods . . . as a woman
Tosses gems in her foam-white hands,
Its wrath—that of ten thousand demons,
Its calm—Time asleep on the sands.

God gave His commands on a mountain,
The echo of His mighty tone—
Still lives . . . in their eternal silence,
And is heard through the heart alone.
                    —*Nora E. Huffman*

CALENDARS

She hangs a calendar upon the wall;
Each year it marks a year, and that is all.
For her the days and nights pass evenly;
Yet years are hours—or eternity.

Days, months, or years, they are as naught;
Of sterner stuff life's calendar is wrought;
Searching the annals of our lives we find
How quickly time and space are spanned by mind.

When pain torments and anguish takes its toll,
Or warring storm clouds burst upon the soul;
When fate has dimmed the light of friendship's ray,
Who does not pass a year in one short day?

Who that has lived, knows not of hours that pass
More quickly than the sand from hour glass,
When poignant loneliness lifts from the heart
As desert day becomes a joy apart?
                                    —*Vira K. Humphreys*

FLOOD TIDE

Sappho, two thousand years ago,
In lovely Lesbos where the sea,
Azure and foam, sobs ceaselessly
Of beauty in its ebb and flow,—
Sappho, in words that linger still
Like distant music on the air,
Proclaimed the rose the fairest fair
Of all the march of flowers that fill
The year.
              The perfumed violet,
Narcissus loved of gods and men,
They stir us with their sweetness yet,
They breathe of longed-for beauty; then
Comes lavish Summer, in her train
The spicy pink, the lily tall,
Blue larkspur by the garden wall;
The nightingale for joy or pain
Pours out her song like golden rain,
And June's flood tide brings in the rose.

Half glimpsed within its armor green,
Each folded bud its silken sheen
Unfurls, white as the mountain snows,
Flushed like the tender dawn of day,
Golden as Autumn sunset, gay
With crimson or vermilion dye,
Haunting us with their mystery.

Sappho, your ashes mingle now
With ashes from the scented bough
Some young Greek lover broke for you
When life was fresh and love was new.

You sang, the music still is ours,
The rose is still the queen of flowers.

—*Flora Louise Hunn*

LIGHTS AND SHADOWS

How like a canvas our lives are placed,
    And by the Master's brush are traced.
Sometimes we see the sun shining so brightly,
    Fleecy clouds float round us ever so lightly.
Our cup of joy is full to o'erflowing,
    And only the silver lining is showing.
Again there are days filled with anguish and pain—
    Long, dreary days with their unceasing rain,
When we yearn, oh, so keenly, for a tomorrow
    That will bring kind relief from a heartbreaking sorrow.
But a picture must have shadows and lights to portray
    The dream of the artist—Lord grant that we may
Be submissive in sorrow and grateful for love,
    That the Great Master Artist our lives may approve.

—*Mrs. Charles Hunoldstein*

IOWAY TO IOWA

From his primal home in the woodland
Of Wisconsin, on the Great Lakes,
A large band wandered southward;
And here the story takes us
To the Mississippi river
At the mouth of the Iowa,
And here they camped on a sandy beach,
And here decided to stay.

'Twas here the little village of Iowaville was known,
Until in a war with the Sacs and the Foxes,
Their power was overthrown,
Their village annihilated,

And the Ioway tribe alone,
Being depleted by warfare,
Were forced to move farther on.
Of a roving, gypsylike nature,
They wandered north, these men,
And here at the Pipestone quarries
Took up their abode again.
'Twas here they resumed their former trade
Of weaving, and fashioning pottery,
For those were the things they made.
They molded bowls of the pipestone clay,
Made peace pipes or calumets,
And for dyes used the native berries and fruits as they could get.
They spun thread from the fibrous roots of trees
And shrubs, and of these wove cloth
For mats, of which they made teepees.
The women did most of this kind of work,
While the men did the hunting and trapping.
But later this band came back again
Led by good chief Mauhaugaw.
They settled on land over near Des Moines,
But life was much the same
Constant warfare with other tribes,
But their heaviest sorrow came
When good old Chief Mauhaugaw
Was murdered by the Sioux—
It caused much confusion in the tribe
This warrior to lose.
But his little son Mahaska
Had now to manhood grown,
So he became their leader,
And proved a worthy one.
But the white man was fast advancing
Within the red man's bounds,
And Mahaska's people must bid farewell
To familiar hunting grounds.

The Great Father at Washington
Would always send his men
To treaty with the Indians, and then—

Give them other tracts of land
To use as their very own;
Thus we see how Iowa
Became the white man's home.
But this early tribe of Indians,
As this story we relate,
Gave to our land the name we bear;
And not only to our State,
But we find the Iowa river,
And Iowa City too,
And the county of Mahaska
For their chief so brave and true.

—May M. Hunt

HE WHO WAITS AT TWILIGHT

Did you ever sit at twilight
By your fireside's warmful glow,
And try to count your blessings?
It's an endless task, and so
You just breathe a prayer of thankfulness,
And sit with half-closed eyes,
And listen to the rain outside,
And the wind that blows and sighs.

You are waiting for familiar steps,
And voices at the door.
The baby builds his magic roads of
Blocks upon the floor.
The evening meal is family hour,
The happiest of the day,
And he who waits at twilight,
Is blessed beyond repay.

—Lillian Crane Hunter

MY SWEETHEART

I sing of love to one I love,
Whose soul is pure as heaven above;
Your image true has kept my feet
From sin and vice when both seemed sweet;

My lips that knew not how to pray
Have learned to bless you every day;
I'll love you, dear, till I depart
This mortal life, my own sweetheart.
                    —*Mrs. Frances Boyd Hurlock*

ARMISTICE DAY

I can hear a sound,
As it comes this way,
Of a martial band—
It is Armistice Day.

In the roll of drums
Where the march is led,
I can hear the voice
Of the brave young dead:

"Peace, peace,"
Like a stifled sigh.
"Peace, peace,"
As the drums go by.

The parade goes on
Up the gala street,
With a blare of band
And a tramp of feet.

But I hear the voice
Of the brave young dead,
In the roll of drums
Where the march is led:

"Peace, peace,"
Like a pleading cry.
"Peace, peace,"
As the drums go by.
                    —*Helen Hutchcraft*

LOVERS' LANE

No more we sit in "Lovers' Lane" with moonlight shining clear,—
We have no time to do so now we have these children dear!
But every time it comes to mind, the same effect is brought,—
My heart speeds up, my pulses waken at the very thought!

Your arm is round me, strong and kind, my head beside your
        chin,—
There is no world of care and woe, but peace like heav'n within.
I sense a surge of happiness as when a robin sings.
The tremor tingles through me that Beethoven music brings.

I know, of course, that Lovers' Lane might stir me bitterly
If you had proved unworthy or had been untrue to me.
It is a tribute to our love,—this sentiment I feel
For Lovers' Lane,—Oh, Lover dear, to think it tested real!
                                        —*Doris W. Inscho*

THE GAZING BALL

All day you hold my garden
Within your silver heart,
Around you in the sunlight
The purple martins dart.

At night all wan and pallid
A ghostly moon you seem,
Where shining stars of fragrance
Amid the shadows gleam.
                            —*Gladys Melville Int-Hout*

ECSTASY

No need have I for drink but my desire for thee,
Nor food require save thy desire for me.
No home have I but thy enclosèd arms,
Thy lips on mine to still the heart's alarms.
Bring me no flow'rs, love's magic incense bowl
With every scent of Araby perfumes my soul.
Sing not to me; for jangling in my ears
Sweet bells of Heav'n ring madly through my fears.

Grieve not that Love must come in beggar's guise;
Thy lips again! 'Tis thus a goddess dies!
Do not awake me, pray, but kiss my closèd eyes;
For Death is sweet if this be Paradise!

—Irma Thompson Ireland

SONGS TO AN UNBELIEVER
MIRACLES

There is no God, in heaven or earth or sea.
"Yet came a little son, to comfort me!"
If he turn evil . . . as the years unroll . . .
"The God within his heart shall save his soul!"

ANY MOTHER OF ANY SON

Within his breast the greatest force on earth
    Now beats and surges.
Must he give way to sorrow or to mirth
    Because it urges?

Will he lay by for fleeting swift embrace
    Before his hour?
Or will he run the race with steadfast face,
    Unslackened power?

There is no God, you say, to give him praise
    At the Great Goal,
No Guide to warn him of the devious ways,
    And save his soul.

No God. So be it then. When I am laid
    Beneath the sod,
My heart for him shall rest there unafraid;
    Himself is God.

—Mabel Lorenz Ives

MOON DAUGHTER

In through the gateway of shimmering moonlight,
Where daisies shone pale by the pathway, she came
On white feet that pressed not the grasses,
While the night wind was crooning her name.

Tenuous, fleet as the starbeams,
Eager and young were her feet,
Like flowing quicksilver her tresses,
And her eyes were so wondrously sweet.

She said, "I was born of your travail,
Earth woman, proud mother of men,
You have called me away from my comrades
In the dream meadows far from your ken.

"For I am your heart's secret yearning,
Though for masculine strength you declare,
And so vainly you boast of men children,
Yet this intimate knowledge we share.

"So I live in the fabric of dreaming
That you weave while you sit all alone,
And I follow your fingers in seeming,
As you do your small tasks one by one.

"I am youth of you, tempered by knowledge,
I rejoice with you, sometimes I weep,
And over the house of your sorrows
My tireless vigilance keep.

"I am yours and you may not disown me
So long as the sand of life runs,
Although denied of you, still I am child of you,
Undaunted mother of sons!"

                                        —*Josephine Grider Jacobs*

THE GREAT AMERICAN HOME

America promised them freedom
And wisdom and wealth and fame.
So out from every country
The bolder spirits came.

They settled in city and hamlet,
In the country and by the sea,
Each filled with a great ambition
For the thing he could do and be.

They builded the church and the schoolhouse,
They molded the voice of the press.
Their President cast one ballot,
And the poor man cast no less.

And each learned of his neighbor something
That was better than he had known.
And life was richer and sweeter
And "Not For Bread Alone."

And the home grew in culture and comfort,
With a vision far brighter each day,
Till the force of its mighty power
No hand on earth could stay.

It was builded on good foundation,
And work and love—aye, and prayer,
And freedom and knowledge and pleasure
Are all represented there.

Oh broadcast it oft from each station,
Engrave it on hardest of stone,
That the heart and the soul of the nation
Is the Great American Home.

—Mrs. F. C. Jahnke

RECOMPENSE

You ask me what this day my hands have wrought—
Some lovely work of art, a picture rare,
A poem, song, or words of lofty thought—
I sigh, well knowing I can show nothing fair.
Then I recall the look within the eyes
Of my small son when to my arms he fled
With aching heart for comfort in his grief,
Because his cherished pet he had found dead!

You ask me what I've given the world today—
What problems grave I've solved; what light discerned
For those whose need is great; how much I know
Of great philosophers or sages learned;

And I stand silent, ignorant, abashed;
Yet something in my breast sings out to me,—
"You've offered solace, shared another's loss,
And what in life surpasses Sympathy?"

—Laura D. Jefferson

MY BUNGALOW

I built for me a bungalow
Upon a terraced hill.
Its low-roofed walls,
Its sunlit rooms
I set myself to fill
With things that were of me a part,
The things which said,
"Read here her heart."

Within my den I placed a desk,
And chair of plain design,
A simple couch
With coverings,
And pillows soft and fine;
A lamp, its stand, a shelf of books—
The books which said,
"Through these she looks."

Upon my walls some pictures hung;
They were not costly—no,
But clear good prints
Of master hands
That wrought for those who know
The spell which beauty casts and holds,
The spell which says,
"This guides and molds."

As tenant in my bungalow
Upon its terraced hill,
I live my life,
I think my thoughts,
I love, I work, I will.
My house, its furnishings—my "I"—
Myself sings on,
"Build—Ask not why?"

—Mamie Cread Jeffress

MUD PUDDLES

Clearing skies reflected,
    Muddy pools;
Wand'ring questions faltered,
    Voiced by fools.
Penetrating depths, O
    May I ask—
Is the infinity
    Behind this mask?

—Nadine Newbill Jenner

OCTOBER IN CONNECTICUT

Oh! October the King of the months is here,
The hills in purple and gold appear,
His goldenrod scepter he holds on high,
And he calls to the breezes that go rollicking by.

"Oh! winds tell the world I hold court these days
On the sun-kissed hills in the soft purple haze."
And his loving subjects haste at his call,
For they all rejoice at the voice of King Fall.

But Jack-in-the-Pulpit will come no more,
For an Indian in scarlet now stands in his door.
The trees turn red at the royal will,
And the blushing sumacs are on every hill.

The sweet fringed gentians from the lowlands near by
Come in loveliest blue that vies with the sky,
And the asters in purple of every shade
Give a royal splendor to hill and glade.

The birches and maples in red and yellow
Stand brilliant and gorgeous in the sunshine mellow,
While the oaks' soft brown sometimes is seen
Burnt deepest red in splashes of green.

Oh! royal October all purple and gold!
Thy wealth and thy glory can never be told!
We bow to thy beauty, thy color, thy glow,
King October we love thee, we can't let thee go!

—Louise B. Olmstead Jennings

IN AN APARTMENT

I live in a new apartment
In the "Gardens" of the city;
The walls are made of parchment,
O, what a tragic pity!

The landlord said it was soundproof
From lowest floor to top roof;
Which means, alas, we've now found out,
It takes in sound but lets none out.

>   So we're all going mad,
>   With the noisy din
>   Of shrieking soprano
>   And thumping piano
>   And shrill violin!

—*Ellen Marie Jensen*

MOONLIGHT AT SEA

I linger on the deck and watch the moon—
The full round moon shine down through mellow night
Upon the sea that in a heavy swoon
Lies all unmindful of the guardian light.
All day thou'st rolled in feverish caprice
And moaned unconscious in thine ample bed,
Thundering in rage against the vessel's side;
        When lo, from out the east
A pale-faced nun with orisons all said
Comes out to watch above thy restless tide.

Thou ridest high, O Moon, above the night,
While I am wondering at thy rounded shape.
I long for fancy and a keener sight
That not one golden arrow may escape.
Thy reign is on the ocean and enchains
An inward vision of a happy past.
The waters break and ripple round the prow
        Like half-forgotten strains
Of tender hopes e'er skies were overcast
With love's sad lesson that I'm learning now.

I lean against the taffrail to look up
Past spars and rigging to a cloudless sky.
Such drafts of balm and beauty do I sup,
All earthly evils I can now defy.
This boundless main is altogether fair—
And though there shines for me no sunny noon,
Content with life's sweet moonlight may I be;
      I could not quite despair
If we for one night, love, might watch the moon
Trace out her golden glory on the sea.

—Gertrude M. Johnson

THE POET

The Poet reads and lives—and learns to feel;
Absorbing words and phrases—links the real
With the slim thread of his imagery;
Himself a crucible then comes to be
Where words and phrases and the lives of men
Do blend—escaping not—save through his pen!

—Marian Phillips Johnson

LIFE

Life is like the purple shadows
   On yonder hills that lie,
Or the flowers in the meadows
   That blossom but to die;
Yes, something like the glistening dewdrops
   After a cooling shower,
Sparkling like jewels in the sun
   Lasting but one short hour.

Life is like a gorgeous rainbow
   Spanning the sky of blue,
Or the flitting airy butterfly as it
   Vanishes in the aerial hue;
Yes, something like a story
   By youth and the aged told,
It may be of pomp and glory,
   Of things that soon are old.

Life is like a mighty river
    Rushing on its way,
As it flows on forever,
    Never ceasing night or day;
Yes, something like the springtime
    Bringing flowers and soft green grass,
Which lasts but a few short months—
    How quickly they do pass.

Life is like a huge book;
    We turn a page each day,
Often turning back,
    But never stopping on our way.
May our lives be like the snowflakes
    Snatched by the burning sun;
When gone will leave marks
    But not stains, when life is done.

                                        —*Marvea Johnson*

RESIGNATION

I prayed: "God, make me useful,
    An aid to those I meet;
O, may I help my students
    To see life's beauty sweet.
I long, O God in heaven,
    To show them things worth-while
And help them meet temptations
    That may their paths beguile."

Then came harsh criticisms
    And stinging words that hurt,
And I would fain avoid them—
    Those cutting things avert—
But still they came upon me
    From sources here and there;
My soul in bitter anguish
    Reached out to God in prayer:

"O, must I thus be tested
   And chastened, Lord, and tried?
Are these, my God, the answers
   To prayers my heart has cried?
Must I, to be most useful,
   Drink deep of sorrow's cup,
That I may aid some other
   When he those drops may sup?

"If then with understanding
   I'll hear another's woe,
And if I can the better
   Show him the way to go,
If thus I'm being fitted
   For service I would do,
I'll bear them all most gladly;
   O, Father, keep me true!"
                      —*Ruth M. Johnson*

A VOICE FROM FLANDERS FIELDS[1]

We did not hate. We did not want to kill.
   We did not want to kill—nor yet to die.
They taught us murder much against our will.
   Such ghastly murder! Can men justify
Themselves for setting us against our kind,
   For throwing on the altar of their power
Our youth, our highest dreams, our lives—to find
   Only grey ashes in the final hour?
They told us we were giving to the world
   Peace, and we dimly thought we understood;
Yet only we, who in war's kiln were hurled,
   Discovered universal brotherhood.
We have found peace out here where we are lying;
   But will men never find peace save by dying?
                      —*Ella Colter Johnston*

[1] Reprinted from *Home & Abroad*, by permission of the publishers.

AN ACROSTIC TO SOROSIS CLUB MEMBERS

Some are little, some are fat,
Often we are told of that.
Regular members all are we . . .
Only go though . . . some for tea.
Studying always, for the smart
Into each of us impart
Something that will help our hearts.

Changing never from the right.
Longing to make each of you bright,
Under some conditions we . . .
Blunder, blunder, can't you see?

Mostly, we are scared to death . . .
Even sometimes lose our breath . . .
Moping slowly with our number;
Best of all, ha! some sure slumber.
Ever ready for the rest,
Right you are, the last is best,
Something good to eat . . . no jest.
                              —*Mrs. Lucille Brock Jones*

LITTLE LOVE SONG[1]

My love is such a tender thing,
I know it couldn't stand
The wear and tear of every day,
The harshness of command.

So I will love you lightly, dear,
And lightly let you go—
It's such a frail, cobwebby thing,
This love of mine, you know.

Perhaps you'll hide its loveliness
Deep in your heart, until
You need its silv'ry radiance,
And know I love you still.
                              —*Katharine W. Jordan*

[1] Reprinted from *Blue Moon*, by permission of the publishers.

ON BEING ASKED TO WRITE AN ORIGINAL POEM

An original poem! Is that all you ask?
Was it in irony you appointed this task?
Or did you think to me had been given
The purest and sweetest gift of Heaven?
Poetry is not an acquired art;
It's to have an understanding heart,
A heart that sees the beauty in all things,
That hears the songs that nature sings,
That feels the deepest feelings one can know
Of faith, love, hope, joy, and woe.
If with this gift of the Gods divine
One can the rhymer's art combine,
Songs will spring spontaneously to birth,
As pure water springs from the hard earth
And leaps down the hill with a bright flow,
Carrying life and gladness to fields below;
Or as flowers push up from dark ground
In fair beauty, sending fragrance around;
Or as the sweet, joyous, ringing notes
Come welling up from songbirds' throats,
Musical, liquid, sweet, and clear,
Telling the world glad summer is near.
Not always will they sing of joy and gladness,
Often it will be of pain and sadness;
For ever through the poets' strain
Is heard the cadence of mournful refrain,
As of falling tears, sobs, and sighs;
For in sadness the sweetest thought lies.
Merry words may be pleasing to the ears—
We remember those longest that move us to tears.
The rhymer may amuse and cause us to smile;
The poet will cheer in hours of deep trial
With love and sympathy kindly given;
For his is the God-given gift of Heaven.

—Alice Judd

LIFE IS LIKE A GOLDEN LYRE

Life is like a Golden Lyre,
  The major strings are Love, Desire;
Then Faith and Hope and Trust and Truth,
The minor strings played in our youth.
  But each string must unbroken be
  To bring forth perfect harmony.
                          —*Rose Carolyn Katterhenry*

RETURNING BLUEBIRDS

When the autumn days are hazy
'Neath a sky of greenish blue,
And the breezes all seem lazy,—
Nothing left for them to do—
When the Southwest seems awaiting
The coming Winter's chill,
When the Summer seems debating
If she shall go from vale and hill—

Comes a cry across the valley,
Comes a flash of sea-blue wings,
And a dozen bluebirds rally
'Mong my rough-stone garden things.
Some perch upon the arbors
Among the roses' rambling vines,
Others call from lofty harbors
Where the grape o'er live oak twines.

My bluebirds all remember,
Through the absent summer days,
That my birdbath, in December,
Full of sparkling water stays.
Then they find my canyon garden
Tucked away 'mong snowless hills,
When their Northern waters harden,
And summer nest with soft snow fills.
                          —*Nancy E. Keahey*

CHILDLESS CHRISTMAS

Mary, from your throne of Grace
Look down through eons of star-gemmed space
On those of us on earth today
Who have no child to watch at play.
Call from your memory's rich store
Again the Magi to adore
Your little Son whose Holy birth
Gave us first Christmas here on earth.
The shepherds watching quiet sheep,
The inn near by, deep locked in sleep;
The great wide sweep of Judah's plain,
The beckoning low-hung Star again—
The lowly stalls, the lowing kine,
With nothing great or grand or fine;
But yet you held against your breast
The Son of God, and by Him blessed.
Though bitter grief was yours—and tears
The bloody Cross of later years—
That night you held, safe from alarms,
The infant Jesus in your arms.
Gethsemane, His stone-sealed tomb
With all its sorrow, all its gloom,
Were of your life but minor part;
A Child once lay against your heart,
The wings of angels brushed your bed,
Their music filled that straw-strewn shed.
You trod the heights, aloof, remote,
His tiny Head cupped 'gainst your throat.
Dear God the Father, throned in Grace,
To Whom there matters time nor space,
Keep close to us on earth today
Who have no child to watch at play.
To us Thy love, dear Lord, instead,
Who put no child tonight to bed.

—*Rowena Millar Kell*

CLUBS

Of Clubs so rich and clubs so rare
There's none so good as Woman's heir
Of Union, State, at home, or far,
The Federated clubs accomplish more.

They urge more courage, a call to service fine,
The joy of work well done; comes a call almost divine
Of art, music, and schools a golden store;
Every work, we always find a place and time for more.

Of Gavels, cups, and emblems fair
Our clubs in Cullman, Ala., have had their share,
But rarest gem that came our way
Was a visit of our loved Mrs. Sipple one day.

Of grace so sweet and charms so rare,
There is no National President who can compare
With Mrs. Sipple's clubs, more worthy, true—
We work for clubs and then for you.

—*Mrs. W. O. Kelley*

DEVOTION

Come kneel at your window like saints of old
And wait for the sun till it turns pure gold.

If you look beyond, where our God still reigns,
You will have more joys and less of the pains.

We should stop to think of the joys we miss,
Of days of worry when we could have bliss.

Let us try to lessen worry and strife,
Make the days sweeter for some other life.

Then kneel at your window facing the east,
Like the saints of old you'll receive a feast.

—*Candace Hurst Kelly*

SONG OF A VINE AND NEST

There's a robin's nest in the wild-grape vine
That hangs on that sagging old porch of mine,
A nest of wondrous and cunning design.
And when on the floor the footsteps fall,
Robin will spring to his nest and call,
And spread out his wings and flutter and squall:—
    "Mine, Mine, these are mine.
    My porch and my nest and my wild-grape vine;
    Mine, mine, these are mine,
        Get away from my nest and my wild-grape vine."

I thin out the iris beside the wall,
And set out the hollyhocks where they can grow tall,
And plant the asters to bloom in the fall.
And Robin sings as he follows me around,
And cocks his head and listens for a sound,
Then pulls a big worm right out of the ground:—
    "Fine, fine, aren't they fine,
    Nice fat worms in this garden of mine;
    Fine, fine, aren't they fine,
        Breakfast for six in the wild-grape vine."

The little birds are as ugly as sin,
Just a nest full of claws and wrinkles of skin
And bills wide open to put worms in.
But Robin sings as he looks at his nest,
And throws back his head and swells out his chest
Till the little red feathers stand out on his breast.
    "Fine, fine, aren't they fine,
    Loveliest nestlings, my mate's and mine,
    My babes in my nest in my wild-grape vine."

L'Envoi

The vine by Autumn's winds undressed,
And fast asleep in Winter's rest,
Clasps Summer's gift it treasured so,
The Robin's nest, half filled with snow.

—*E. Grace Kimberly*

EASTER DAWN

Lily bulbs, that in the earth
  Slept through months of winter's cold,
Break their clods—a glorious birth—
    Soon their pure white blooms unfold.
      Springtime green is on the lawn—
      Easter dawn!

Silken cerements, misty, gray,
  Within a weathered chrysalis
Held a moth. Resplendent, gay,
    She bursts her bonds and finds her bliss;
      Fairy creature, winging on—
      Easter dawn!

Watchers waiting at the tomb
  Where their Lord was laid with tears,
See how joy disperses gloom
    As the risen Christ appears!
      Night's sad vigil past and gone—
      Easter dawn!

              —*Caroline M. Kinder*

MY AIRSHIP

I'm traveling in my Airship
Above the world so high!
I see so many pictures,
As I go passing by;
I see the worn and weary,
The paths so rough, they've trod,
I see the youth, lighthearted,
In flowers that gaily nod.

I see the grave and thoughtful,
And next the young, so gay;
And now brave men and women,
And then the child at play.
The youth is at the altar,
The older ones at prayer,
I gaze on the moving picture,
With many a lesson there.

I rise above the drifting cloud,
Perfection now I view,
I see a land of Promise,
And things of age, made new;
My Airship slowly lowers,
I touch the earth again;
There are many roads marked "Duty,"
And I join the march of men.

—*Edna Fuller Kirk*

GONE [1]

You are much more vivid
Than you were before
That strange day they carried you
Through the open door.

Queer that I remember
All the things you said
Ever so much better,
Now that you are dead.

Every day and hour,
All the things I do
Are with the intention
Just of pleasing you.

Thinking of you always,
I can see your face,
When I turn to touch you,
Oh, there's empty space!

—*Mary Wallace Kirk*

A MAN

If I could only be the man
That my kid brother thinks I am,
I'd be a wonder, sure 'tis true,
I'd be a man full through and through.

[1]Reprinted from *Blue Moon*, by permission of the publishers.

I'd have the knowledge of the age,
I'd have the wisdom of a sage,
The skill and grace of every art,
With strength and worth deep in my heart.

Kid brother, now in faith to you
I'll have to strive my best to do;
To keep that faith and trust my aim,
And never bow thy head in shame.

Thanks, thanks to thee my brother small
For faith that trusts and asks my all;
A banner bright 'twill float before,
Bring out my best, and then some more.
                                          —*Mrs. Victor Kirk*

TWO BIRDS

Two birds were singing in an apple tree
With but a tiny, fluttering leaf between,
Yet separated as by spanless sea—
Two birds upon the boughs of waving green.

For one was singing of an empty nest
And still, dead mate, and nestlings ne'er to be;
A ceaseless grief and pain dwelt in his breast,
A world of sadness in his melody.

The other sang of love, the old, old song,
So glad, so rich, the very air seemed sweet
And vibrant with the bliss that swept along
In rapturous paeans, jubilant, complete.

Two birds sat silent in an apple tree,
The one in sorrow at the other's pain,
And fearful lest his own love-dream should flee
And hush his music to a minor strain.
                                          —*Alice Pilcher Kirkendall*

DEPRESSION WITHOUT THE "DIE" IN IT

"Why is your heart in panic, pray?
Press on! There's yet another day . . ."
Though icy winds their bugles blow
Above the blanket of deep snow—
A cardinal cheerful and bright,
Without a crumb, or food in sight,
Has no depression in his song . . .
"Press on! Press on! It won't be long!"
You brilliant bird, you truly spoke,
And in my heart an echo woke . . .
The victory goes to the strong—
"Press on, have faith, press on!"

—*Frances R. Klopfenstein*

AN EPITOME

God's winds lift high to barren rock
A seed that clings, and laurel flings
Its splendor down a mountainside.
He lets a grain of genius fall
Into the mire and Lo! a fire—
An illumination world-wide.

Man, the provider, sows his seed
In fertile soil with eager toil,
That harvests him may gratify.
Material are the crops he seeks—
His very need incurring greed
That lets the finer things go by.

A woman plants the seed of joy
Anywhere; she breathes a prayer
And fences it in with love.
She plants for beauty, service, faith,
Nor cares who reaps the ripened heaps—
The owlet or the cooing dove.

—*Kate Robertson Knauer*

"LITTLE MOTHER OF THE NAVY"

Your life is crowded with eventful things,
Strong words of cheer, and stirring songs of glee;
Your voice is like a silver bell that rings
In harmony,—to prove your thought is free.

I love to see you walk the busy street,
Greeting inquiring strangers with a smile,
A friend to every Service man you meet,
Whose thoughts of you enrich each homing mile.

To wayfarers you open wide your door,
And all who need your help are ushered in;
You cheer each heart, relinquished faith restore;
Each wanderer feels your sympathy akin.

We hail the one whose hearthstone welcomes all,
Comrade, friend, companion is your name;
You lend a helping hand to great and small,
In sacrifice your selfless acts proclaim.

—*Jessee Inwood Knoblock*

LONGING

If I had the wings of the morning,
    I would fly far away
To the top of some high mountain,
    And there sit me down for a day.

I would watch the golden sunbeams
    Breaking through clouds of gray,
Bringing light to the countryside,
    Giving birth to a new day.

I would hark to the song of the sparrow,
    The lark, the robin, the wren,
Singing their greetings to morning
    Over and over again.

With the gleaming waters below me,
    With the beautiful blue sky above,
I would list to the wind through the treetops
    Whispering its message of love.

Far from the World's busy tumult
   Strife and turmoil cease;
I would commune with Nature,
   I would find rest and peace.

I would seek Truth and find it
   On this hill so far away,
I would have time to be thankful for life,
   I would find time to pray.

All the day long would I rest there
   Free from toil and care,
Drinking in its beauty,
   Breathing the glorious air.

Then night would drop her mantle,
   The stars would come out to play,
The moon would ride high above me,
   And moonbeams dance and be gay.

There's magic on a night like this,
   And under its mystic spell
It would give me faith that somewhere
   God lives and all is well.

As I winged my way homeward
   Away from Nature's Shrine,
I would be taking with me
   Something akin to divine.

Then I would thank my Maker
   That I had been spared this day,
And that at last I'd found my soul
   On that hilltop far away.

                    —Fannie M. Kuhl

UNWRITTEN MUSIC

So many lovely notes come to my ear
   From brook and bird—
That oft midst toil and carping care
   My soul is stirred.

The sound of rain upon a shingled roof
    Soothes me to sleep,
While whispering winds‧through darkened pines
    Their vigils keep.

Caressing "coo" of pigeons on an oaken beam—
    The drowsy "tweet"
Of nestling chicks beneath their mother's wing,
    So soft and sweet.

The rhythmic beat of eager wings
    Across the sun,
The hoot of owl at eventide,
    When day is done.

The carefree laughter of a child
    Can often lift
The weary load of saddened years
    That downward drift.

Unwritten music, pulsing sweet and low,
    When muted string
Would seem ofttimes e'en gently brushed
    By angel's wing.

My heart awakes to eager longings,
    And to yearn
To keep my soul attuned to things
    That breathe and burn.

The busy hum of bees in summer gardens
    Gay with flowers,
Where bird notes keep me willingly enslaved,
    Enchanted hours.

The rustle of the falling autumn leaves
    In woodland way,
When down the old familiar path
    My footsteps stray.

And from the dewy grass of evening
    Crickets lone
Chirp mournfully of sunny hours,
    With summer flown.

The cadence of the moaning winter wind,
　　While safe and warm
I sit in chimney nook, protected
　　From the storm.

But lo—from boggy marsh, wee heralds pipe
　　Their message clear,
And soon from budding bush a robin sings,
　　And spring is here!

　　　　　　　　　　　—Laura M. Ladley

FRIENDSHIP

I shall remember the tenderness
Of thoughts no sound will ever express
In a garden by the sea;
For your flowers spoke what your eyes had spoken,
While dusk fell, and time was broken
Out of eternity.

　　　　　　　　　　—Louise Burton Laidlaw

AD INTERIM

I think when I look across the street
At that strange old gabled house,
How relieved it feels now they've all emerged
And left it to itself.

The rugs sprawl, oh, so comfortably
And sleepily stretch themselves;
No brushes beat, no brooms go swaying,
No tramping feet go scurrying.

The poor old lounge can settle down
Without its weekly pounding.
The cushions, too, have a chance to breathe,
And the halls have stopped resounding.

Houses, they say, to some look sad
When humans are forced to leave,
But I've looked again at this gabled house,
And I fail to see it grieve.

　　　　　　　　　　　—Helen C. Laird

THE WREATH ON THE DOOR

There's a wreath on the door
Of holly and pine,
The little red berries
With green intertwine,
And I know as I pass
That there's much joy inside,
For the wreath on the door
Bespeaks Christmastide.

There's a wreath on the door
Of galax and white.
The perfumes of flowers
With the green leaves unite
To tell as I pass
That there's sadness in there,
And that wreath on the door
Whispers low, "vacant chair."

Now the wreath, as the ring
From traditions of old,
Is symbol of endless,
The eternal, we're told;
And whether the wreath
Is of galax or holly,
Whether inside be grief,
Or hearts that are jolly,
May it say to the world
As it hangs on our door,
"The Christ Child is born,
Oh come and adore."

—*Sara F. Lane*

MORNING IN THE HILLS

'Mongst the hills of Indiana
Where but Nature has her way,
And the vision of her grandeur
Melts our troubles all away,
There is quiet, peace, and beauty
That would cure us of our ills—
If we'd go out in the morning
'Mongst those Indiana hills!

There through haze of early morning
With the quiet that it knows
Comes the dawn so young and tender
Where the straggling brooklet flows;
But we get a clearer vision
Of the new day, peaceful, fair,
O'er the hills and through the valleys
When the mists begin to clear.

Cabins dotted o'er the landscape
Send their threads of smoke on high
As a tiny silver ribbon
Reaching up to meet the sky,
And the bobwhite in the valley
Gives a call that through me thrills,
As his mate will answer clearly
O'er those Indiana hills!

Not a trace of noise or bustle
From the city's glare and din
Penetrates this peace and quiet
Nor may hope to enter in.
Nature takes my hand and leads me
Up and down o'er rocks and rills,
Where the land is filled with beauties
'Mongst those Indiana hills!

—*Mary Larkin-Cook*

CRISIS

A flash from the sky on the crest of the wave,
The line of the mist on the flame in the brush.
Hammering floods, wild gusts that rush
Like a blast near the stone-paved mouth of a cave.

Fear chills the soul like the cave walls cold.
Yet the floods, soon a mist, the mist burned by flame,
The flame but a flash, gone as it came,
Life's ocean, love's earth, and their Jester, Gold.

—*Georgette Grenier Laserte*

FLOWERS

Roses of red and iris blue,
Flowers of various kinds and hues
Have come to my door in ages past
Only to wither, never to last.

Orchids and lilies, smilax and thyme,
All from a garden where memories twine.
But the flowers most precious, kind friend and dear,
Are the *words* from your garden you phoned to me here.
                    —*Mrs. Roberta Campbell Lawson*

MISSISSIPPI FEDERATION

Hark! What music now comes ringing,
Swaying softly, then so clear?
'Tis the song of Mississippi,
Sung by Federation dear.
Mississippi Federation! Join it now,
'Tis not too late,
Though organized at Kosciusko   ·
In eighteen ninety-eight.

Mississippi Federation
Binds our hearts with loyalty,
Reaching out with friendly handclasp
Wheresoe'er the need may be.
Cotton blossom and the boll,
Pins you see on every hand,
Green and white, the colors flying,
Symbols of this mighty band.

Federation state officials
Ever busy at their task,
With their wisdom, strength untiring,
Standing there before the mast.
Seven districts have their leaders,
Each to hold the standard high.
Zones and clubs then follow after,
Striving thus to simplify.

Let us now with growing interest
For department tribute pause,
Each a loyal unit working
Everywhere to boost the cause.
American Home department problems,
Surely these will interest all;
Finance, thrift, and life insurance,
Tasks to solve by great and small.

Citizenship, how necessary;
We must always stand for right.
Law observance, immigration,
For the highest standards fight.
Now are hearts becoming anxious
The eighteenth amendment to preserve.
Bravely think it, bravely talk it,
In this way your country serve.

Literature, suggestive items
On all Federation work;
Without these to guide our footsteps,
Surely we might often shirk.
Music, how we thrill to music,
Strikes a keynote in each heart;
Songs for home, for church, for nation,
Each for beauty plays a part.

Art, its educative value
Links us to the world today;
Pottery, pictures, for our children
Beautify the common way.
Education, so creative;
Weaker ones are made more fit.
Give material gifts to aid them;
When you can, give scholarships.

International Relations,
This a vital subject, too;
Love of God and peace of nations,
Here is work for you to do.

Peace on earth! The angels sang it
Centuries ago, 'tis true;
We must strive for peace, to have it,
Let's stand by and see it through.

Legislation, use your influence,
Officials now must stand the test;
Be it local, state, or nation,
Expect each one to do his best.
Press, Publicity, so important,
Makes us all as one to think.
Praise for these department workers;
From their tasks they never shrink.

Public welfare, this a broad field,
Includes Indian Welfare, too.
Community needs, and child sufferings,
To all of these our duty do.
Conservation, last but not least,
Preserve earth's beauty where we can;
Shrubs, flowers, birds, and dreamy forests
Glorify this earth for man.

What a breadth of service find we;
In these lines let's also mention
Contests, honor points, and finance,
Institutes, and Club Extension.
As first President, Mrs. Hebron
From your memory do not sever;
First to strive for Federation,
Hers the first, great, brave endeavor.

Hark! What music now comes ringing,
Swaying softly, then so clear?
'Tis the song of Mississippi,
Sung by Federation dear.
Mississippi Federation!
Pledge your hearts and hands anew.
To the General Federation;
For its causes, you stand true.

—*Mrs. Shep Ledbetter*

HOUSE VERSUS HOME

A house and a home are different, you see,
And on this subject I'm sure we'll agree,
When I reason with you as it was reasoned with me.

A house is built of lumber and brick,
And it doesn't take long to complete the trick;
But a home is built of sorrows and joys,
And the happy faces of girls and boys,
And a mother and father who willingly share
All the ups and downs—and all of the care
For these girls and boys.

When you enter the door of the house you will see
Everything in its place as nice as can be,
But entering the door of the home you will find
On the floor toys and books that were left behind,—
Now, this is a home, but don't go away,
For you are just as welcome as the flowers in May.
                                        —*Laura Lee*

FAITH

Autumn,—and the trees are stripped
Of summer vestments proudly borne;
Autumn, and the earth, still-lipped,
Regards her garments, stained and torn.

Naked the trees against the sky,
Braced to the bitter winds that blow;
With gnarled branches lifted high
They wait the winter's gift of snow.

Thus, in the Autumn of my years,
Facing with certainty the cold
Of chilling age, my life appears
But an old story, newly told.

Winter, and death; but somewhere, soon,
I shall know spring, and rouse from sleep,
I too shall know some lovelier June;
Oh faithless heart, why weep? Why weep?
                                        —*Mildred Bentley Lee*

OUR CLUB CREED

Lord, the newness of the day
Calls us to the untried way.
May we, when face to face in our Club meeting,
Be not hasty in judgment, but gentle in greeting.

All our faultfinding take away,
And any pretense or prejudice, we pray.
From us all pettiness wilt Thou keep,
So that thoughts of self we will not seek.

Let us be unafraid, for all things take time,
Be broad-minded, generous, always kind;
Be straightforward, serene, and calm;
Our impulses better, with no thought of harm.

Help us to realize that differences create
Thoughts of jealousy, strife, and hate.
Let our words and deeds be so done
That in big things of life we are as one.

May we strive always ever to be
Large in thought, more like Thee.
To us the gift of peace restore—
Touch our hearts with goodness once more.

Let us take today, and do our part
As our part is given,
For that's the way to woman's heart;
That's the way to Heaven.

—Mrs. Marion Le Flore

THE STORM KING TRAIL

Looming dark against the sky,
The great thunder cloud
As he passed the mountain by
Spread his garment wide,
And hov'ring low to rest
Over the Storm King's crest,
Beckoned the little rain maidens
To come to his breast.

They, heaving a gentle sigh,
Gathered their misty veils about them,
And caught in the folds of his robe
Floated far away with him.
All save a few tardy ones
Who, left behind, with tears streaming
Have watered the countryside,
Leaving it fresh and gleaming.

—Grace Patchen Leggett

PUERTO RICO

Puerto Rico,
Isle of mountains and deep valleys,
Rich in lore of Spanish days,
Once was but a tiny sand grain
Slipped from out the hands of Nature,
Rested on the blue Caribbean.
Such a tiny runaway!
Nature, all-forgiving, smiled;
Puerto Rico, understanding, thrived.
Child of Destiny!
Fertile fields with stores of gold,
Sugar cane of apple green,
Laden boughs of coffee trees,
Fruits, the like unknown of old,
Made a garden of wealth untold.
Tiny Isle
Wove a crown of native blooms,
Bound them gently with the love vine,
Interspersed with bits of blues
Gathered from the deep sea's bosom.
Gift of child to Mother Nature.
With lavish hand
Return was given, by wave of magic wand;
A land of sunshine, love, and flowers,
Hopes fulfilled, and lilting hearts.
Happiness, with gilded wings,
Played so gently the harp strings,
That reverberated joys
Lived and shared in fair
Borinquen.   *—Verona Watson Lehmer*

TWO THOUGHTS ON YOUTH

THE PESSIMIST

Full of slang,
Full of jazz,
Full of giddy laughter,
With ne'er a thought for things gone by,
Nor what may be hereafter.
Straight to perdition, so they say,
The present age is going,
If we may judge the harvest
By what our youth are sowing.

THE OPTIMIST

Full of sweetness,
Full of grace,
Full of the joy of living;
A sweet smile here, a soft touch there,
That's what makes life worth living.
Straight to our hearts with frank appeal
The present age is going,
For we enjoy the harvest
Of love our youth are sowing.

—*Retta Irwin Leichliter*

MINNESOTA LANDSCAPE

The fields flow with fireweed;
  the birches
    on the hillrise
Sing a psalmody of summer weather;
  wintergreen and bunchberry
    hide their scarlet earrings
      among the brake fern,
And goldenrod waves many a saffron feather.

The pines spread dark wings,
  veiling
    the forest floor,

Where the fawn runs with velvet feet,
  stirring up the bronze needles
  until their sweet aroma
  drifts out
Where sun and shadow meet.

The landscape sways with motion,
  rocking rhythmically
  in a cerulean cradle;
Shadows move ahead of wands of light;
  the singing dance of morning
  slows to the beating march of noon,
  flows into adagio
At the coming of the night.

—Louise Leighton

ART

Art is that mystic, forceful thing
That takes mere words and makes them sing!

It is the urge and that alone
That keeps the sculptor at his stone

Until he sees his dream arise
In finished form before his eyes;

While to the dancer's joyous feet
It lends a charm with grace replete.

Art looks on life—a tangled mess—
And changes it to loveliness.

—Adeline Evans Leiser

CHRISTMAS IN FLORIDA

Oh! sunny day, oh! balmy day,
  The mockers trill a roundelay.
Your brow is by soft winds caressed,
  The sun sinks swiftly to its rest.
And now another yuletide fades in Florida.

—Marian Leland

REVERIE

Oh, to live the life of a Helper,
By doing the things worth-while,
To boost when boosting is needed,
To walk with the traveler a mile,
To live for the good of others,
And to crown each deed with a smile!

Just to feel that I am fulfilling
In some way the Lord's command
By helping a fainting brother
With an outstretched willing hand,
Would bring me joy and contentment
That comes from a life well planned.

This, then, would my heritage be:
A life by the side of the road
In touch with the Heavenly Master,
Always ready to help with the load
Of a faltering fellow traveler
Who might pass by my humble abode.

—*Mrs. Maud Lemmon*

PRAYER

Guide me through the day, dear Father,
Guide me through the day,
For without thy guidance, Father,
My feet would surely stray.

Hold me by the hand, dear Father,
Hold me by the hand;
Let not my heart by Satan's darts
Be pierced, but hold my hand.

Help me do thy will, dear Father,
Help me do thy will,
That thy words of praise, "Thou hast well done,"
Will linger with me still.

Lead me gently on, dear Father,
Lead me gently on,
And when my work is ended,
Dear Father, lead me home.

—*Lutie Price Leslie*

THE BROOK

Oh! I wonder, now I ponder,
Let me glide along;
I am ever happy
Singing my song.

Gliding gently round the mossy mound,
Now I toss a pebble;
On and on I go,
Singing, singing ever as the ripples flow.

Leaping! dashing! wondering!
Down the mountainside,
I shall reach the river
Ere the eventide.

The breeze speaks to the wild flowers
As I pass them by,
Gliding swiftly on my way
To the river I will play.

—*Adia James Lewis*

MORNING

The sun peeps o'er the treetops
And drives the mists away,
The dewdrops on the grass blades
Sparkle like jewels today;
The humming birds sup nectar
From hyacinth and rose,
The redbird in the peach tree
Bids farewell to repose.

The little pigs awakened
From slumber in the sty
Are busy getting breakfast,
While larks are soaring high;
From Morpheus' arms I struggle
To hear the call of one
Who coos and squirms and wiggles
In joy that night is gone.

—*Nell Tillotson Liddell*

ABSENT

Two sons I have away from home,
One in the North, one South;
Their absence sears my lonely heart
Like grainfields seared in drouth.

Their letters come, so dear, so sweet,
Quite often, yet too few;
They flood my heart with happiness
Like parched grass drenched with dew.

Vacation time, when they come home,
My heart forgets its pain
In drinking in each word they say
Like dry earth drinking rain.

—*Virginia Hart Lide*

INDIVIDUALIST

I stood beside an undulating sea
At morning, when a tempered, soft light lay
Upon a scene at peace, not grave nor gay,
Yet magic in the call it made to me.
It was a sea of grass on Texas plain;
Its whitecaps, cattle topping every hill,
Its only ship in harbor idly still,
A distant house beside a field of grain.

What bold adventurous rover anchored here?
What hopes, what aims, what greeds had sent him hence?
Resistant of restraints, a pioneer,
Inherent in his blood some social sense
Resentful of the crowd's demands on self
Or time or thought or, maybe, only pelf.

—Alice Lindsey

THE LAND OF "MIGHT HAVE BEEN"

Why go about with a troubled heart,
Why add to the dreadful din
That ever comes from that lonely spot,
The land of the "Might Have Been"?
'Tis a lonely land, 'tis a dreary land
Filled with wrecks of blasted dreams,
Where hope ne'er enters, grief ne'er leaves,
And the light of love ne'er beams.

'Tis a land that is strewn with blasted hopes
And moistened with bitter tears,
That is filled with sorrow and discontent,
With misery, grief, and fears;
And calling ever with anxious voice
It bids you enter in,
Till you're caught in the darkness that ever reigns
In the land of the "Might Have Been."

Leave this lonely spot, give the voice no heed,
But value the present hour,
Which filled with deeds of real worth
Takes from discontent its power;
For though there's despair along your way,
There is also much of bliss—
When you turn from the land of "Might Have Been"
To the land of "Really Is."

—Pearl Linkhart

CALM

From out the great Eternal I reach to take my own,
The Atom that is only me I place upon a throne.
To the vast "Unknown" I raise my eyes,
   I have no name or creed,
But in the hour of quiet thought
   It fills my greatest need.
I can and I will is written in every luminous ray,
The world is a little better because I live today.
                —*Grace Miner Lippincott*

CALIFORNIA COLOR

Black the smoke of Lassen's fire,
Black the walls that end the quest
To pierce strange Mono's heaving breast
And quickly quell her mad desire.

Gray the wing of gull in flight,
Gray of fog from sea-born bowers,
Gray of Mission walls and towers,
Gray—Kaweah's crannied height.

White is the foam of ocean's waves,
Restless, roaring, and resounding,
Loma's point to Del Norte pounding
In Big Lagoon and Jolla's caves.

Green of spring's fine Wedgwood tracing
Appears on Fresno's fruitful vines,
Lacy leafiness forms designs
To aid in nature's gracing.

Azure deep tints Tahoe's lake,
Nestled where the mountains mold
Their peaks into a cup to hold
Heaven's blue for human's sake.

Red of redbud and of Toyon,
Spear of snow plant so amazing,
O'er the snow its color blazing,
Beckoning from winter's canyon.

Glittering sheaves of gilded grain,
Glowing fields of poppies golden,
To the sun both are beholden
For their burnished, brilliant stain.

Lupines just inside the Gate
In royal hue deck Tamal's land.
Shasta's crest to silvery strand
The spectrum of our sunburst State.

—Martha W. Little

A WINTER SEA

I love the sea, its mystery,
And surging tides have talked to me.
The rush and roar of surf tossed high
Till blue of water meets blue of sky,
But I cannot leave my inland dwelling
To watch the tides receding, swelling;
So old King Winter brings to me
His imitation of the sea.
By my north door he likes to blow
A miniature wave of purest snow;
A downy crest of no mean height
He whirls on the South for my delight.
The meadow broad where we cut sweet hay
Is now a still, white, frozen bay.
Wind roars like surf on my icy strand,
Sleet strikes the panes and sounds like sand.
And winter holds for me a charm
On my snow-blocked New England farm.

—Grace R. Lloyd

RIVALRY

The opalescent sails
Of barks adrift enchanted seas
Are like white-winged birds
In flight . . .

The deepening skies
Are resplendent with colors
Daubed from the brush of some
Jealous god . . .
I wonder
If nature is not enviously rivaling
The brilliance of that white hour
When genius
Takes wings . . .

                                        —*Aileene Lockhart*

VISITING

'Tis fine to go a-visiting
    And spend a day or two
With friends I long have known and loved
    'Mid scenes all fresh and new.
But the finest part of visiting
    To me, I freely own,
Is when I pack my things again
    And take the long road home.

My mind goes on ahead of me
    Along the homeward way,
I think of things that must be done
    And should be done today.
I see the house and every room
    The way I left it last,
And wonder if the little chicks
    Have had a two days' fast.

There may be dishes in the sink
    And ashes on the floor,
The beds unmade and all about
    Dust thickly scattered o'er,
But I'm so glad to be at home
    Among my household gods,
I'm even glad to start again
    Those long-despised odd jobs.

With thoughts still with the friends I've left
   And hands that know their task,
I spend a busy happy day
   As full as one could ask.
For home is just the dearest place
   That I will ever see,
And my folks just the nicest folks
   'Cause they belong to me.

I like to go a-visiting
   And spend a little while,
But I like coming home again
   Where nothing cramps my style.
The finest part of visiting
   To me, I'll have to own,
Is when I pack my things again
   And take the long road home.
                —*Anna Patten Lockwood*

SPRING

A flash of blue in the lilac hedge,
A robin on the housetop's edge
   Sing—Spring is here!

The tulips through the molded leaves
Pushing their way to sun and breeze
   Say—Spring is here!

The rosy buds on my almond tree
Burst into lovely bloom and see
   That—Spring is here!

The gentle rain on my windowpane
Whispers softly the sweet refrain,
   Ah—Spring is here!

And though the spring of my life is past,
My soul is not sad nor yet downcast;
For have I not seen the flash of blue,
The bursting buds and the tulips too?

So my heart joins in the glad refrain
Of birds and flowers and gentle rain,
Spring—sweet spring—is here again.
                                        —*Hazel Funk Lockwood*

MY LADY OF THE ROSES

She dwells within a mansion fair
    Where sunlight soft reposes,
How wonderful for me she'd care,
    My Lady of the roses.

Though others come and humbly kneel
    To sue for smile or favor,
To me she's true through woe or weal,
    Her love will never waver.

Though fortune frowns and fate's behest
    Sorrow and pain imposes,
I'll not complain, to me is left
    My Lady of the roses.

And when some day in death's embrace
    My silent form reposes,
May angels guard with tender grace
    My Lady of the roses.
                                        —*Grace Johnson Lomon*

OUR LOVELY PIONEER

In the club there is a lady,
    And her hair is silvery gray,
But her smile is just as winsome
    As it was on that first day.
Yes, that first day—we say it proudly,
    For it meant so much to all,
When the yearbook was completed
    And she answered first roll call.

Through the years she has been faithful,
    Faithful to her holy trust;
Earnest, hopeful, wise, and tactful,
    And we've always found her just.

Twenty years! Oh, sisters ponder
  How inspiring the career
Of our faithful, dear, club lady,
  Yes, our lovely pioneer.

        —Elva N. Lovell

ETERNITY

Some day the stars will all be gone,
  Blown out by God;
Some day the trees will sweep the sky
  No more nor nod
Against the wind.
I'll stop for just one last long look,
Last listening to a mocking brook,
Before I step in through the door
And close it after, evermore.

        —Frances Stockwell Lovell

BROTHERHOOD

Ah, pity the poor, Good Brother!
They lie a-shiver with the cold,
Half waking through the bitter night.
Reluctantly they watch the dawn
Of an unwelcome day, whose sun,
Barred by frost-thickened windowpanes,
Sends scarce a beam of light and warmth
Into their homes so comfortless.

Sadly they rise, and in the thin
Habiliments of poverty,
Bereft of pride in work well done
And wage for service given, they light
Scant fires of charity and eat,
In bitterness of heart, its bread.

And true it is this need not be,
Had we not wandered far astray
From Thine own law of love divine,
"Thy neighbor love as thine own self."
More holy and still more Thine own,
"As I loved you, each other love."

And still we cry the cry of Cain,
"Am I my brother's keeper?" I?
And ask, as asked that one of Thee,
"Who is my neighbor?" Who, indeed!

Ah! cleanse our selfish hearts and fill
Our souls with purest love of Thee,
That we may know in truth our kin,
And love our neighbor perfectly.
—*Mabel Brackett Lovell*

GLAMOUR

A row of lilies stretching white
Through garden dusk out into the night;
That was the way for an eager child
To places far and sweet and wild.

Shimmer of moonlight on waving grain,
A far, faint sound as of falling rain—
For a breathless moment,—could it be?
Led the child to the rim of the sea.

She wandered once to a woodland glade,
The grass was dappled sun and shade;
There she saw, with lilt and swing
The fairies dance in a magic ring.

A row of fir trees standing stark
Against the house in the fragrant dark,
Called to the woman—she came alone,
"Alien feet tread the old hearthstone."

The windows behind the firs gleamed white,
Though she saw in the house no single light;
But the firs ever beckoned and called, "Come home,
We have waited long for our own to come."
—*Phebe Beach Lovell*

TABLEAU

Orchids in your boudoir,
   Roses in the hall,
Pansies in a yellow vase
   When I come to call.

Iris in your garden,
   Moss among the rocks,
Asters by the garden fence,
   And some four-o'clocks.

Air is full of fragrance,
   Perfume rich and rare,
Mingled with the sunshine
   Jewels in your hair.

Flowers in your garden
   Blooming 'neath the sun,
Keep their rarest perfume
   Waiting till I come.

—R. Geraldine Lown

PEACE

What? Pity her!
That she has dared to slip away from suffering;
That she has found a peace
Nothing can check or mar;
That she can rest with folded hands
Among green, growing things
And know the mystery of night winds sweeping
Through tall, dark pines
That watch beside her sleeping?
You say her face was sad and drawn,
You pity her!
But I know that sleep caught her lips in smiling;
Why do your lips lament
Her sculptured peace?

—Lillian Lowry

TO A MOCKINGBIRD

Little bird upon my sill,
　　How I love to feel your thrill!
Happy home up in a tree,
　　Pretty sight for child to see.

When the years round 'bout you pass,
　　And your family's en masse,
Song and twitter all afloat
　　That has come from your dear throat,
I shall call to those who pass—
　　Other birds now on the grass,
From your throat has come pure joy
　　Like the whistle of a boy.

Praise to God who sent you here,
　　Just to wipe away a fear
From a troubled heart that's sad,
　　Gloom dispelled and fear made glad.
　　　　　　　　　　—Pearl H. Luebke

HILL AND SEA

Lost in the blue of distant hills
A slowly sinking sun now spills
Its crimson color in the sea,
Whose bosom throbs with mystery;
A sea who quickly hides her face
With wind-blown, pale Venetian lace.
O jeweled Hills! O salt-white sea!
Your beauty wrings the heart of me!
　　　　　　　　　　—Lou Mallory Luke

GEMS OF TODAY

At dawn

When the dew still sparkles
On each tiny grass and flower,
You eagerly rise with a thought for the day,
　　A hope for this quiet hour.

When countless lives are resting
From labors Time must cease,
You breathe a prayer for the waking world—
    Its love, its joy, its peace.

At noon

When the sun above you
Covers all with cloth of gold,
Your faith bejeweled, gleaming,
    Like flowers of the morning unfold—
You stand before your Master,
With a tuneful song to Him
Who opens wide his portal,
    And you joyfully enter in.

At dusk

When the glory of sunset
Enshrouds all the earth like a veil,
And a mystic peace from heaven guides you on
    To the end of the trail—
Your heart beats high in thanks
For joys you long have sought;
Abiding hope, calm faith, and endless love
    Are gems that to you are brought.
                —*Florence O. Luker*

THE LIBRARY SPEAKS

I stand upon my little hill,
A mass of brick and stone,
And yet I am a vital thing
With a mission all my own.

I hold within my silent heart
A store of wisdom deep,
Which you, by reaching out your hands,
May have to use and keep.

And more than this I have at heart
A fond and deep desire
To be a help in anything
To which you may aspire.

I hold the best of everything
In History, Science, Art,
And stand in eager willingness
This knowledge to impart.

Men would forget the Great of yore
And all their valiant deeds;
So I will keep them on my shelf
For everyone who reads.

Discoveries of every age,
And tales from every land,
I have in language clear and plain
That all may understand.

Great Artists too, with brush and pen
In History took their parts
And gave me pictures, poems, prose,
The choicest of their arts.

But if you tire of lore so deep
And would relax the mind,
I have the choicest fiction
It is possible to find.

So you who view me as I stand,
Don't pass nor turn about,
For on my door, so near your path,
The latchstring will be out.

You who are growing old in years
Are cherished friends and dear,
And I will open wide my door
To bid you welcome here.

You have brought many volumes
To place upon my shelves,
And I know things that you have done
To make History, yourselves.

And middle-aged, who hurry on
With such a rushing pace,
Just drop your cares and read awhile
Beside my fireplace.

And children on your way to school—
A happy, careless throng—
I love to hear your laughter
And your bits of merry song.

But come inside! You're very young,
And life has just begun;
And *I* hold all your lessons,
All your fairy tales and fun.

So come as often as you can
And spend some time with me,
For you'll grow old as I grow old,
And lifelong friends we'll be.

So old and young, come gather here
Your leisure to beguile,
And I will furnish fact or fun
To make the time worth while.

And I will stand, year in, year out,
Upon my little hill.
Just *use* me, and give me the chance
My mission to fulfill.

—*Elizabeth Welton Lumpkin*

A PRAIRIE MIRACLE

The river's dwindled to a creek under the red sun's glare;
The corn leaves curl and crumble; thick dust chokes up the air;
Like shattered bits of a rainbow lie petals of wild rose;
And worn with futile waiting, lilies their chalice close.

Grim pastures, dry and barren,
Mock at the lean, gaunt stock;
While weird and eery comes the cry
Of blackbird, dove, and hawk.

But up from the Western skyline, mountains of black clouds
loom,
And out of the brooding hush echoes the thunder's boom.
With a roar comes the Southwestern, driven by flaming lash,
Dashing asunder the clouds with crackle and groan and crash!

And lo! the portals are opened
With miracle again!
Old Earth, o'erfilled with pregnant hope,
Relives that scene at Nain.

—*Grace Welsh Lutgen*

HOMESPUN

My robe I wrought of sorrow,
    Sewn with little tears and sighs,
I hid it from my neighbors
    Lest some might sympathize.

My cloak I spun of gladness,
    Daffodil dawns and eves,
The bluebird's song, the robin's call,
    Shimmer of light on leaves.

A golden hour's transit,
    A planet's frosty beam,
Laughter of a little child
    Awakening from a dream.

Folding them close about me,
    I set off up the street,
Thinking I will be different
    From any one I meet.

Tilting my cap of fancy,
    I watched the passers-by,
And was surprised to see them
    Attired much as I.

—*Carrie Ward Lyon*

CRYSTALLIZATION[1]

The tears that belong to the poet,
His magic skill has wrought
Into pearls of joy or of sadness,
The crystals of his thought.

[1] Reprinted from the *Poet's Forum*, by permission of the publishers.

And when in the heart of another
The pearl once more appears,
The wonderful art of the poet
Has melted it back to tears.

—Mabel Lyon

YOUR ACCOUNTING

If you've walked with Wisdom—known the way,
Of this my friend, you're sure—
That when you come to The Great Day
Naught else but Justice can endure;
For this we know—let come what may—
Who does God's work, will get God's pay.

So after all 'tis well to share
This world as best we may,
Life's choicest gifts and blessings rare;
We've such a little while to stay;
Then ne'er forget—let come what may—
Who does God's work, must get God's pay.

If you've learned of better things than clay,
If your soul has looked above,
If you've walked the paths of Virtue's way,
If you've scattered naught but Love,
Your sure reward on your Great Day—
You've done God's work—You'll get God's *Pay!*

—Emme Maak

BEAUTY MARKS AN URGE

The grass returns to spears of brilliant green,
And lilacs tip their branches with gay plumes,
On lively trees bird choruses convene
To warble songs through orchards' choice perfumes.

Now earth is eager, life reflects her mood,
For wounds that deepened in the wintertime
Assuage, as Spring with flower and feathered brood
Proclaims renascent joy in ardent pantomime.

Beauty marks an urge ancient as the sun,
In caroling of birds, in budded rod;
And Spring with earth a joyous thing has done . . .
Beauty is as old as the love of God.

—Hallie Davis Maas

AT SLUMBER TIME

So unafraid we trust our loved to sleep
When evening shadows fall and day is done,
Content to know they will awake at dawn
And greet us when the morning has begun.

We light the candle as the hour grows late,
We smile and say, "Sleep well, dear one, good night!"
Then stand and watch them as they climb the stair
Till face and form have passed beyond our sight.

We catch the sound of footfalls as they go,
And then the gentle closing of a door
Above us, then a silence drops between
As softly as a shadow on the floor.

We go our way to rest and feel no fear,
We know they sleep to dream as we shall do,
Forgetting all the weariness of toil
Till day puts out the stars and skies grow blue.

And yet when Death's calm hour of slumber comes
To fold our loved within its rest, we weep,
We question what the solemn mystery is
That walls them from us in unwaking sleep.

We fear the silence that no cry can break,
No fond caress reach through its hush supreme
To call the sleeper back when morning comes
To fold away the night's soft robe of dream.

Oh, would we had the perfect faith to say,
When our belovèd go beyond our sight
Up Death's dim stair to enter into rest,
"They do but sleep to waken with the light!"

—Mae Wallace MacCastline

PIXY HEART

My hands are in the kitchen
　　Doing homely things;
My heart is on the moorland
　　Shaping fairy rings.

My lips recite drab pages
　　Of household rights and wrongs;
My little witching heart-voice
　　Is trilling fairy songs.

My staid feet, shod in leather,
　　Tread solemn paths of clay;
My heart, in crystal slippers,
　　Lilts down a rainbow way.

I sew discreet blue gingham
　　For frocks of doubtful grace;
My heart trims gowns of gossamer
　　With Queen Anne's lace.

Perhaps the pans are brighter
　　Touched by a fairy gleam;
Perhaps the bread is lighter
　　When mingled with a dream.

My course is plainly charted
　　For-ever-and-a-day . . .
What ho! This pixy heart of mine
　　Has up and run away!
　　　　　　　　　—Mirza French Mackay

CANDLELIGHT

There is a potency in candlelight:

I see a great cathedral where there burn
Tall candles in a dim and flickering glow,
Still figures kneeling, while low voices give
Their murmured prayers—these rise and softly go.

A banquet board is spread, and 'neath soft shades
Of rose and gold a filtered light streams out
To play upon the scene of Beauty rare,
With Wit and Romance in a merry bout.

Within a quiet chamber quiet lies
A form all peaceful in the last deep sleep,
Guarded by tapers with a mellow sheen,
That seem so hallowed by the watch they keep.

—*Nora Hefley Mahon*

MY MOTHER'S ROCKING CHAIR

I loved my mother's rocking chair,
    So cheery and so bright;
'Twas small and round and painted red,
    It was my chief delight.

The seat was deep, the back was round,
    It fit you, oh, so snug;
I loved to rock in mother's arms,
    She'd hold me tight and hug
Me, oh, so close up to her heart;
    Then all my fears would soon depart.

I would love to see once more, my dear,
    That dear old rocking chair,
To be a child in mother's arms,
    To feel the comfort there.
And that old kitchen, the old blue clock,
    The winding wooden stair,
But memory dear has painted clear
    A picture, oh, so fair
Of my mother and her kitchen and
    The little rocking chair.

—*Marcella Drennan Malarky*

TIME

As I glided down the valley of time,
I felt a strange sweet sense of peace;
I bid adieu to yesterday,
Tomorrow I cannot see.

Oh! Time as you glide so swiftly by,
More precious art thou than gold,
Swifter by far than the swiftest steed.
Oh! Time what must thou be, that we cleave to thee so eagerly?

Glide on, oh Time, in your flight.
No sorrow in the bygone days,
No hope in the future years
Can rob me of the joy and peace of the golden present, Now.
                                        —*Bertha Osler Malcolm*

AT THE END OF THE DAY

My desk is always littered
With things I want to keep;
They should be cleared away
Before I go to sleep.

Announcements of events gone by
To tell of death or birth,
A greeting from a distant friend;
These really have no worth.

A picture of a romping pup,
A withered wedding rose,
A daughter's little copy book;
I've many more of those.

A husband's useless, loving gift,
A small son's trial at art;
Of no value to the hand or mind,
Their merit's in the heart.

My life is always baffled
By things I want to do;
They cannot be attained
Before my life is through.

My mind would steer a steady course
Directly toward the goal;
My heart stops at so many ports
For cargo for the soul.
                                        —*Iowa Marshall Maplethorpe*

THE LONG JOURNEY

A ghostly caravan of women bowed
Are dragging weary feet through slewy sand.
They journey on and on in dour complaint,
Yet ever kneel for burdens, not their own;
And through eternity they travel, (like
To camels) whining, yet with sour content,
Yet after all, they are the mothers of men.
The woman and the camel baffle them
(Despite their power and mental strength).
Refractory-complaint is woman's trait.
With supercilious, subtle, dumb aspect
She weirdly plods her way fore'er detached.

—*Susan R. Marsh*

THE GRANDCHILD

When baby feet go pit-a-patter
And the sound of childish chatter
Sweetly falls upon my ears,
Then I travel down the years
And live again days of the past
When baby fingers held me fast.

O baby girl! With your hair of gold,
You'll comfort me when I am old—
Your childish ways, the things you say
Fill me with rapture day by day,
I feel you'll always be a part,
Next to your mother, in my heart.

—*Pearl M. Marshall*

WHAT MOTHER SAID

"Close your eyes," our mother said,
"Take a deep breath, my dear,
See, the sliver's nearly out,
And you haven't shed a tear."

Close your eyes, trust, don't look,
Breathe a deep breath, a prayer—
That was the source of mother's strength
When things were hard to bear.

Slivers—or hearts all broken and sore—
It always helped somehow;
So "close your eyes and take a deep breath,"
We say to our children now.

—Mabel Standley Marston

MY ROAD LEADS TO YOU

"This is my road"—I heard a woman say,
And down the winding trail she went her way.

"This is my road"—a pretty maiden cried;
Down the bridal path she went a happy bride.

"This is my road"—said a darling child,
Gathering bright flowers in a garden wild.

"This is my road"—what I say is true,
My road is the road which leads me to you.

—Clara Tull Martin

SONNET TO MONADNOCK

O sentinel of Peterboro hills,
Half-slumbering power, unattempted might,
Calm watcher of the moon-awakened night,
Thy vigilance serenity instills.
The centuries will leave thee unperturbed,
As does the secret whisper of the rain,
The exhortation of the wind, the pain
Of winter storm, or press of settling bird.

The hand of Time is full, her foot is fleet.
Our youth is but a hope and a surmise.
Futurity may darken in our eyes
When we have seen the ash replace the heat.
Yet the eternal summit still appears
Sweetened by the seasoning of years.

—Eleanor Beckman Martin

HER POEM

She looked to find a poem,
For her heart was all a-song,
And she longed to find expression
To pass the joy along.

But it played—a thing elusive,
Like a floating thistledown;
So she turned to little duties
As daily she had found.

She put a tiny house to rights
And made it cherry bright.
She set a bowl of blooming bulbs
Within the window's light.

She answered fifty questions
For a busy little brain,
She kissed away a troubled tear
And made a circus train.

She served an appetizing meal
On quaint old Quimper ware,
And half forgot the poem thing
To rumple up his hair.

She watched a glowing sunset,
And then a white star shone.
From heaven's blue a message came,
"Your poem—'tis your home."

—Eva Jones Martin

FROM A CAR WINDOW

Woodlands and prairies all rolling and green,
And telephone poles that seem whizzing right by,
Then acres of Indian corn can be seen,
And a view of a church spire with cross in the sky.

The train now must follow the course of a stream;
The scene's ever changing—now lands that are bare,
With mountains so distant that cloudlike they seem,
Then rocky formations that tower in the air.

Onrushing with whistle so shrill through the night,
With whispering voices and creaking of brake.
A sunrise on peaks that are dazzling and white
Is seen o'er the forests, again in a lake.

A stop at each station with clanging of bell,
With ever new faces, while traveling on,
Each speaking a welcome or lingering farewell—
Thus briefly our lives perhaps touch—then they're gone.
—*Leona Bolt Martin*

A WOMAN'S WISH

I wish I might be like the rose
Who gathers beauty as she grows;
The rose who, drinking sun and air,
Breathes out her love life without care;

Like the rose who lives her day
Spreading her magic for display
Freely to those who pass her door,
Giving her all—knowing no more.

I wish I might be like the rose
Who gathers beauty as she grows,
And when she goes, fades quietly,
Leaving a fragrant memory . . .
—*Ella Mason*

RESIGNATION

No more against life's cruel bars
    My pinions will I beat,
But like a wise imprisoned bird
    I'll perch with steady feet

Upon my swing and sing my song,
    And through encagèd bars
I'll gaze upon earth's loveliness
    Beneath the wondrous stars.

No more my pinions will I beat,
  But look on meadows green;
Then soon my bars I'll cease to see,
  And life will grow serene.

               —Malvina Yerger Mayes

FALLEN LEAVES

I strolled o'er wooded, wind-swept hills
  'Mong bare and naked trees,
And walked as in loose drifted snow
  Through brown, soft, rustling leaves.

I felt a wee bit sad at heart,
  I missed the colors gay
Of autumn leaves upon the trees,
  When last I passed this way.

Now, all those gorgeous colored leaves
  Lie scattered on the ground;
Few hints of previous wondrous tints
  On any can be found.

They're caught by every passing breeze
  And circled high in air,
To fall again and huddle close
  At the feet of trees so bare.

And thus, dear leaves, your mission fill;
  As much your part to be
A shelter for all tender roots,
  As swaying high in tree.

Soon, floating low, some soft grey clouds
  Will send a cover warm
Of snowflakes, light as down itself,
  To shield you from all storm.

Then, when the Springtime comes again
  And cold wind disappears;
All leaves and flowers will lovelier be
  Because of you, my dears.

               —Dora Dickson McBroom

GEORGE WASHINGTON—A PORTRAIT

We do not think of him as fair of face,
With ostentatious dress in ribboned wig and lace,
But one whose brow was furrowed deep with thought
And scarred with many a battle fought.
His stately mien and austere grace
Hid much of that Titanic force
Which ever gently turned, or backward
Cast in wrath the unceasing tide of wrong.
With men and measures, statesmen, friends,
He urged the cause of right; untimed,
And like the everlasting hills he stands,
A soul of adamant, undaunted and sublime.
                              —*Minnie Parker McCown*

A LOVER

I am in love with so many things:
A cricket that chirps, a bird that sings;

A tree that is green in a garden small,
A creeping grass, the iris tall;

A baby's dimples, your eyes of blue,
A rainy day and the morning dew;

A country road, a tiny brook,
The star Altair and a "poetry book."

So much to love, to have, to hold,
I have scarcely time for growing old.
                              —*Marta S. McCracken*

JOHN AND I

We have jogged along together
Through fair and stormy weather,
          John and I.

We've had our ups and downs,
We've had our smiles and frowns,
          John and I.

We've had sickness, we've had health,
We've had everything but wealth,
       John and I.

We've had good times that were snappy
When we both were very happy,
       John and I.

We have had some sadness too
When we both felt very blue,
       John and I.

Just thirty-nine harvest moons we've seen;
Some years brought fat, some years brought lean
       To John and I.

We've seen sorrow, we've seen joy
Trying to raise a girl and boy,
       John and I.

So we've climbed the hill together hand in hand,
And we'll journey on together to the better land,
       John and I.

                    —*Mrs. John McElroy*

NATURE'S SONG OF GEORGIA

Down in sunny southland
Nature tells the story
Of its treasure store in Georgia
That is yet to claim great glory.

The wind goes whispering through the trees
And bids them be content,
So good and greatly woods
Shall give the Nation recompense.

The waters of the rivers laugh
As they come tumbling down,
To think that they pass hills of clay
In which a fortune may be found.

The ocean waves ever knocking
Against the Georgia coast,
Would have her offer made well known
That one may claim and boast.

The sun and wind agree
That since ole Georgia has a share
In most of Nature's royal gifts
That they put all their climates there.

Georgia gives so many themes
For the birds to sing about;
Songsters stay the whole year through—
Then they never sing them out.

—*Vera McElveen*

PAUSE ERE LIFE HAS SPENT ITS COURSE

The sun gives life to this wondrous land!
   All might live and not despair,
Receiving riches from bounteous hand,
   Did men not suffer from man-made care.

Of worldly wealth we're given a measure
   Of what we crave—nothing more.
Deep in the soul lies greater treasure,
   Buried from sight in the heart's inner core.

The man who lives with a curse on his lips,
   Not knowing the worth of golden days,
Misses the goal, while he tightly grips
   His binding chains till flesh decays.

Pause ere life has spent its course,
   Its wheels in action swiftly turning.
Little remains but sad remorse
   If we see not the light steadily burning.

Days and years roll on forever,
   Man at best lives not for long;
Search your heart for the golden treasure,
   Make Peace and Love your helpful song.

—*Blanche Baldwin McGaw*

NIGHT'S BEAUTIES

The ground is covered with moonlight
   Shining on the snow,
And the stars up in the heavens
   Twinkle, twinkle so;
The lights are out in the houses—
   For folks are fast asleep,
While I kneel at my window
   And all the night's beauty seek.
                —*Gertrude Yates McGiffert*

MUTE

I cannot speak the thoughts
That crowd my throat to aching;
I cannot speak the dreams
That fill my heart to breaking.

Yet when in spring I see the pear tree keeping
Her fragrant, snowy tapers lifted high;
Or sometimes, when I watch a baby sleeping;
Or when an old man smiling totters by;
Or sometimes, when a butterfly goes winging
Its fragile way across a windy sky;
Or sometimes, when I hear a young girl singing—
It seems that I must speak, or I shall die!
                —*Nelle Graves McGill*

MEMORIES

You cannot take from me the memories of old,
As they come to me through the mist.
The prattle and charm of the little ones come,
And with them come triumph and bliss.
We loved them so much and each little ill
Was easily healed with a kiss.
And as they go forth in their homes to abide,
I pray, they let *God* be their Saviour and guide.

I cherish the thought of the days gone by,
My heart has been steadfast and true.
There's still one sweet thought that I cherish the most,
The love of the things that bring pleasure to you.
—*Mrs. R. E. McLaughlin*

ADOLESCENCE

Wistful, cruel, tender, gruff,
Each in turn you seem to be;
Baby, sage, roisterer, bluff—
All of these you seem to me.

Wonderings, thrills, longings, fears,
With all of these your soul is rife
As the age of man draws near.
Such a puzzling thing is life!
—*Mabel Ward McQuaid*

PHOENIX
To my loved ones

In time I'll leave this worn-out form,
With sunken eye and whitened hair
And withered cheek that seem to mask
The radiant youth that once shone there.

When that time comes, farewells still near,
Give not my form an earthy bed
Where worm and mold impatient wait
And Death's own seal will mark my head.

Let cleansing flame remove the mask
And set me free in silver ash,
To drift like smoke from winging plane
Flown high above the lightning's flash.

Quite unafraid shall I then swing
Between blue sky and blooming earth,
And riding high and shining winds,
Exultant, trace the world's whole girth.

The rainbow's arch will fold me in,
And rest I'll find in cool white bars
That ring the moon when skies are pale
And gauzy streamers drape the stars.

For years untold shall I be part
Of day's and night's prismatic tone;
And you shall see, not rosy dawn,
But cheeks now warm against your own;

Not dusky clouds across the sun—
My blowing hair—you know it well;
Not green-blue sky above the west,
But eyes where love will always dwell.

My voice you'll hear in little winds;
My lips you'll see in sunsets red;
If through the years we see and hear
Old loves, we know they are not dead!
—*Ida Carothers Merriam*

IN SUMMERTIME

A marsh bird swinging on a slender reed,
A fragrance faint, elusive in the air;
Blue sky and reedy lake, swift fleecy clouds,
Long drowsy days that were so sweet and fair.

In fitful dreams, when winter winds blow cold,
And birds have flown, and the blue lake is gray,
I shall remember all those happy hours
That seem so near and yet so far away.

And I shall hear the music of the marsh,
And see white lilies wooed by dragonflies,
Clusters of stately purple hyacinths,
And over all the azure of the skies.

I shall look with longing, till once more
Those magic hours return and bring to me
The loveliness of gracious summer days,
And a blue lake, a glowing pageantry.
—*Mary Royce Merriman*

COURIER

Today a robin heralded the spring,
From scarlet scrip proclaimed
The season's birth, a new faith's christening.
"The king is dead," he cried. "Long live the king!"
A tulip stirred, and flamed.

—*Maud Woodward Merritt*

THOUGHTS IN A BEAUTY SHOP

Quiet and busy hands,
Perhaps a word or two,
"How do you like your nails?"
"Shall we try an oil shampoo?"

What do they think all day,
These girls who work with care,
Dolling a beauty up,
Making my lady fair?

What is the difference here,
Isn't it all the same?
Isn't it living the life,
Aren't we playing a game?

What will it matter at last
Whether she worked and I played?
Isn't our life all set,
Aren't our circles made?

"O! am I through so soon?"
"Thank you, it's very nice."
"O yes, I'll come again."
(My thoughts have been worth the price).

—*Maude R. Meyer*

PHOENIX

A city of the desert,
A part of our great Southwest;
Its magical spell has won us,
Of charm it is possessed.

We love its glorious sunsets,
　Its skies of azure blue,
Its purple-tinted mountains,
　Its flowers of every hue.
So here's a toast to Phoenix,
　By nature richly blessed,
This city of the desert,
　A part of our great Southwest.
　　　　　　　—*Cora Holbrook Milchrist*

LONE LITTLE HOUSE ON THE DESERT

Oh lone little house on the desert,
　Why do you look so sad?
You once were filled with laughter,
　Do you mourn for a little lad?

The vines still creep round your doorway,
　The cactus blooms in the yard,
But where are the folk who came to live
　'Neath your friendly arms, now marred?

Did gold in the hills allure them
　And fill their breasts with hope?
Or was it visions of orange groves
　And date palms on the slope?

Did loneliness of the desert
　Dampen their ardor so gay?
Or did ghosts of wandering Ho-ho-kam
　Frighten them all away?

The red and gold of the sunset
　Still hang o'er the brow of the hill,
On guard stand the giant sahuaro
　Like sentinels lone and still.

But no one stands at the portal
　To welcome the good and the bad,
Oh lone little house on the desert,
　Tell us your secret so sad.
　　　　　　　—*Blanche Powell Miller*

CONSECRATION

Me you may lose, but the spirit of me
   Keep in the faith that I gave it;
Me you may blame, but I let you see
   New vistas of life, so why save it?
Use me for a pattern to fashion your love,
   And some girl, than I, you'll set above.

I had ideals, but now I've become
   A woman more real, more fine;
I was ultragood, too far above some
   To know their shoes could be mine.
Fear, disillusion, tragedy, pain;
   These have I known, yet not in vain—

I'd like to think that I could give
   To you the art of learning to live.
                —*Estelle Wiepking Miller*

OLD STREET

There is a solitude in this great space,
  A silence that has birth in these old trees,
  That hovering above refuse the breeze
Admittance there to brush the ancient face
Of buildings younger by an age than they,
  These trees that once were young by quiet lanes
  Where violets looked up, and sudden rains
Reached to the ground long fingers to repay
The dry earth for its futile blossoming.
  And now in this unbroken cloud of leaves,
  Beneath this weight a rising race conceives,
Comes an old promise of a vanished spring,
A promise that is even now stillborn
  And never challenges the hidden truth
  That age may dimly recognize, but youth
Will never know, or guessing, hold to scorn
Of later things; and they deny its pleas
  Unnoticing, as youth may draw its cart
  Across the silence of an old man's heart
And never know the severed memories.
                —*Helen Janet Miller*

WINGS

My thoughts are like the wild things
That flash across a pond:
Like gleam of fin in sunlight,
Or mating call beyond,

Where eyes glint from ambush
And branches vaguely stir,
Where paws pad softly
And bright wings whir.

I would not bring one captive forth
With metre's handcuffs on it,
Impaled upon a simile,
Or caged within a sonnet;

I would not catch and fetter it
The imprisoned host among,
Though you should be forgotten,
Though you should go unsung.

—*Jessie S. Miner*

THE HAPPY PILGRIM

I still salute you, Life, send what you may
Of sorrow's sheaf, the rough hour and the dark.
For I do cherish yet a potent spark
Of youth's spent beacon, flaming yesterdays,
Brightness of little casual joys astray,
Fresh Violets, enchanting rain—that lark
At heaven's gate—and memories that mark
With morning gleams the milestones of my way.
Nothing can daunt the spirit given to Mirth,
No crashing tower of dreams, no cause forlorn,
Nor imminent "Halt!" where the dim outposts are
Edging the last grim barriers of Earth.
Send storm! Send night! Joy's henchman bred as born
Needs but the tiniest rift to see a star.

—*Lulu W. Mitchell*

AFTERWARDS

A soft wind caressing the leaves of a tree—
Gone, leaving no trace save a memory.

A white-winged ship reaching a sheltered bay,
Storm-tossed, treasure-laden, from a weary way.

A lark singing, soaring into the sky,
Bearing its paean of praise on high.

A tiny star blending its living ray
With the glorious whiteness of the Milky Way.
    Think thus of me if I should die today.
              —*Nancy Red Montgomery*

TO A MODERN POET

I find that I have lost my taste
For queer jade bowls and frustration.
Your pale emotions are a waste
Whose songs to slow-fed rivers run.

For I have seen a woman's face
When unsought travail bore her down,
Or heard a redbird's rising grace
A thousand morning paeans crown.

In sunny windows I have seen
Some red and amber jellies glow,
And opal wheat against the green
Where lovely, lovely shadows go.

And so I like a virile song,
Or one so quiet and so still
That my tired heart can go along
And wait for God beyond a hill.
              —*Elizabeth Monyhan*

PRAIRIE STARS[1]

How many ages have these silent stars
Dotted the darkness of this firmament?
How many generations have been blent
With the lost blood of desperate border wars,
And dust that flashed in burnished scimitars
Of waving grass before its hour was spent?
The ancient glacier's frozen malcontent
Once rolled this way beneath that same red Mars.
Then what am I who pause a moment here,
One with the wind and night, yet not of them?
One with the earth, yet strangely separate
This breath, this heartbeat, this ephemeral tear.
A thousand, thousand summers past my fate
These stars shall gild this prairie's diadem!
                                        —*Minnie Hite Moody*

WILD PROPHECY[2]

Hear me, Lords of the upper air,
Cloudy keepers of time and space,
You who hold in your broad embrace
The peace of God and the world's despair;
You whose windy halls lie far
And firm upon the ether's edge,
Whose towers lift from heaven's ledge,
Whose doors have neither lock nor bar;
Hearken, masters, for I would tell
Of a vagrant whisper, an eerie sound
Fleet as mercury on the ground—
Syllables I could scarcely spell.

Heed me and help me, Lords, I pray,
For a voice has come to my waking ear,
A splintering cry so swift, so near,
It has brought the stars to my floor today.

[1] Reprinted from *Frontier and Midland*, by permission of the publishers.
[2] Reprinted from *Afterwhere*, by permission of The Poets Press.

It has pierced the marrow and bone of me,
And whither it went or whence it came
The blood in my body has turned to flame
While my heart beats time to a prophecy.
To a prophecy both wild and fair
Of that bold hour when farthest space
Shall yield its code to the human race—
Our Moment linked with the Afterwhere.

Oh, marvel of the astonished morn!
Oh, signal out of the stratosphere
When she whose name I hold most dear—
From whose brave body I was born—
Shall summon me from that blue height,
Shall call my name, release my load,
Her beacon white upon the road,
Flooding the darkened path with light!
Hear me, kings of the upper air,
Lordly keepers of time and tide;
Your star-stitched banners, blowing wide,
Spell courage when your children dare!

My vow is lightning-swift and strong;
My pledge is hot upon the wind;
New knowledge leaps within my mind—
Love tells me it will not be long!

—*Angela Morgan*
POET LAUREATE
GENERAL FEDERATION OF WOMEN'S CLUBS

MY CUP IS NEARLY EMPTY

My cup is nearly empty now
    Of bitter draughts and sweet.
The sips at first just quenched the thirst,
    The depths were still to meet.
But drop by drop the contents cleared
    Until the vision gleamed
With life and beauty, hope and cheer;
    Each quaff more precious seemed.

And when the last drop shall be drained,
   I'm sure of not a fetter,
For joy and sadness mingling strange
   Have made the drinking better.
My cup is nearly empty now,
   More precious is each sip,
And sweeter far each drop, I trow,
   As my cup I daily tip.

                    —*Beulah Russell Morgan*

I THANK THEE

The face of a child beamed with joy
When t'was given a pretty toy.
She took the gift, ran off to play,
One more pleasure had come her way.
She had no special thought or care
How this gift might have gotten there.
You think, such careless untrained ways,
Because this child forgot to say;
        I thank thee.

So many gifts are ours each day,
So much to gladden all our ways,
We take these joys and go along
On life's way with a merry song,
Perhaps with never a thought or care
How these gifts might have gotten there.
The little child forgot, 'tis true,
But have these words been said by you?
        I thank Thee.

                    —*Mrs. Elsie Morlan*

TWILIGHT

From out my casement window low I leant,
Wrapped in fond mem'ries of a day's content;
I watched night softly folding down,
Stars peeping forth, a living crown.

Birds their cradle songs were crooning,
Blooms in cloying scent were swooning,
Waves crisped the sea, a long tryst keeping
With shores that even now were sleeping.

Peace flowed over me, evening air grew chill,
And every beating pulse of life was still;
Yet as this lambent beauty drifted by,
In ecstasy I breathed a long-drawn sigh,

And whispered in the darkness circling me,

"Wait, fragrant night,
Come not too soon.
Pause, waning light,
Reflecting yon pale moon—
Give me my little hour—
Twilight, I love thee."
—*Clara Whittaker Morrissey*

READ A BOOK A WEEK

If I were king of Zululand, a grand and noble Sheik,
I'd have one hobby all my own and read a book a week.

Were I a mermaid of the sea and dwelt in caverns deep,
I'd have a cozy in a rock and read a book a week.

Were I a spirit of the air, my lodge a mountain peak,
I'd sit on clouds on sunny days and read a book a week.

Were I a dame of ample means with home my friends would seek,
I'd try to influence everyone to read a book a week.

If I could head a Woman's Club with members bold or meek,
I'd make the slogan of my term to read a book a week.

Were I the head of C. L. U., I'd on the common speak;
I'd send the last man to his work and read a book a week.

Were I the leader of the land, a Harding, so to speak,
I'd set the pace for every man and read a book a week.

But I'm a maid of tender years, must work that I may eat,
But I take some minutes every day and read a book a week.
—*Mrs. Helen S. Morse*

TO THE BLUE, HIGH MOUNTAIN
As Pike's Peak was formerly called

The Japanese have Fujiyama, we
Have you in snow-clad majesty;
Remote, you are unceasingly
Uplifted for our sight against the blue
Of Colorado sky's most vivid hue.

Changeless you stand, the same yet not the same
From morning's dawn to evening's painted flame,
Lovely and lonely, deaf to our acclaim;
All lights and shadows play along your crest,
Changing your face, though you remain at rest.

Now lapis lazuli in clear moonglow
Your beauty to your worshippers may show
Purpling to darkness where the slope dips low;
Aquamarine the heavens o'er your head
Are breathless wonder for the rapt gaze spread.

Or gloomily above our homesteads warm
Dark blue you brood in shadowed time of storm,
Etched sharp with snow to outline your clear form;
And yet, oh dreamlike peak, we love you best
In common garb of snow and sunshine dressed:

Fair in the early light your slopes seem brown,
Darkling and rich beneath your snowy crown,
Changing to blue as the high sun slips down,
Plunging in splendor to its nightly tryst,
And leaves you veiled in filmy clouds of mist,
White-capped above a sea of amethyst!
                                        —*Rebecca Emery Morton*

A CLUBWOMAN'S PRAYER

Build of my life a structure fair,
Make large the rooms and pure the air,
Sink the foundations deep and wide,
God the Architect—Christ, the Guide!

Make strong its walls, and anchor fast
To withstand storm and tempest's blast;
Raise up its columns with Thy Love
Until they reach to Thee above!

Give to me a far-flung view
To sift the false out from the true!
To help me see in toil and care
The beauty that lies hidden there.

One room for Trust and Charity,
Faith and Wisdom's clarity;
One for Forbearance, one for Mirth;
In one to Joy and Peace give birth.

Put Sympathy, e'en Sorrow there,
For Life metes out to each his share.
And mingling all with Love,
Approve my mansion from above.

And when I leave my mansion door,
As my short day of life is o'er,
May the golden rays of the setting sun
Shine on a beauty just begun!
                    —*Rebecca L. Moseley*

MOTHER LOVE

E'en though the earth should pass away
    And all that God had e'er ordained—
The realms of space all starless be,
    And Chaos rule where Order'd reigned—
No deep, dark night would hover o'er,
For still there'd be, below, above,
A tender haze of mauve and rose,
    The afterglow of mother love!
                    —*Ruby M. Moses*

GARDEN DREAMS[1]

Moonlight rests white fingers
On my garden's breast,
The wind says—"Hush 'tis sleeping,
Quiet is its rest."

[1] Reprinted from *Home Friend Magazine*, by permission of the publishers.

But O, I know, beneath the snow,
Like soaring wings its dreams alight,
Waking every flowering grace
Long hidden from our sight.

                                                    —*Anne Murry Movius*

MY WESTERN HOME

My heart turns sick with longing
  For my primal western home,
Built by the hands of the pioneer
  Near the canyons where the antelope roam.
For there were no ghosts of pain, nor evil thoughts,
  When Night her sable mantle threw,
Only the hearth fire's friendly gleam,
  With incense from the burning cedar, too.

From night-dark hills, range beyond range,
  Tall singing pines made patterns 'gainst the sky,
And the village lay adream beneath a roof of stars
  Faintly gleaming from afar, on high.
And there stood the silent Sawtooth mountains—
  White Stone Castles built by God,
And below, the valley of winding Lost River
  With the cottonwood trees' friendly nod.

                                                    —*Eva W. Mullen*

"AS A LITTLE CHILD"

'Tis told that where the Carpenter once wrought,
There bloomed a perfect, pure white rose alone,
Till gathered by a crippled child, and brought
Where blossoms from the royal gardens shone
In fairylike array, seeking a prize.
The child with rapture laid his off'ring there,
And felt his gift must surely draw all eyes—
In waxen beauty there was none so fair.

"Whence came this rose? We know it not," they cried,
And clutched anew their robes of wealth and power;
Could Nazareth bring forth the perfect flower?

An old man touched it tenderly and sighed;
The sunshine kissed its petals where it lay;
But from the child a crutch had dropped away.
                                    —*Ida Norton Munson*

THE TEAKETTLE SONG

Oft, late at night, when all are asleep,
Through the still house I silently creep.
Back to my kitchen I love to go;
There on the fire the bright coals glow,
Shadows dance and little lights play
On the ceiling and floor in a fanciful way;
And I list to a song that my kitchen brings,
The wee, weird song that the teakettle sings.

I linger awhile and muse of the times
This song has been sung in many climes,
At firesides great, or humble and small,
But the same queer song sung to them all
Since long years ago, when the center of home
Was an open fireplace and a sacred hearthstone.
Such thoughts as these my kitchen brings,
And the wee, weird song that the teakettle sings.
                                    —*Olive Lavena Murphy*

KEEPING STORE

Out of the land of "make-believe"
Memories I now retrieve.
    When I was only four,
    I played "keeping store"
Under the old sweet apple tree.

Those "apples" were dress goods rare,
Their "quality" none could compare,
    Those luscious groceries, too,
    Were cleverly sold through
The saleslady—some "debonnaire."

Not only big sales to transact,
But it took courtesy to attract
  Old Tige and Lizzie cat,—
  They'd invariably spat
Over a bargain—then it took tact.
                     —Amanda Muterspaugh

LOVE SANG FROM OVER YONDER

Love sang to me afar—I did not understand.
I would not be a slave nor bow to Love's command . . .
  Then Love came close and strong, caught me in his embrace—
  Oh sudden sweet his song and beautiful his face.

"What art thou Love? I cannot know!
Yet thou hast substance fine as snow—
  And thou hast gracious form and face—
  But how canst thou speed here through Space?"

From out a light-year's day I hear,
And strain to catch Love's whisper clear:—
  "Love hath no bounds, no age, no place,
  Unsought—like light his rapid pace.

"For I am Love and I love thee,
Though planet-lives apart are we.
  I come to thee as to a shrine,
  For love I serve thee—dearest, mine!

"Did not a cool breeze fan thy cheek
When thou wast struggling, worn and weak?
  Did not a flashing wave of joy
  Uplift thy soul? 'Twas my envoy.

"No sacrifice (if glad thou art)
Can be too great for me—dear heart!
  Dost thou forget—when lone and sad—
  Came lesser loves to make thee glad?

"'Twas e'er the great love that I bear
Sent lesser loves thy love to share.
  No limit be there to true love,
  That Selfless roves where'er we rove."
                    —Florence E. D. Muzzy

DESERT MOTHER

Her husband had been gone for weeks,
And now she knew that she must die
Before his wagon rumbled home,
None but the children standing by.

Folk rarely passed the lonely place.
The eldest child was nearly ten;
She mothered Janet, Dick, and Tom,
As busy as a little wren.

"If you should wake and find me gone
Some morning soon," she told the girl,
"You must not go to look for me
Till daddy comes," and stroked a curl.

"Just wash the plates and bring the wood,
And keep the children fed and clean,
And watch for daddy every day,
My darling little Josephine."

The children slept, the night was dark,
She slipped away without a sound,—
The children waked, the days went on,
The desert sun was red and round.

When daddy came, the search began;
Upon the plain he found her clay,
And wondered at the mother love
That gave her strength to go away.

—Berta Hart Nance

A HOUSE THAT'S A HOME

A house that's a home has a soul;
It breathes and it laughs and sighs,
It shares with its owners their joys,
And for their sorrows it cries.

A house that's a home can convey
To the visitor who stops for a while
Thoughts and wishes the owners have,
And a house can be grave or can smile.

Once I went into an old house
Where folks had lived and had gone,
And I could almost hear it talk
Of the sights it had looked upon.

The walls seemed to want to tell me
Of the things that they had seen,
And the ceilings bent to whisper
From their lofty heights serene.

I knew I should hear a story
If that old door could but speak,
And the high old latticed window
Had a romance in its creak.

The passage that led from the kitchen
To a room with a window seat
Seemed to give forth a friendly echo
Of the patter of many feet.

The quietness of the bedrooms
Up the long and winding stair
Registered a careful memory
Of folks who had rested there.

Then up in the dusty attic
Where discarded things were thrown,
Where children played on rainy days,
What joy that place must have known!

I would always choose an old house
That is used to folks and their ways;
It reaches out to welcome one
With experience of bygone days.

                                        —*Irma Jeffers Nelson*

THE LONESOME HILL

Low I hear the night wind
Round the wintry eaves,
Calling back its joy-time
Like a heart that grieves.

'Tis a voice of Nature
Sounding in my ear,
Bidding me remember,
Sighing out its fear;

Life and Love are parted,
But they hold me still,
As I follow visions
Up the lonesome hill.

Always one beside me
Though I walk alone;
In my heart is sounding
Ever one sweet tone;

So I look not backward
O'er the length'ning years—
'Tis the sunset gateway
That the vision clears—

'Tis the glory throbbing
Through the twilight chill—
There where Love is waiting
Past the lonesome hill.

—Lillias C. Nevin

OLD LOVER

How could I know that all the ashes strewn
Over past years were cov'ring hidden fires
Eager to burn again in mounting flames,
Consuming me with all the old desires?

I, who had lived the years in quietness,
Housewifely, circumspect, and near content—
What warning had I that your slightest touch
Would start the flame that left me clean forspent?

I am so tired—I cannot fight this fire;
I am so weak I cannot bear this pain;
I love you, spite of all the years between.
Why did you come? When will you come again?
                                    —*Mabel Newman*

REPOSE

Oh Hours,
So overfilled
With clam'rous cogent chores,
When shall I find voluptuous
Repose?

Yet stay—
Perhaps too soon,
My duties all complete,
I shall be vainly desolate
For toil.
                                    —*Martha Newsom*

CHRISTMAS SECRETS

"Say, fellers, how is it at your house,
    'Bout this time o' year?
Is everything so mysterious,
    And does everybody act queer?

"Why, mother wears the sweetest smile,
    Don't say a word to me,
Like her thoughts were long way off;
    I wonder what it could be?

"Dad calls mother on the phone,
    Mother talks so low,
Seems awful 'fraid I'll listen;
    Gee, I don't want to know.

"Even gran'ma's acting queer,
    Says I mustn't pry,
That little pitchers have big ears.
    Naw, I ain't going to cry.

"Big brother Jim last night
    Came walking in the door,
With the oddest done-up package
    I ever saw before.

"When I asked him 'Let me see,'
    He grinned and ran upstairs;
I wouldn't have hurt his old bundle,
    Say, does he think I care?

"Even little sister Sue
    Goes snooping all about,
Caught her peeking in my closet;
    You bet I jerked her out.

"'Cause way back in the corner
    I've hid a heap of things.
S'sh, Christmas presents, don't tell.
    I wish the days had wings.

"Say fellers, I never thought,
    Bet you I know why
All the folks are acting funny,
    Why gee, so am I.

"And so we all are mighty queer
    As we tiptoe round about,
We're each afraid the other
    Will find our Christmas secrets out."
                            —*Bertha E. Nicholas*

COLORADO

The poets have sung the praises
Of the "Road to Mandalay,"
Of the land of the midnight sun,
And the lights along Broadway,

Of the awful cold of the Yukon,
And the "grandeur that was Rome";
Would that I could write an epic—
T'would do justice to my home!

My home is *Colorado*,
A state though young in years,
Carved out of the golden west
By the sturdy pioneers!

Where the arid land was conquered,
Crops wrung from the virgin soil,
Where the fickle goddess Ceres
Bows to the hand of toil.

Where the old man of the mountains
Gives of his wealth untold,
He shares his buried treasure—
His silver and his gold!

Pure air and great wide spaces,
Fine cattle roam the plains—
What matters sordid Wall Street,
Its losses or its gains?

My state where all are equal
Of high or of lowly birth—
A land of opportunity,
Where a man can prove his worth.

So come to Colorado,
Don't wait until next year;
Here, with freedom, love, and service,
You'll find heaven very near.
                                        —*Gertrude Florence Nichols*

MY SIX LITTLE BOYS

Oh my little ones around me
    With their clinging baby hands,
How they fondle and caress me,
    Life is sweet when they are near me;
I would stay Time's hand to hold them
    And to keep them—always children.

For they look to me and trust me,
   Blindly follow and adore me,
Thinking I could do no wrong;
   For am not I their mother
Whom they look to as their queen,
   And I to them as subjects loving?

They cannot be my babies always—
   One day they must reach man's estate.
Till then, may God's protecting angels
   Watch o'er and guide my children's feet,
As they're tempted, sorely tried—
   May God in Heaven be their guide

And lead them in the paths of peace,
   Teach them love and charity—
Give them Health and manly beauty—
   Clothed in Hearts of Righteousness.
If this—within my boys I gain—
   My life has not been lived in vain.

                —*Kathleen Moody Nolen*

ANOTHER DAY

Each morn I greet the rising sun
With thankfulness, and pray
That greater wisdom may be mine
Than I had yesterday.

The thoughtless blunders I have made,
The unkind words I've spoken,
The vows of better things I'd do,
Made only to be broken,

The thoughts that to my mind will come
Unbidden and unsought,
The myriad things I would forget—
What anguish have they brought!

Mistakes of other days are past;
Why live them o'er again?
The thought brings only wretchedness,
Unhappiness, and pain.

How futile, in the light of morn,
Remorse that robs of sleep!
Regrets so vain, so hopeless are;
What avail the tears I weep?

The yesterdays have passed away;
Their sorrow's a thing apart.
And as the morning comes anew,
I make another start.

I'll live this one day to the full;
No others may be mine.
I'm thankful for the dewy morn
When hopes my fears entwine.

And as I greet the rising sun
With thankfulness, I pray
That somewhat better I may be
Than I was yesterday.

—*Jeannette Hazelton Norman*

COMFORT

No, my boy, you are not away,
You are by my side the livelong day.
I feel your touch, I see your face
Reflected in everything about the place.
I see you as a baby tot;
Ah no! I haven't so soon forgot
Those years when all hope and joy
Seemed to center around my baby boy.
Then, so very soon, you were six
And off to school, and out to mix
With other lads, and to learn the way
Of the world, and wonder at new mysteries each day;
The while at home I waited and hoped and prayed
That from your learning great plans were being laid.
Then, in a few short years, or months it seems,
You were a big grown-up lad in your teens,
Helping at daily tasks, and at night
Delving into books, and living with men of might

THE GOOD SHIP "PRAYER"

At sundown I shall launch a boat in space.
  Its cargo will consist of all the care
  Of one more earth-bound day. My ship is "Prayer."
Its port? 'Tis destined for the Throne of Grace!
And though I cannot see my Saviour's face,
  My sunset supplications reach Him There.
  The argosy returns both rich and fair,
Well laden with His soul-sustaining grace.

The calm expectant hush at close of day
  Has power to charm my spirit all its own;
    For strength and confidence around me flow,
And "Prayer" will sail upon its parting ray.
  The sweetest benediction I have known
    Is drawn from out the sunset's golden glow.
                    —Martha Fay O'Neal

REVELATION

If we could climb together, hand in hand,
To some high hill, windswept and free
From lowland mists, and there behold undimmed
The miracle of dawn;

If we could break the petty chains that bind
Our steps to middle ways, and seek the heights,
With what clear vision we could see
The shackles of today.

We'd fling behind us envy, wrath, and woe;
The sordid weight of cares we would discard;
Unburdened by false pomp, we'd face
The splendor of the sun.

The icy pride that held our hearts enthralled
Would melt, and malice be dissolved.
The rancor of old wounds would heal,
Our love untrammeled stand revealed,
That each might know.

If we could climb together to God's morn
And fearless face the radiance of dawn.
                    —Lila Todd O'Niell

LIFE

Eternal strife is on.
    Ere long we'll all be gone;
For as swift seasons roll,
    Each takes a telling toll.
Then our departing soul
    Finds a sublimer goal.

—*Mrs. Emily Oredson*

SPRING

Out in God's brilliant sunshine
The grass is restful green,
Spirea in the garden shines
With a glimmering sheen.

The birdbath awaits the robins
Who from the treetops fly,
While near by stands the sundial
Where sunny hours go by.

The rose blooms on the rose-vine
Along the garden wall.
Mignonette, her neighbor, sings,
"Miss Rose, I've come to call."

The snowball nods her pretty head
To the tulips, not far away .
And all the flowers hear it said
That Spring has come to stay.

—*Grace Fitzgerald Orr*

FAITH

Love wraps us round like a soft grey mist,
    A diaphanous veil whose filmy mesh
Is fragile as a spider's weaving.
    This love of ours can be as cold,
Penetrating as the Winter's fog,
    Searing as the fiery blasts of Summer,
Strong as the trees of mighty forests,
    High as heaven-reaching mountains;

Through eons it shall hold us close in bondage sweet,
   Yet free as the winds that blow.
Though we have passed the Portal grim,
   And the forms we knew are into dust—
Love shall live and shine, a scintillating star;
   For Life is Love and Love is Infinite.

                —*Naomi G. Orr*

PRICE

A jewel,
They said,
The little poem.
Perfect.
A thing
Of art.
They
Could not know,
The price
Of it, though,
Was the
Poet's
Broken heart.

                —*Virginia Keating Orton*

PEACE

Good Phoebus, speed thy chariot wheels,
And quick-recurring cycles swing,
When man with man will clasp a hand,
And War shall be an unknown thing.

                —*Florence Tucker Osmun*

QUEEN CREEK CANYON

About me rose chaos of peak on peak;
High above all, towered Apache Leap—
Crags of weathered granite grim,
The floor of the chasm, shadowy, dim,
Hundreds of feet below—

And I said, "The God who builded this,
The Heaven-kissed dome and the deep abyss
That has stood for eons, and that shall stand
After the days of transient man,
Marks the sparrows fall."

—*Virginia Weigel Page*

A SHOWER

See, the clouds in troops are must'ring
    While the sky seems overcast;
'Mid the hurry and the scurry
    Go wee cloudlets scamp'ring past.
Now a golden streak of lightning
    Pierces through the leaden sky—
Flashes follow one another
    Leading dashing raindrops by;
Sunshine comes, and raindrops falter,
    Then in serried lines draw near,
And a rainbow spans the heavens,
    Brilliant, beautiful, and clear.

—*Mabel Ethleen Palmer*

MILKING

Thrum, thrum, thrum! With a spurt and a splash,
Into the bucket the white streams flash.

High overhead the cottonwood leaves
Dance tiptoe in the evening breeze.

Is that a dryad peeping there?
Or the golden gleam of a fairy's hair?

So, boss, so! Don't stir one hoof!
There's a hungry babe 'neath yon brown roof.

A pat on old bossy—smooth as silk!
Thanks, faithful friend, for fresh rich milk!

Milk for dear grandmother in the house,
Milk for the kitten—just dined on mouse.

Milk for your calfie, whose bright round eyes
Gaze from its pen in quaint surprise.

Long grow the shadows, down sinks the sun;
Loiter to pasture—milking's done!
—*Ellen Daniels Panter*

WE'LL MOTHER THE TOWN WITH MOTHER

Our little ones demand us,
We mother them at home;
We've time for but a look-in
When club days come.

Our mothers mothered us,
But now may lonely be,
Although they're busy mothering
A whole community.

Soon our clinging children
Older will be grown;
Then hand in hand with mother
We'll mother all the town.

Oh, sisters of our club life,
We need each other all!
Our hearts grow warmer, happier,
At the "Come to order!" call.
—*Ada Cora Park*

THE MASTER HAND

As union with Arcturus releases astral fire,
So the torch of Shakespeare reveals the flaming soul.
Grim Tragedy slays Comedy,
The "damned spot" of blood remains;
Muffled death knells, grievous tears
Condemn falsettos of a tinkling joy
When villains drain the Circean cup of revelry.

Brier rose and eglantine perfume the Paradise
Of lovers met by stealth to pledge their secret vows;

Yet love embittered turns to hate,
Funeral meats grace nuptial feast.
Clutching his irresolute prey,
Halting Will confuses Time. The envenomed snake
Ever palsies dynamic forces of the mind.

"To be?" that question is the loadstone of tangled doubt;
Avarice demands the crown, lights burn low, crazed men die;
Crises, traced through complex lives,
Kindle fires in virile man,
Fires that smolder, flame, destroy.
Recorded is the epic of long centuries;
Amazed, we find true portraits of our mirrored selves.
                                        —*Julia Edna Parker*

MODERN BABEL

At twilight, when the sun is low,
I look upon a Babel bright
Across a harbor that I know,
At twilight.

Bewildering splendor to the sight!
There all the works, in sunset's glow,
Of God and man, don robes of light.

The jeweled spires skyward go.
A diamond city, mountain height;
Below, the rivers deep green flow
At twilight.

At twilight, fog upon the Bay;
That Titian city, masked in night,
Will vanish utterly away
At twilight.

Instead, the fog horn, wakeful wight,
Will shriek its warning, there to stay
The ocean greyhound in its plight.

Oh, jeweled city, set in jet!
Where all the world both come and go;
That is a fog, should you forget!
At twilight.
                                        —*Helen M. Parsons*

HER GARDEN

God made for her a garden,
And gave to her gentle care
All of the lovely flowers
That He had planted there.

The flowers grew and flourished,
Her garden was fair to see,
And never were blossoms tended
With more love and loyalty.

She guarded them and shielded them
From the wintry wind that blows;
She cherished the modest violet
As she did the stately rose.

The fragrance of her flowers
Was scattered far and wide,
Beyond the walls of her garden
Through all the countryside.

The perfume from their blossoms
Spread happiness and cheer;
Their color carried sunshine
To places dull and drear.

But ere life's summer was over
And autumn's chill had come,
God left her garden untended
And called His gardener home.

Her flowers neither stop their blooming
Nor cease their fragrance to shed,
For when she worked in her garden
'Twas by His hand she was led.

Her spirit still lives among them
In the deeds of good she wrought—
In the garden that God gave her—
In the lives of those she taught.

—*Ruby Bransford Pearce*

RESURRECTION

This day in March I walk the hills
   All sodden with the first spring rain;
The soft air stirs the stiff brown grass
   Like waving grain.

The kildeer's anxious, peevish cry
   Comes sharply from the blue abyss;
The bluebird's sweet, caressing call
   Falls like a kiss.

Beyond the woodland, smoky dim,
   The sun's red ball in gray mist sinks.
The horned lark's trill as frolic sounds
   As bobolink's.

And on a sunny western bank,
   Where summer's furry mosses creep,
Hepatica's soft gray-green buds
   Have waked from sleep.

Then comes a flash of azure wings
   Beneath the elm tree's bare, brown arch;
I feel the throb of summer's pulse,
   This day in March.
                           —Florence A. Pepoon

TWO PATHS

The flaming sun sank down the western sky,
Leaving behind a trail of brilliant hue:
Crimson and orange, rose and amethyst,
Which, slowly fading, turned to silver blue.
Twilight found me near a lonely wood,
Dim was the pathway in the waning light,
Black shadows crept along the mossy ground,
And like a pall descending, came the night.
I had been told this byway dark to shun,
I had been warned that danger lurked ahead;
But stubbornly I went my foolish way,
Nor did I care where others had been led.

I stumbled on past ghostly trees
Standing like sentinels tall and stark;
Their arms seemed reaching out to clasp me
As I sped onward through the dark.
Soft moving creatures crept beside me,
Blazing eyes from shapeless forms did glare,
While mist from the marshy ground arose
To fill with chilly clouds the air.
Alone at midnight in a dreary forest,
The inky blackness all about me laid,
And as I fled along the tangled pathway—
                    I was afraid.

Another path, another setting sun,
When all the sky was full of dazzling light:
Pink and purple, gold and heliotrope,
As daylight softly faded into night.
Twilight, and my way was up a mountain;
From rock to rock I climbed the narrow way.
Soft clouds were lazily drifting overhead,
And one bright star proclaimed the close of day.
I plodded on as other stars appeared,
Glittering gems in a curtain of blue.
The moon arose and her bright radiance
Turned to a silver carpet the evening dew.
Giant trees along the way were standing,
Their arms outstretched my way to guide,
And over stones and sand a brook was laughing,
As it went its happy way to meet the tide.
At last I reached the summit of the mountain,
Entranced, I stood the world and sky between;
The cool, clean air swept all about me;
In awe I gazed upon the wondrous scene.
Above, the glory of the bending heavens,
Below, the earth with silver moonlight sprayed.
Alone at midnight upon a mountain peak—
                    But I was not afraid.
                    —*Mrs. Edgar A. Perkins, Sr.*

A BLACKBIRD SINGING AT DAWN

"What bird sings now, an hour before the day?
  Into my very heart that sweet note rings,—
O Diarmid, my son!" the Abbot said:
  "Daybreak is near; in darkness the bird sings."

Answered the monk: "It is the blackbird's song,
  My father; in the second month, each night
Wears chill before the dawn; then, the bird sings,—
  Praising our God for light, *before* the Light."

The Abbot Kemak's eyes o'erflowed with tears;
  "In these sweet praises, God's great love I mark
To me:—to teach me faith beyond my fears,—
  How bravely sings the bird, while yet 'tis dark.

"A bit of earth in feathers! yet there springs
  A fount of Song attuned to Love Divine:
Answering the Call of joy, his praise he brings,
  His morning Hymn; my God, Thou shalt have mine!"
                 —*Martha Elvira Pettus*

LIFE

Why fret about what we are here for,—
Whence came we, or whither we go?
We're here;—there's an Infinite Power,—
And that much we surely do know.

You ask about life; let us ponder:
As all with our world is not right,
It may be that God, our Creator,
Is testing our faith and our might.

"Who loses his life, he shall find it,"
Seems to us a queer paradox;
Yet he who makes service a habit
Doesn't fret about Pandora's box.

Don't worry, or fume, or get morbid;
Some Power made the lily and rose:
Before you ask what we are here for,—
Tell me how the wild flower grows.

Why probe into the Infinite?
Why gaze at the burning hot sun?
It doesn't change them for one minute,
Nor answer your questions, not one!

We people of earth in our living
Are part of a pattern and plan,—
With sunshine and shadow both blending,
A picture not visioned by man!

Through prayer we get something sustaining,
As plants from the sun and the soil;
List closely, we also get guidance,
Adverse circumstances to foil.

As to "where," when this life is over,—
What state, or condition, or home;
Let that be the least of your worries;
Live right, and let God's part alone!

So leave to our Heavenly Father
The questions of destiny deep;
And lend a hand here to our brother,—
Be reverent, and helpful, and sweet.
                              —*Beulah Wyatt Phillips*

THE REACHES OF A SONG

My weathered house looks very small,
Inconsequent to one who toils
With a rule to measure just how tall
The reaches of a dream-built wall—
How far the patient ivy coils
Above a chimney pedestal;

Who marks with calculating eyes
The stanchion's length, the width of gird—
But overlooks a nest that lies
In sheltered eaves, the swift uprise
Of bubbling joy a homing bird
Throws to the roof of morning skies;

Nor sees the gold of ripening grain
Spread by the autumn hours of day
Upon each small square casement pane.
Who measures thus, can he explain
Why walls grow high when dreamers pray—
Broad when their songs defy the rain?—

Why little flaming joys that throng
About my hearthstone all declare:
None earth-bound know the height of prayer,
Or the wide reaches of a song!

—*Gertie Stewart Phillips*

MY GARDEN

Come with me to my garden
On a sunny day in June,
Worship in my chapel,
Peacefully commune;
Moss-grown stones the altar,
Singing birds the choir,
Incense from the flowers,
You yourself the prior.
No orthodox religion,
No creed you need declare;
Just thank God for the beauty
Of gardens everywhere.

—*Harriet Duff Phillips*

THE STARRY HEIGHTS

At this dark pass we part, our ways divide.
I shall not say that you remain behind,
But I go on, not back, and you will find
I am not like Lot's wife. You may decide

To walk this way with me and be my guide
   Along this hilly path, and be resigned
   To travel on with me. I have in mind
The starry heights I reached with one who died.

I never thought to tarry where the grime
   Of muddy waters creeps to foul the earth.
      Above on that high hill I know a place
Where melodies, with lilt of song and rhyme,
   Intone sweet music I would hear. No dearth
      Of joy is there to cloud a happy face.
                              —*Marie Tello Phillips*

CAREFREE WAY

Let's leave our cares and travel along
   The sunny path of Carefree Way;
Let us pause and tarry here awhile,
   Be joyous, happy while we may.

Clasp my hand, dear friend, and come with me,
   And we will find a magic nook
Along some bubbling meadow stream,
   Or by the fireside with a book.

Let's forget our cares and dream a bit,
   There's happiness for you and me;
So just pass your happy thought along,
   And walk the Carefree Way with me.
                              —*Elsie K. Pierce*

WALL STREET WAIL

Up and down where Wall Street is a-rumbling,
   Grim and gruff, the gory bears go growling,
Tearing trade to tatters, every tumbling
   Horrors down upon the horde that's howling.

Up and down, too, devious paths a-weaving,
   Burly, battered bulls go stamping, stalking,
Hopeful horns impatient for the heaving,
   When our debt commissions finish talking.

Lowly little lambkins are a-frisking,
   Midst great hooves and claws are nibbling, nipping;
Timid tiny tails forever whisking,
   Where angels fear to tread they're blithely skipping.

A rare request I'll make in this connection,—
   Gods of the ticker, pray you, grant me hearing,—
I am a fool to think *I* rate protection,
   But—let this woolly lamb escape the shearing.
                    —*Enid Crawford Pierce*

THE MYSTERY

But yesterday you walked beside me, dear,
Your eyes, well loved, looked love returned to mine—
And yet today you lie so silent there,
Ah me, 'tis ever thus with life's glad wine!

But yesterday—'tis years ago, I wean,
Seen through the haze of agonizing grief.
Oh yesterday, could I have only seen
Death stealing by, like a strong, silent thief.

Oh vain the wish, and vainer still regret!
For who can by one second stop the sun,
When moving on he rises but to set—
From morn till eve on his appointed course to run.

Oh Death, Thou great, mysterious, dreadful thing,
Must Thou, forsooth, take all that we hold dear?
Thou drawest o'er the world Thy sable wing,
And leav'st us with our grief—a memory, and a prayer.
                    —*Claudia A. Pinckney*

SCRAPS

I have among my treasures a book I hold most dear,
Though judged by standard measures, it would not pass, I fear.
No gilt or rich embossing its simple covers claim;
You ask "Why so engrossing—this book without a name?"

Its pages are a history, bringing me smiles or tears;
Odd bits of fact or mystery, treasured throughout the years.
Rare gems of verse or story that touched responsive heart,
Snapshots in all their glory, in which I played a part.

And as I turn from page to page, each one to mem'ry dear,
Come visions of a mystic age, and bygone days seem near.
Once more I'm with the merry band I knew in days of yore,
Though some are in the "Better Land" and known to earth no
   more.

Again we dance with bare brown feet the wooded paths along,
Carefree and happy, blithe and fleet, the summer day—a song.
Another page brings wintertime, with fire-log's cheery glow,
Or—skimming to the sleigh-bells' chime, across the moon-lit
   snow.

And so this time-worn volume seems to link me with the past,
And thrills me with the old-time dreams, too beautiful to last.
Then do not gaze with scornful eye upon my humble "scraps."
But follow suit, and by and by you'll feel the same—perhaps.
                                        —*Agnes Stowell Pinkney*

IN A GARDEN

There is magic in a garden,
Mellow sunshine, growing things,
Soft warm earth, and cool green shadows
Cast a spell, and all life sings.

In a garden, calm and tranquil,
Milling thoughts grow tranquil too;
Something checks their wild momentum,
Reason, serene, now reigns anew.

There the heart forgets its sadness,
Hopes long dead revive again,
Heavy burdens strangely lighten,
Peace slips in where grief has lain.

Little worries, daily pin pricks,
Vexing trifles, magnified,
Slowly, gently fade and dwindle,
Paltry fears are laid aside.

For a garden is not flowers,
Light and shadow, leaves and sod,
But a place of peace and quiet,
Love and labor, faith and God.

—Mamie Gray Pinkston

TRIUMPH

You pity me, you strong who go your ways
Out in the world, that cloistered I should be,
Cut off, apart from all you joy in. Ah!
You little weigh the world wherein I dwell,
My world which stretches vaster far than yours,
And will enlarge when this material earth
To unknown shape and substance is transformed.

My realm is boundless, ocean without shore,
And earth without circumference. Here I lie
And grasp your plans and ways as cannot you
Yourselves. Not doing, clearer still my seeing;
Apart from motives, interests, rivalries
That stir your actions, I but plainer view
Their workings in the happenings of your lives.

My realm is boundless; thought is limited
By naught but force of its own origin;
Within my enfeebled body, mind springs up,
Plays like the fountain that will not be choked,
Cleared crystal by the great revealer, Pain,
Descrying to my soul the meanings once
Seen but as darkly through a glass or hid.

And ah, the spirit-whisperings that fan
My narrow bed, an altar whereon meet
The outstretched wings of golden cherubim!

My flesh, the ready sacrifice, but waits
Consuming by the fires celestial, whence
My soul-incense its triumph shall proclaim
Up to the throne of Him who breathed its life!

For you, ye kindly ones whose footsteps find
The stairway leading to my chamber door,
Twice blessed here your ministerings! Can they
Who walk the ways of men know as I know
Your heartaches? When you come with gifts and cheer
And your eyes say to mine, "I too am needy;
Soul, give thou to me!"

Lost years? An empty life? This old world still
Learns not the values of the One that saith,
"Who loseth life shall find it!" We forget;
Earth-blind our eyes, too much in ways of men.
So then, O world beyond my windows,
Pity not the one who but looks on;
And you, ye friendly hearts that watch and love,
Pity me not!

—*Sally Macon Garland Pippen*

RECOMPENSE

I used to wonder what the Master meant
    When He said, "Thy cloak also"; and then, "Go
With him twain." I think I did resent
    The sacrifice in the commands. But now I know
Eternal Wisdom uttered them, for I have done
    These things; and at that journey's end
My heart took wings, and since has flown
    To heights undreamed. The lofty trend
Has given me assurance of His power
    To give another cloak. He knows my plights
And will provide. The second mile's dark hour—
    The price I paid for dreamless sleep and quiet nights.
—*Mary Wimborough Ploughe*

GARDENS OF THE MIND

Flowers are the magic bit of leaven
That brings to earth the fragrant breath of heaven;
Messengers of love and beauty rare,
Spreading perfumed gladness everywhere.
We may have the flowers if we will,
Blooming on our mental window sill;
Or, if we prefer the noxious weed,
We have but to plant that kind of seed.

Flowers grow where thoughts are pure and kind,
In these fertile gardens of the mind;
Thorns and thistles from the seeds of strife
Crowd the lovely flowers from our life.
Heaven's richest treasures ours to use;
We can make our Eden if we choose.
Weeds or flowers—which then shall it be
For our gardens in eternity?
                                            —*Lillian Irvine Pollock*

PRAYER FOR PEACE

Grant us surcease, we pray, from cosmic strife,
   Let us have quiet for reflective space.
   Mankind, now conflict-weary, would replace
All vestiges of grimness which the knife
Of Hate has scarred so deeply, with fresh life—
   Would summon plaintive loveliness and grace
   And kindlier ways of thinking to a race
Desirous never more to march to fife.

War reaped its harvest. Those whom we held best
   Were first to quaff the seething cup and die.
In silence they courageously fared west,
   Who loved the radiant earth, the sapphire sky—
Brooke, John McCrea, Joyce Kilmer, and the rest.
   God, give our younger sons no battle-cry!
                                            —*Mabel Posegate*

THE SNOWFLAKE'S FAREWELL

A snowflake sailed through the frosty air,
Pure and glistening, and fashioned rare,
And it kissed the cheek of a maiden fair,
And straightway became a tear.

For the glow and the warmth of the maiden's cheek
Were like breath of June, and of roses sweet;
And with farewell kiss did the snowflake weep,
For it thought that the Summer was here.

—*M. Eugenia Potter*

MOTHERS' EYES

Immortal blue, so gentle, holy, true,—
The blue that was the color of her eyes!
If I should run the gamut of each hue,
I'd choose the dearest, noblest shade, the blue
Of murmuring seas beneath October skies.

For ragged robin and the indigo,
That rival sapphire wings of butterflies,
For far-off hills and shadows on the snow
I thank the Lord, but thank him most to know
The blue, blue tenderness of mother eyes.

—*Diana Kearny Powell*

PURPOSE

To seek things glad and beautiful,
That is our creed;
To lift us from sordid things,
To fill the need
Of loyal womanhood, in earnestness
To feel quick stir of wonder at loveliness.

To be strong in faith, in deed,
Benignity;
To be master of circumstance;
Exist to be
Of greater service, of greater worth,
A richer living on this fertile earth.

—*Winnie Lita Price*

ATELIER

Moonfrost burnishes the sculptured trees
Unmoved beneath the chiseling
Of bats that gouge with sharpened wing
The rough-edged shadows.
Steel on stone . . .
Pale splintered chips fall free
Where powdered moths flake noiselessly.
Cold steel on stone . . .
Faint shimmering sparks
Are struck. The fireflies with eerie light
As tremulous as a distant shout
Curve briefly in bright
Swooning arcs,
Then flicker out.

Moonfrost burnishes the sculptured trees.
No whispering drapery of breeze
Disturbs the stark intensity of night.
Only the drone of far-off surf,
The mallet's muffled pound,
And from the rumpled canvas of the turf
The crickets' sound,
Echoing steel on stone,
Cold steel on stone . . .
Interminably.

—*Helen Danforth Prudden*

THE BOBOLINK'S SONG

You flew far above me,
Beneath the sun's crown,
Broadcasting your music
Through country and town.
It came from your station—
The big sky-space of blue,
As if harps of angels
Were broadcasting too.

There was no announcement
Nor static to annoy,
It fell from the heavens—
A symphony of joy.

—Sara V. Prueser

HOPE

When friends shall lay me gently down
Beneath the sheltering clay,
I hope the joyous birds will sing
In hedges by the way.

I hope the sun will brightly shine
And lovely buds unfold,
The day my soul shall pass within
Those gates of pearl and gold.

I hope no friend will pause to weep
Beside my narrow bed,
Because my heart that loved them so
To brighter realms has fled.

And if dear hands should lay bright flowers
Above my quiet breast,
Remembering their love for me,
How sweetly would I rest.

I still shall love you fond and true,
Though I shall give no sign,
And waving grasses spread between
Your faces dear, and mine.

—Jessie Hubbard Pruett

THE OLD RAIL FENCE

I never see a gray rail fence,
With angles in and out,
But that I ponder o'er and o'er
Just how it came about:

Who felled the Chestnut, monarch grand?
Who cleft the heart of Oak?
Who split the rails, so uniform,
With sure and steady stroke?

Who "laid the worm" with vision true,
O'er hill and dale and plain,
So that who builded on this base
Had worry ne'er again?

Who knew to balance angles so
That though the fence built tall,
It served not only pioneer,
But sons, descendants all?

So may we choose our timbers strong
The fence of life to make!
So may we lay the pattern down
For who come in our wake;

And may our lives be balanced so,
Though angles sharp there be,
We'll calmly stand secure and strong,
So he who runs may see

Just silver gray, the crown of age,
Enduring work through all,
And know that each can thus build life,
Whatever fate befall.

                              —*Martha Grassham Purcell*

GIFTS AND SINS

The simplest things are best
For peace of mind, for rest.
A cottage small, a lovely tree,
A dog, some books, friends for tea.
Plain foods, fresh air for health,
A field, a brook are wealth!
Sunrise, sunsets, the sea,
Clouds in the sky, a soaring bird,
Moonlight, are free.
These are some gifts of God.

Creeds that have killed the Christ
In Christianity,
Greed, avarice, revenge,
Vice, cowardice, and strife:
The things that cripple life
Are crime.
Help, with a sparing hand,
Malicious gossip fanned,
Excesses to intemperance,
Intolerance:
These are the sins of men.

—*Edna Eades Puryear*

AIR MAIL

I was one with space.
The long horizon's rim
Was brushed with flaming clouds
Like the wings of a Seraphim.

I was one with vastness,
The field of limitless blue,
Alone with cosmic wonder,
With sky and atom of dew.

When up toward heaven was lifted
The crunching engine that brings
Our lettered lines—they're speeding
On time, and shod with wings!

And space became a mountain
The pilot must ascend,
And I was one with time
Expecting words from a friend.

—*Anna Hawks Putnam*

ATAVISM

This mad longing, this wild hunger,
Are they but an ugly scar
From the days when life was younger,
Left to prove us what we are?

Left to prove that we inherit
From the tiger and the ape,
That behind each hard-won merit
Lurks a savage, crouching shape?

Still, behind the brainpan shallow,
Farther back than primal slime,
Is a sound that yet shall hallow
Man's long climb through space and time;

Back of fang and cruel fingers,
Softly rustle angel wings,
And the hymn of heaven lingers
On Creation's golden strings.
                                        —*Grace Brown Putnam*

THE UNIVERSAL RHYTHM

There's music in the measured beat
    Of heart, of wind, of rain;
Its harp strings are the pulse,
    The trees, the windowpane.

In all this measured beat
    We feel on land and sea,
The Universal Rhythm sings,
    I am at one with Thee.

If you would keep in tune
    With this joyous Rhythm of life,
Then lend your ears to God's music
    And shut out all the strife.
                                        —*Bess Munson Quier*

SUNSET

I wander near the river's brim, the sun is sinking
    low,
The sky is tinged with colors soft, the whole world
    seems aglow;
A velvet silence covers all with peace and sweet
    repose,

And as I gaze into the West, Heaven's gates seem
to unclose.
And while I muse, it seems to me that in the
sunset's glow
I read a message sent from God to us who wait
below—
That our life here on earth soon ends, but at our
close of day
The good we've done lives after us to brighten
someone's way.

—Melicent Athleen Quinn

HUMMINGBIRD

On fairy wing
Enchanting thing;
In flower cup
For magic sup,
Or poised in play
On rainbow spray—
Then suddenly
And whizzingly,
With vivid flash
Elusive dash
To sweet retreat,
Wee, lichened, neat;
Exquisite place
Of down and lace,
A cradle hung
For tiny young.

He's lived who's seen
This midget's sheen,
And watched him brave
Fierce, hawklike knave;
Or nicely fluff
His gleaming ruff
In raindrop pool
On roseleaf cool.

The darling sprite!

—Jess Campbell Rae

MARCH

In mullioned pools of wildwood bowers
    Belated ice still lingers;
Corsage bouquets of last year's flowers
    Are clutched in earth's cold fingers.

—Bertha Raffetto

A MOTHER'S PRAYER

Oh grant, dear Lord, that I may be
    The mother that was meant for me.
Help me be patient, kind, and true,
    No bitter words or petty acts to rue.
May my love be the kind to strengthen, keep,
    Making for what is rich and deep.
Never the kind to fiercely hold
    Young lives to mine as they unfold,
Blighting the wholeness theirs should be.
  Grant me, dear Lord, to keep them free,
Free from a selfish, strangling yoke
    That would hamper their souls, their hearts provoke.
Keep me, dear Lord, from the martyr fair
    Who demands through all the lion's share.
Teach me, dear Father, myself to forget;
    With keen vision seeing their needs—and yet
Being able to help, but never intrude,
    Fitting each act to their varying mood.
With understanding mind and sympathetic heart,
    May I ever be able to do my part.
But, hardest of all, may the strength be mine
    To forget myself, lest the fetters bind,
Fetters so delicate, strong, yet frail.
    O, God, grant my prayer; may I not fail,
Fail to be all that my children need,
    Yet never lost to the fateful greed
That saps the strength of many a son
    Who might have fullest honors won,
Had he not sacrificed too much
    Responding to a mother's touch.
Oh grant, dear Lord, that I may be
    The mother that was meant for me.

—Blanche Banta Ramsey

DORCAS

A little head of curly gold-brown hair
  I used to pass at morning on my way,
With blue-gray eyes and baby smile—and there
    A new light seemed to shine upon the day,
      And all the hours were bright.

She will not wave her little flower-like hand
  At me again, or flirt her gray-blue eyes—
And yet I know I only understand
    In part the aching emptiness that lies
      In lives so near her own.

Now morning brings us but the memory
  Of other mornings when we saw her smile;
But lingering light through all our lives shall be,
    Because we had her here a little while—
      A bit of Heaven itself.

So while we grieve that she is gone away,
  We cannot feel the tiny girl is dead;
We know we'll read life's mystery some day
    Limned in the sunshine of that gold-brown head,
      When tears are wiped away.
                    —Bessie Clark Randle

BLIND TOILERS

It is not sad that they must ever toil,
  It is not sad that lives grow old and break,
Never to wash away the grime and soil,
  But sad that drowsy souls may never wake.

Sad never to soar—or climb a lofty height,
  Never to see—or feel—or think—or grow,
Never wisdom to make a wrong thing right,
  To claim a star—or hear the east wind blow.

Never to feed upon some healing dream,
  To fill the soul with visions deep and real,
To walk from out the muddy human stream,
  Drop beast-like burdens he would cease to feel.

As unpeopled houses fall into sad decay,
　　So the blind toiler in his listless plod
At last becomes an empty heap of clay;
　　Dim grow his footprints on the sullen sod.

　　　　　　　　　　　　　　　　　—*Marguerite Ray*

HOMELAND

Who would forget Ohio?
Her hills romp to their old mother—
The Appalachian;
Can you say when they are loveliest—
In the spring when pearled with dogwood's white?
In the autumn as they burn like huge fire opals?
Or in winter diademed with snow?
And after all
There is the peace of summer's green;
Would you not have the peace of these hills
In your heart?
And a majesty like that which sweeps
The course of her name-river?
As the winds blow, you may be calm
Or stormy, like her great lake—Erie—
But to the homeland you are constant
As her ancient hills!
Who could forget Ohio?

　　　　　　　　　　　　　　　　　—*Monna Merle Ray*

OKLAHOMA

Oklahoma, youngest state of the West,
Arrogant you are,
Billowed on beautiful time-worn ridges
And valleys of fertile green.
You proudly and boastfully laud your own quick growth
　　into wealth.
You show your shining milk teeth to the world,
You bite,

You kill, while guarding your claims.
Your oil fields,
Of a million tanks,
Of unlimited latticed rigging lifted
Vauntingly to the sky,
Proclaim your source of wealth.
Without a "Thank you, God,"
You pump, pump, pump,
And pour out a stream of liquid dollars
From God's storehouse, unwittingly given by indifferent
   potentates and flung
At the Indian's feet!
Oklahoma! You claim an aristocracy of wealth!
You flaunt it red before uncultured eyes.
How dare you! 'Tis maddeningly multiplied.
The spirit of Christ goes grievingly among your powerful
   steel machinery of pipes and bars
That knows no day or hour of rest.
He hears your creed,
That money talks,
Dollars first and then perhaps the soul,
That nothing counts against the clink of the silver wheels.
Ah! money-mad you are!
But, some day
Your uncovered streams
Will cease.
What then?
Oklahoma.

—Stella B. Redding

HUNTER'S MOON

Unleash the hounds,
We hunt tonight.
The moon still sleeps,
But long before
The hounds have "treed,"
She'll mount the sky
On wingèd steed.

We wait the tryst,
And rake the straw
To glowing flame.
We know the while
This woodland flare
Can rival not
The huntress fair.

Through leafy shade
A new light gleams.
The resinous flame
Grows pale indeed.
The huntress rides!
Away to hounds,
Far music glides.

—*Marie E. Reddy*

A THOUGHT

A little here, a little there,
Just gath'ring as we go,
And save each little scrap with care;
That's how kind thoughts will grow.

Don't mind the petty things of life,
They're not worth a useless sigh.
We're here for more than worldly strife;
Just laugh, and pass them by.

A kind deed may be a little thing,
But means so very much;
A little tune we sometimes sing
Oft gives a helpful touch.

Just march along, head up high,
Sow kindness as you go,
And life on airy wings will fly.
We reap just what we sow.

—*Gertrude Reed*

FOREST POOL

I had forgotten Nature's depth of calm
Until I wandered here. The world of men
Had wrapped its muffling greyness like a veil
About my once-perceptive sense and soul.

I had not thought a forest pool could be
So round, and green, and still, and intimate
With my neglected deeper realm of thought.
It lies there at my feet, a thing discovered,
Shallow with oozing moss and dim reflections
Of straight grey trunks, smooth and each aloof
From his fellow, yet stiffly glad of company.
The silver-threaded wings of dragonflies
Shimmer above grasses; and white-frocked children
Play at hide-and-seek, now crouching by trees,
Now tiptoeing over leaves. Beyond the pool
Stretches an aisle of misty sunlit green,
Where lazy leaves hover continually;
Afar floats a golden haze of Elysian Field.

The stillness is so deep I cannot breathe;
An unspent sigh weighs heavy on my breast;
My limbs are strangely numb and far away;
My thought, afloat in air, entwined in trees.

Half-dreaded remembrance wakes; I seem to know
That puzzled friends await beyond the wood,
That they will whirl me loudly back again
To city clamor, thoughtless talk, the din
Of taxi horns, persisting on one shrill note,
And quarrels over choosing hats and tulle.
Yet I shall turn and never gaze behind,
I'll walk to meet them down the clean-swept path
And answer eager queries. Yet deep within
Is buried the green stillness of my pool.

—Rosalie Regen

AN APPEAL

Oh Women of America. Arise!
Pull down the dusty cobwebs from the skies,
That we may once more clearly see the stars.
Make no more sacrifices unto Mars;
They leave such very deep and bitter scars.

Oh World! Who blotted out the very sun?
Our Pilgrim Fathers' work, is it undone?
Whence come these bootleggers and racketeers?
For this we must endure all Europe's sneers.

Let's drive them out! Be this our very goal,
As one drives mortal sin from out the soul.
They are the dregs, the scum of our great melting pot.
The broth more wholesome clear! We must not rot!
Our glorious land deserves a better lot.

Oh rescue from oblivion our high ideals,
And lift our country up. Make our appeals
To touch the latent good in all of us.
Oh help us, lest we grovel in the dust
Of filthy things—of greed and shame and lust.

Let's contemplate our great men of the past.
Those mighty ones would surely look aghast
At what we have become—their work undone.
We—in our self-sufficient vanity,
Forget their deeds of valor,—but
Delight to show their frail humanity.

Strive hard for peace upon this blessed earth,
And foster happiness and love and mirth,
No task to shun, when once our work's begun.
Clubwomen of this mighty Federation!
Let's lift our banners high, and
Build again a mighty nation!

—*F. Isabelle Goodwin Reid*

I OPEN MY WINDOWS TO THE MORN

I open my windows to the morn;
The day, new-born, God gives to me
Unlived, and fraught with mystery.

There come soft rushings as of wings,
The fragrant breath of lovely things,
As though the angels of the night
Were passing in their homeward flight.

And trailing bridal veil of mist,
Morn shyly moves to keep love's tryst,
A wreath of star flow'rs in her hair,
And jewels of dew the night left there.

With wingèd steeds her lover bold
Rides in a coach of rose and gold,
And bending to receive her kiss
Wraps round her robes of amethyst.

He rides in flame of fire-lit hearth,
And morn rides with him; while the earth,
Pulsating with the joy of birth,
Wings song across the hills and leas
And flings winds sighing through the trees
To play her lovely symphonies.

I gaze on my belovèd; sleep
Ascending from her soul doth creep
Midst clouds translucent on his way
Till night shall dusk another day.
Her eyes, bemused with dreams, unclose;
Her cheeks, like petals of a rose,
Are dimpled with bewitchery
Where lips, half parted, smile at me.

Against a sky of marigolds
A cloak of purple cloud enfolds
The laughing light of my new day.
And then, like fairies at their play,
There comes a mist of silver rain
Aglow like some cathedral pane.

And there is borne upon my ear
A choir boy's chanting, sweet and clear—
The thrush is singing to the morn
That gave to us our day, newborn,
And ev'ry little living thing
Makes vibrant stir amidst the sod.
I open the windows of my soul
And stand there, face to face, with *God.*

—*Louise Loflin Reiley*

AWAKENING

The vase is broken and it lies in bits—
A shattered dream of beauty at my feet;
The Potter's careful work—the glazier's task
All gone for naught. About the room there flits
Pale dust from crumbling petals of a rose
That blossom'd in its clasp. Not hers to ask
The why of living or if death be sweet—
Hers but to blossom for a day and leave
A fragrance clinging round a broken vase—
This, ev'n tragedy cannot erase;
An echo yet for some lost happiness—
A golden mem'ry for the soul's reprieve.

O dream, that one man formed from senseless clay!
Beauty lives on forever, and its loveliness
Recks not the blossom space of one short day.
Up from the ruins rises sweet perfume—
Sweeter than flowers in their radiant bloom—
More poignant than the last, long bitterness
Of candles burning in a darkened room.

—*Kate Hassell Reynolds*

PINE-CLAD HILLS

I hope that I shall live forever, here,
    Upon these pine-clad hills,
Their beauty snares my soul;

I love them 'neath mantillas of the mist,
Or in the dawn, resplendent and sun-kissed,
   When Spring fulfills
Her promises of immortality.

Yet, if I may not live forever, here,
   Upon these pine-clad hills
Where peace and beauty dwell,
I would, wind-blown, return in silver rain
To wake the violets and dogwood again,
   When Spring fulfills
Her promises of immortality.

—Elizabeth Davis Richards

LEAVING HARBOR

A sandy beach, shell-strewn, where jellyfish
Sprawl glistening silverly; white-gleaming foam
Fast melts in underlapping waves whose lips
Caress the waiting stretch of sand. Far off
In fascinating groups gay whitecaps flash,
Shrill sea gulls swoop and rise upon swift wings
Against a sullen sun; in silhouette
A lighthouse, steadfast, strong, holds tireless watch.
Then slowly . . . slowly . . . on that pathless field
Of sombre blue—majestic, brave, serene,—
Face toward the vast unseen—unhurried, poised,
Prepared to meet whate'er may lie beyond,—
A fearless, stately ship puts out to sea!

—Isla Paschal Richardson

EARN A DOLLAR

By promise I was held
To make something
That I could sell;
So bread I made
Called "Boston Brown"
And sold to friends
Within our Town.
One loaf so round
Brought in one dime,

And ten were ordered
Just in time
For me to bring
My dollar here.
My bread, they said,
It had no peer.

—*Clara Lynn Rickard*

AUX ÉTOILES

One day I wrote a little song
And sang it as I passed along,
But no one heard—the World of Men
Had other things to do, just then
To listen, so in blind dismay
I threw my trifling song away.

But the West Wind, whispering near,
Caught up my song and bore it clear
Through furtive shades and somber night
To some unfathomed, cloudy height,
And sang it softly through the trees
To misty moon, and mounting breeze,
Until it reached the trembling stars;
And in its lilting, magic bars
I heard all Nature's melodies
Of crooning winds and whispering trees,
And knew it, then, more glorious far,
Because my song had reached a star!
Had sung in Nature's symphony
Its plaintive, lilting melody.

It came to me, quite clearly, then;
How little is the World of Men!

—*Leona Train Rienow*

IN COMMEMORATION OF SON'S
TWENTY-FIRST BIRTHDAY

'Twas a weary bird
   That came to a stop,
With never a word
   At the chimney top.

'Twas a mammoth bird,
   Yet he settled down,
While no sound was heard
   In the little town.

A moment he stood,
   Then his wings he flopped;
As he flew to the wood,
   A small bundle dropped.

Down the chimney it fell,
   This bundle so small,
And you never could tell
   It was falling at all.

It landed so lightly
   On a bed dainty white,
This bundle wrapped tightly,
   In the dead of the night.

A moment it lay there
   As still as could be,
Right out of the Nowhere,
   And right here to me.

And then a voice said—
   "This must be for you."
And I saw a small head,
   And I knew it was true.

The big bird you see,—
   (Stork was his name)
Dropped this bundle to me,
   So that's why it came.

There was nothing to do,
   Because it was here,
And the bundle was *you*,—
   Mother's so thankful, dear.

But now you can see
   I smile through the tears;
Since you came to me,
   It is twenty-one years.

The reason I smiled,—
    It is easy to see,
Because a wee child
    The stork brought to me.

The cause of the tears,—
    That is easy to know;
'Tis because of the years,
    It was so long ago.
                          —*Mrs. Caddie J. Riley*

BABYHOOD

A baby nestles in my arms,
His face in innocence clad—
Eyes somewhat wistful,
A pure, dimpled, little lad.
In so short a time
You have become so very dear.
God only knows what we would do,
Were you not here.
Each task only makes you dearer,
Every tear makes us love you more,
Your smiles add happiness to us;
You were a gift sent to our door.
                          —*Mrs. George Ringhofer*

PROCESSION

Where thou, immortal Mother, trod the way
From Truth's dethronement unto Calvary
Beside the rood—too blind with grief to see
The Light beyond, too reft of hope to pray
For mercy from the crowding enemy—
Uncounted women, destined to obey
The call to sacrifice upon a day
Of wrath, have followed, and will follow thee.

As thou didst know few joys unmarred by strife,
Few triumphs from soul-travail separate,
So they must drink the mingled cup of life,
And under star and cross in patience wait
Upon the Lord, who share at last with thee
The fullness of celestial victory.

—Helen Pursell Roads

POETRY WEEK

How fitting that a few short days
From out the busy year
Should be devoted to the muse that plays
Upon the strings,
Caught by the keener ear,
Tuned to the hidden things
Of inmost life that sings
And is immortal.

While listening to poetic lay
Sung by the Laurel-crowned,
A timid, shrinking, helpless soul must stay
Earth-bound;
Because no all-discerning eye can see
Prospective poet—in the lines that he
Poured from his heart.

—Elizabeth B. Robb

WELCOME, HUSBANDS

We extend to you a welcome hearty
To this our anniversary party.
We hope you'll enjoy everything that we do,
For it's all with the thought of pleasing you.
We'll be just as informal as we know how,
And, of course, won't expect you to act like a high-brow.
There is a story going round,
That on our husband's garments not one button can be found.
We thought they were there, but I guess they wasn't.
So what could we do but hand you a pin with a smile and a kiss?

And you know quite well, that button you didn't even miss.
So don't you worry, for we're not caring
How many pins instead of buttons you are wearing.
For we're busy as busy can be,
We study early and we study late,
Just to be able to keep up at your gait.
And yet we appreciate, far more than you know, all the nice
   things on us you bestow.

—Mrs. Marcella Robinson

A MOTHER BEFORE A MILITARY MONUMENT[1]

Was it for this I braved a pathless, dark,
And chilling void, in travail while the hiss
Of Death grew loud and near; from that abyss
To stumble back, enfolding in the arc
Of love-warm arms an infant life—a spark
I fanned to ruddy glow? Was it for this
I succored childish needs—healed with a kiss
Each wound that left on flesh or pride its mark?

Ah yes, for this I led my stalwart son
In paths of rectitude; abhorring vice
And choosing honor's way, he tossed the draft
That brimmed Youth's cup. Bereft and old, I run
Through War's red ledger—scan the costly price
I paid for laurel wreath and marble shaft.

—Winnie Lynch Rockett

YOUR LAMP OF FRIENDSHIP

Hold high your lamp of friendship
As you travel the rugged road,
Let it shine along the path
As I bear with grace my load.
Then strength will be given me
To endure with a cheery smile,
For your lamp will guide my feet
Along many a weary mile.

—Flora C. Rosenberg

[1]Reprinted from *World Affairs*, by permission of the publishers.

A PASTEL

A gentle hill clad all in velvet green,
Close 'broidered o'er with dandelions' gold
And violets that loving leaves enfold;
Here gnarled apple trees have gracious grown
With rosy-petaled loveliness full blown,
And now in dainty shower the blossoms fall
Through softly fragrant air, whence comes the call
And joyous lilt of bird choirs, still unseen.

—Delle Oglesbee Ross

CATECHISM FOR THE CLUBWOMAN

What do you see in the women you meet
In your club life, day after day?
Are you impartial and kindly of heart,
And just, when their motives you weigh?
Do you realize that most of them
Are doing their best to make good?
And give them credit for all they achieve
In this glorious Sisterhood?

Have you sympathy, and a friendly eye
For the woman who strives in vain?
Do you give her a lift along the way
To the post she hopes to attain?
And when she fails, have you been at her side,
And have let her know that you care?
And have you thought that "the last may be first,"
In the Sisterhood, Over There?

So if you have made a success of things,
And have gone to the top with speed,
Be gracious, and offer a helping hand
To the one not destined to lead;
Give her warm words of praise, remembering
That she, too, "hath done what she could,"
For the "mite" of all, not the strength of a few,
Makes this glorious Sisterhood.

—Margaret Wheeler Ross

BEGGARS

Like Eve I coveted untasted things,
　　To travel far in distant, magic lands;
I craved the easy comfort fortune brings,
　　And cursed the rings of bondage on my hands.
I felt disheartened, discontented, poor,
　　And railed at fate, that I should lack so much;
A beggar knocked upon my kitchen door,
　　A crippled beggar, leaning on a crutch.

Great flecks of sleet were clinging to his beard,
　　As humbly this poor beggar bowed his head;
The hopeless tears of age his eyelids seared,
　　"I roved the earth, and now I plead for bread."
Mine was a beggared soul, conjuring pain,
　　His, but a twisted body in the rain.

—*Bessie Maas Rowe*

GOOD NIGHT

　Good night, mother.
I gently close those eyes which once themselves
Of their own will were opened and were closed,
Which laughed with me and laughed when I was sad.
I kiss them now with lips that trembling say—
　"Good night, mother."

　Good night, mother,
Good night. And when tomorrow's dawning breaks
And my own eyes shall open where you are,
I'll see again the laughter in your eyes;
For you will kiss mine into life again,
And I'll be glad for I need never say—
　"Good night, mother."

—*Laureame M. Royer*

THE GARDEN OF LIFE

There are beautiful walks in the garden of life,
Where the sweetest of rose-passions grow,—
But there's a higher plane, past passion and pain,
Where lilies grow,—row upon row!

There is joy that is pain in the rose-scented walks,
You reach wildly,—and would hold them forever;—
But one stroll 'mid the lilies, where only the soul talks,
And the rose-path—cannot hold you—no, never!
                                        —*Lynn K. Rumell*

MY MOTHER'S QUILT

My mother cut the pieces,
And sewed them one by one
Into a beautiful pattern,
Until the quilt was done.

Some were bright and glowing,
Others a duller shade,
But all brought out the colors
Of flowers, down in our glade.

I see her face before me
With eyes and cheeks aglow,
Threading her needle swiftly,
Which made the quilt grow.

She sewed the pieces together,
Then placed them on the white,
And beneath her nimble fingers
Several blocks were done by night.

At last the quilt was finished,
Quilted in stitches fine,
And breathlessly we both looked on
That handiwork of love-time.
                                        —*Margaret Rushmer*

OUR YESTERDAYS

We take the brook path slanting down the hill,
And sit us down beside a wood fire's glow;
The cheery flames reach high but soon burn low,
As do our dreams that life does not fulfill.

In smoke-drifts through the blue dusk, cold and still,
We can see a whole life's visioning go—
Hear splintering of dreams that we would know,
Mingle with the wail of the Whippoorwill.

What does it matter if our yesterdays
Held but a portion of the April sun?
What does it matter if we can but find
Among drab years of dull and misty greys,
The handclasp of a friend—this lovely one
Of flaming hue brightens a weary mind.

                                          —Lillis L. Russell

HOLLYHOCK TIME

The bees are droning all the day,
The birds are singing loud and gay,
"'Tis hollyhock time in Iowa."
Beside each walk and garden wall
They stand like sentinels straight and tall,
And in each nook, and by the winding road
They bend in beauty beneath their load.
And as we pass they nod and say,
"Have faith in God, be kind today;
'Tis hollyhock time in Iowa."

                                          —Mrs. Oliver J. Saltsgiver

LANCASTER

I came to live in a storybook town,
Where the streets (very queer) run uphill and down,
And North and South and East and West;
I know by this time you have guessed

That the houses too, all straight and fine,
Like soldiers true, stand in a line,
And seem to say, "We look quite prim,
But open the door and come right in.

"We will show you things that were bright and new
When our British Mother got into a stew,
And made us so mad, we threw the tea
Out of Boston harbor right into the sea."

Some of the folks in this storybook town
Are given to wearing a cap and gown;
The caps are white, but the gowns, dear me,
Are colors not worn by you or me.

On the King's Highway in the Land of Penn,
You can find this town, and then, ah then,
By the red rose sign I know you will see
I have told this tale as it looks to me.

—*Sarah Steele Sample*

REDBUD TIME

Deep in my heart is a feeling,
Something that seems to entwine
Your heartstrings and my heartstrings
Together when it's redbud time.
Soft spring breeze and new-born leaves,
Winding roads and humming bees
Are only a few of Nature's jewels
Under the skies of blue.
Snowy white clouds that float where they may,
A sinking sun closing the day,
The appealing song of the whippoorwill,
Babbling brooks that are never still.
Oh come again in this time sublime
And we'll be together in redbud time.

—*Bertha Capper Sanders*

A HEART SONG

On my ear there fell a cry of hate!
And it filled my soul with gloom,
For torture seemed to be part of it—and despair.
But ere the gloom possessed me wholly—quite,
I heard a Mother singing to her child.
All the gates of Heaven seemed to open wide
As the song burst forth upon the air;
It breathed of love, of love Divine!
A Mother's heart was singing to its Child.

—*Elizabeth Rial Sargent*

RECOMPENSE

I've been where the mountains majestically stand
    In contours against the skies,
I've seen them enveloped in hazy mists;
    Aloof in grandeur they rise.
These, and the azure of placid lakes,
    Or mirrors of silver sheen;
I've seen them and vales in beauty stretch,
    Where rivers move serene.

But God in his infinite wisdom
    Knows what is best for me,
He gives me the prairies low and wide
    Where balmy winds sweep free,
Where verdant fields like billows roll
    And cornfields, rustling low.
What more is wealth than all of these;
    Beloved Kansas, I love it so.

I love it for splendrous sunsets,
    And the rosy-tinted morn,
For the glory of flowery meadows
    That cooling streams adorn,
O pray! what's more enchanting
    Than the cardinals' sweet refrain?
Dear to my heart are the myriad pools
    After the last long rain.

As I stand upon these great plateaus
    To view this broad expanse,
The horizon seems so far away
    At that momentary glance.
There are zephyrs wafted here and there
    That fate decreed for me.
O! for the charms of Kansas,
    Where 'tis my abode to be.

                                    —*Lora Evans Sauer*

DESTINY

We are born! And our Destiny
Is like a Leaf upon a Tree!
Life's slender stem, but clings at God's Command!
Swayed by His Will, and in the Hollow of His Hand!
—*Helen A. Saxe*

ODE TO HOUSECLEANING

Housecleaning has begun for this springtime,
  We're busy day and night,
Storing, discarding, and keeping
  The things we've stored with a might.

We sort them over so carefully,
  Keeping them year after year,
Lest once we ever discard them,
  They'll be needed—O, yes, my dear!

Ceilings and walls must be papered
  And cleaned with our favorite brand—
Smoky City, Climax, or Cleveland—
  Advertised the best in the land.

Clothespresses, drawers, and the woodwork,
  Each must be cleaned in its turn;
Everything cleaned with a vengeance
  From top to the bottom most stern.

Bad temper, broken nails, and picked stockings,
  Hands made grimy with oil,
Husbands sedated, children berated
  Must each play a part in the toil.

As we clean from the top of the ladder,
  There's a prayer that we breathe in our heart,
"Dear God, thank Thee for only one springtime—
  The time for the cleaning to start."
—*Louise Wilt Sayre*

PRAYER

Dear God, if I should die and then
Long afterward be born again,
I beg You set my spirit free
To live as a bird or flower or bee,
In some bright vale or fragrant glen.

To dwell in the deep of a woodland pool,
Lying calm and mysterious, dark and cool,
Near a fallen tree or a bed of moss
With bits of insect life skating across,
This would gladden the heart of any fool.

Or just to be born as a lump of sod,
A seemingly useless, worthless clod;
Yet it would nourish lush growing things,
It would hum with the beat of tiny wings,
And be blest by Your Footstep some holy day, God.

This last is the best. A tall green tree,
A pool, a flower, a bird, or bee
Can pass in a breath. But eternal rebirth
Would be the lot of the bit of earth.
This is my prayer. Dear God, grant it me.
                              —*Adelaide Foerch Schinzel*

BLIND SPOTS

They said that he was first to fall
When there was war;
But wondered why grief still remained
Long after there was built
A monument to honor him.

It was years before they knew
That they had failed to see
The One who died before he fell;
That Truth dies first the deadliest death
When there is War.
                              —*Lois Ethleen Schmidt*

THE BLESSED RAIN

The rain, sweet balm to nature,
Is falling, falling fast;
It washed away the banks of snow,
And now the winter's past.
The spring invites her flowers out,
The grass is green again;
But how, I ask, could all this be
Without the blessed rain?

We hear a song of gladness,
Sometimes a song of pain,
And oft a little sadness comes
With the falling rain.

But nature hears a wakening call,
She lifts her head again,
And with her beauty thanks the Lord
For all the blessed rain.

—Jennie Schmitz

A SIMILE

The burry housing of the fruit
Is not its essence.
For 'neath the rough-spun outer shield
And stonelike sheltering, wise
The kernel lies.

Through seasons' change, in preparation,
Protected well from harmful contacts bold,
The secret lies.
No confidence of creatures
Well guarded, deep within its cell.

And then this modest little kernel
On journey goes
Quite near its mother earth's repose.
And changing moons and
Shifting tides, its life fruit bears.

With me, enjoy this simile
Of souls encased
Who soar, like kernels planted deep,
To greater majesty and longer years,
Leaving their burry shells for higher tiers.
                                        —*Mrs. Emma M. Schwartz*

WAITING

How slow the red sun sinks in the silent west,
And the fog that creeps from the marsh on phantom feet,
Cloaking ravine and crevice, waits to greet the night
And hold his great black horses, while as guest
He lingers in the valley; so on quest
The slow fog slides across the stubbled wheat,
Leaving a sea of ghosts forgotten by his feet,
Making a path of dreams as night rides west.

And still I watch from the barren hills for you,
Watch till the winding road has writhed alive
In coils and turns, a trail without an end,
Watch till the fog that swallows all shall rend
And show the road; a hundred times this drive
The night has ridden west, but never you.
                                        —*Mary Elizabeth Schwartz*

OUR FAMILY DOCTOR

Our Fambly Doctor tells kids things
That's plain old stories; still I see
He sits in church and nods and sings
Like all the Deacons do; and he
Can even leave if someone sick
Says, "Doctor! Get a Doctor quick."

My Mother once was sick a spell
And said our Doc was out of date.
She went to see a Doctor Snell
With city style and city rate.
When she came home, she sure was sick
And screamed, "I want our Doctor quick."

Our Fambly Doctor gives Pa oil
And salts and pills, and sticks his skin.
It makes him cuss and fairly boil
And vow the Doc can't come again.
But next time he is feelin' sick,
He yells, "Go call the Doctor quick."

Our Fambly Doctor worked all day
And night when folks was havin' Flu.
If there was some that couldn't pay,
He'd try to ease their suff'ring too.
I think our Doctor serves so gran',
He's cop'ing from the Jesus Man.

—Flo Hampton Scott

WHEN JOHN TURNS ON THE RADIO

When John turns on the radio,
He gets all settled in his chair,
And draws his smoker up quite near.
I speak to him—he does not hear,
But looks at me with vacant stare,
And acts just like I wasn't there,
When John turns on the radio.

I go and find myself a seat,
And listen to the music sweet;
But soon my feet start keeping time
To those sweet tunes;
We both get up and start to dance,
It thrills us so,
When John turns on the radio.

Sometimes when winter nights are cold and clear,
That lovely music seems so near,
We just feel satisfied to sit and hear
Those gems that come from far and near.
We have front seats at every show,
When John turns on the radio.

—Geneva Harris Scott

RETURNED

This is the path I traveled when a child.
The house has aged, I have been long away;
Stripped of its past, the flowers growing wild,
Yet dignified in grandeur with decay.
At this descent we coasted down the hill,
Where earth has washed away from lack of care;
Ravines unknown, where brooks can sing at will;
As dusk descends, old joy turns to despair.
Beyond the low stone fence that long has stood,
I faintly hear the tinkling of a bell,
And cry of nighthawk in the distant wood,
Familiar sounds of old, the twilight knell.
I journey back along this broken slope,
Shorn of old love, unburdened of my hope.

—*Rose M. Scott*

THE GARDEN

I want to live in a garden
In the sunlight and the air,
Beside the grasses and the trees
And all the flowers fair.

I want to grow beside them
And help them day by day,
Since they help me and make my life
Happier every way!

The world began with a garden
In Eden, long, long ago;
The Saviour of men had a garden
Where He for peace could go.

I love to watch the miracle
When blossoms bud and blow;
I'm nearer to God in a garden,
Than any place I know!

—*Mary Chisholm Seager*

SONG FOR A YEAR

Wrapped in silver and gold,
When the year and my heart were young,
There was never a song so welcome,
There was never a song so sung.

"Always and ever," I caroled,
"Till the rivers of earth run dry."
(Only the old or weary
Believe that songs must die.)

Silenced the rippling measure . . .
What will the New Year bring?
Ghost of a young love's passion,
Or another song to sing?

—*Sadie Fuller Seagrave*

SHIPS AT ANCHOR

They know the vagabondage of the seas—
Those ships that swing at anchor in the bay,
With flags that flutter on a lazy breeze
From masts that lean in such a friendly way,
As though they gossiped of that far-gone day
When decks ran flame, and fierce men fought for gold;
Or of great virgin, forest lands, when they
Held their green council in some Arden old;
O, they are wise! those ships that swing at ease,
Home—from the vagabondage of the seas!

These are but poet-fancies—what I hear
Are hawsers straining, and the swish of spray—
A sailor singing, as he mends his gear,
Of lips that lure him back to old Cathay.—
We talk of Venice and its barges gay,
Of lurid sunsets over Singapore,
Of pearls, and ports where I may never stray
Who love the sea—and its enchanting lore;
But here, I cull such treasure as I may
From those old ships at anchor in the bay.

—*Alice Marston Seaman*

THE SCHOOL

The school to me a dovecot is,
　　As from my lofty fell,
I see the birdlings on the green
　　And hear the old school bell.

At early morn the flock files in,
　　So ribbon-wise and fair,
Who knows what skill the schoolhouse holds,
　　What future fame is there?

Like happy larks their voices blend
　　In morning melody,
I cannot think of sweeter sounds
　　Nor fairer sights to see.

At playtime hour I see them flit,
　　These birds of yours and mine,
Go running up and down the hills,
　　And in and out in line.

These flitting, happy, birdlike things!
　　If only they could stay
With hearts forever light as now,
　　As free from care alway!

With lessons done, the birdlings fly
　　Back to the warm home nest.
Another day,—another flight,
　　And back to home, and—rest.

God bless the patient, kindly ones,
　　Into whose tender care
We send our precious treasures,
　　And know them safe while there.

　　　　　　　　　—*Carrie I. Segerstrom*

GRANDMA'S BIBLE

Grandma's Bible is old and worn,
Page after page is yellowed and torn.
Every torn page she loved so well,
What a story they all could tell

Of days and nights spent in her hand,
Reading things she did not understand,
But believing unquestioned every word
As the sweetest stories she ever heard.

Nothing to tell from whence it came,
Nothing, but her own dear, faded name;
"Fanny Robinson" can still be seen,
"Born January 24, 1814."

Ninety times she read it through,
Straight through, and every time new
With meaning, while at her knee
Stood her children, then carefree,

One after another, learning there
The lessons she had read with care;
They never loved it as much as she,
The greatest of all books to her and to me.

For now it is mine; all old and torn,
Dilapidated, pages missing and worn.
But if I knew well all it still holds,
What a world of meaning it would unfold.

Ninety times The Book she read,
Once for each year of her life, she said.
A long life of labor and sacrifice,
"St. Fanny" they called her, "pearls without price."

Grandma's Bible inspiration be
To poor, unhappy, struggling me.
Let Grandma's thumb-worn Bible show
Her influence and love of long ago.
                    —*Leafa Dorne Seibert*

BEDSIDE FLOWERS

Delphiniums make me dream of realms afar;
Their heavenly blue suggests a land of dreamy splendor,
Of floating gently on a bed of clouds
In painless ecstasy, in freedom from all care;

All troubles gone, no monthly bills to meet,
No dinners to prepare, no dusting, cleaning up, nor anything,
Just resting on a cloud in heaven's blue.

But roses bring me back to earth again;
Their fragrance lures, and makes me wish
To conquer lassitude and aches and pains;
To conquer self and live awhile,
Accomplish things, get busy, hum,
Live, breathe, and love;
Be there when children call,
Fulfill each day the task imposed,
And make life brighter for my belov'd.
                                                    —*Marie Sercombe*

A WISE COUNSELOR

If you're up against a problem
    And the world's not going right,
If you've racked your brain to solve it
    And the end's not yet in sight,
You surely need a counselor
    To help you in your fight.
        —Ask a woman.

When your life becomes a burden
    And you're longing for a friend,
And the job that you have tackled
    Seems though 'twill never end,
Don't forget there's someone near you
    Whose thoughts with yours will blend;
        —'Tis a woman.

If your heart is filled with sadness
    And has been for many a day,
And the gloom that's settled o'er you,
    (Will it never pass away?)
See how quickly all will vanish
    If the right one has a say;
        —'Tis a woman.
                                                    —*Maggie Shades*

LYING AWAKE

'Tis fun
To lie awake
At night,
And watch the stars
All shining bright.

I should be sleeping
But I'm not—
I'm lying here
Upon my cot
Watching the stars
Up in the sky.

They're up so high
That each one seems
A little dot—
A tiny,
Round,
Bright yellow spot.

I wink at them,
They blink at me,
And we
Have greatest fun,
You see;
As I lie here
Upon my cot—
I should be sleeping
But—I'm not!

—Gertrude Kurzenknabe Shaffer

ON THE HEIGHTS

The pine trees tall
　　Their boughs fling high
On hilltop heights
　　Against the sky.

The evening breeze
　　Blows soft and low.
The sun reflects
　　A golden glow.

Upon this pinnacle
　We gather now
To celebrate
　A marriage vow.

Young hearts and true
　In happy union live.
Gladys and Gerald twain,
　Each to the other give.

May your eyes look up
　The heights to view,
And high hopes last
　Your whole life through.

                                            —Ines V. Shaffer

THE FIRST FROST

The World has changed her dress,
She's garbed in silv'ry white;
Filmy, gauzy, lovely thing,—
She donned it in the night.
The first fall frost is on the ground,
And silver glitters all around.

The World has changed her dress
From one of warmest brown,
To preen herself in white,
A queenly, showy gown.
But when she donned the lovely dress,
The flowers bowed in deep distress.

The World has changed her dress
To one of royal lace;
Chilly in majestic mien,
She stands with regal grace.
But plant life all around, we see,
Has paid the modiste's frightful fee.

                                            —Edith H. Shank

LOVE'S SONG

A song lay hidden in the folds
Of Baby's own attire;
The soft and dainty little things
Enkindled into fire
A spark within my breast.

Then as I washed them carefully
With water in a tub,
I heard the song of sweetest notes
In rhythm with each rub,
A Mother's love expressed!

—Wealthy Sheetz

THE CALL OF THE WILD

Let my spirit fly as the wild geese fly;
Let my grey pinions aspire to the beckoning sky,
My dead hopes scatter like dry leaves to earth
Forever dead. Within my heart quicken a new birth—
The past forgotten—the marsh, the reedy lake,
The tumult of other symphonies—love's slake—
Ask no reward; seek no recompense;
Only to follow the call that challenges hence
The wild grey pinions—know how great it is to be.
The selfsame voice that guides the geese, guide me!

—Daisy Sherman

THINGS

Her little workbox—needle, thread,
A bit of floss of brightest red,

The thimble bright, which did not know
Upon which finger it should go;

The last crude stitches which were made
Before the busy hands were stayed;

The crumpled handkerchief once pressed
By dainty fingers now at rest.

Was that a teardrop glistening there
Among these cherished treasures rare?

Ah! Why should I be moved by things,
When my little girl has wings?
                              —*Ada Simpson Sherwood*

FIRE

Thou flame of the soul, O thou fountain of life
That stimulates action and instigates strife;
That warms the cold-hearted and soothes every chill,
And stirs to emotion and makes the eyes fill;
That sends a force coursing through every vein
And brings form and beauty to vision again;
That lights and enlightens the earth and the soul
And makes of the heavens a glittering bowl;
That moves souls to passion of anger and lust
And lifts the heart Godward and fills it with trust;
That plays zigzag notes on the heavenly lyre
And makes the clouds boom like a masculine choir;
That drives powerful engines through sea, air, and land,
And burns into ashes the structure of hands;
That sweeps clean prairies and forests and hills,
And bursts wide the mountains and hot lava spills;
That draws from our bodies their moisture and salts
And makes of us but crumbling dust in our vaults;
That fills earth and soul with a beautiful light
That living without would make eternal night.

L'Envoi

Thou flame of the soul, O thou fountain of fire,
Thou canst make of the earth paradise, or a pyre.
'Tis no wonder that thou wast a great god of old,
For 'twould seem that 'tis thou that the earth doth control.
                              —*Emma Reed Shoaff*

I HAVE KNOWN BEAUTY

"I have known Beauty," the poet said in glee,
"I have seen it in the swaying of a slim birch tree."

"I have known Beauty," the lover said in pride,
"The woman I love with my son at her side."

"I have known Beauty," the mother said in pain,
"Happy little feet that will never dance again."

"I have known Beauty," the man-child said with grace,
"Patient, tired, wrinkled, old—my mother's face."
—*Isabel Brown Shurtleff*

FAREWELL, OLD YEAR

Farewell, farewell, Old Year;
You go from me
And with you take
That which I cannot hold,
The sacred key of all the past.
I would not call you back,
Yet I with love and fear
Still will cling to you, Old Year,
While these few moments last.

One year ago I greeted you
In all your new-born glory,
And resolved that true to you I'd be,
True to myself and others.
Was I?
Oh let me not look back
Or I will see
That all my resolutions were as chaff
And count for naught,
Although I sometimes tried to be
The strong man God intended me.

I hear Time calling, and I sigh,
For well I know, Old Year, you soon will die,
And I for my mistake
Must retribution make.
What can I give, Old Year,
What will you take?

Love, Truth, and Charity you bid me keep
And bind them to my soul,
Then go and seek
The key to manhood's goal;
'Tis hard and steep, you say;
The crags and cliffs are high and deep.
I will while there find time to weep alone—
And for the past, Old Year, atone.
You bid me keep all these;
What will you take?
I ask again, for I must give—
While yet, Old Year, you live,
You'll take from me only a promise rare
That I the crown you give to me shall wear.
Old year! Do as you will with me.
"The crown," you say, "is Sweet Humility."
Farewell, farewell, Old Year,
I've found at last the goal,
That which was lost, my soul, my soul.

                                        —*Florence L. Sidley*

THE FOUNTAIN IN THE RAIN

When the storm clouds loose their torrents,
    Whipping garden, hill, and plain,
There is courage, staunch and loyal
    In the fountain in the rain.

Shorn of all its rainbow colors,
    All its lacy, opal spray,
Beaten back in heavy splashes,
    Vanquished quite its elfin play,

Straight it leaps to meet the downpour
   Like a silver dart of light,
Bounding skyward through the deluge,
   Springing—thrusting with its might.

May I meet life's stormy weather—
   Sure the sun will shine again—
With a bounding spirit ever
   Like the fountain in the rain.
               —Katharine R. Siegert

REVERSE PITY

Your life so full of joyous things,
You seek to pity me, who bring
No tale of travel lore to sing
To winter groups; who never climbed
The wondrous Alps, or saw the Nile;
Whose journeys were not timed, as yours
To bow before the Midnight Sun,
Or Parthenon of ancient Rome,
Or Taj Mahal, the final home
And perfect shrine of India's queen.

I beg you spare your pity, friend!
My life to me is full of joy.
Two splendid children are my own—
A daughter and a boy;
A tiny vine-swept home,
A helpmate, understanding, true.
With them, in soul, I've journeyed far
On earthly globe and alien star.
In tiny craft, with cooling breeze
We've sailed across the Aegean seas—
At nightfall we have softly tread
O'er Macedonian battlefields—
Sometimes red with blood.
And we have stopped to tell
The crippled soldiers, lying as they fell,
Of God's illimitable Love.

I beg you spare your pity, friend—
'Tis I who pity you.
               —Georgia Blaney Skaer

ADVERSITY

To the thorns of life I'm more indebted
Than am I to the roses sweet.
They will not let me lie contented
While round me there are tasks to meet.

They prod me on to nobler action
Nor long allow me quiet ease,
But keep on pricking at my conscience,
And often drive me to my knees.

—*Ruth Smeltzer*

PLUS OR MINUS

Are you a plus or minus quantity,
    An asset or a liability?
Do you add or just subtract
    From the trend of human progress?

What is your excuse for being
    If your duties you are fleeing?
Do you contribute happiness,
    Or merely pad your own success?

Is your life a life of giving,
    Or is your mission taking?
Have you earned your right to be,
    Or do you always think of "Me"?

Don't be a minus, be a plus!
    Don't you lean, but give support,
Help the helpless, lead the blind,
    Lend a hand, and be a sport!

—*Alma Smith*

GIVE ME GAY COURAGE

Give me a magic belief
In the beauty and adventure of life,
Give me a gay courage
To meet its sorrow and strife.

Give me a calm content
Which comes with service and giving.
Give me a happiness and faith
Which comes with the joy of living.

And with all these gifts
Thy Love and Guidance lend,
That I may be given a gay courage
To meet the sunset's end.

—Edith M. Smith

RELICS

Down narrow streets through dim lights may be seen,
At early hours of morn of every day,
A tiny old man, always clad in gray
Of ancient cut, with cap of velveteen.
Though bent his body, his black eyes are keen
And note with interest all along his way,
But never let a thing his steps delay,
Until the shop's portals are passed between.

This shop of antique relics gathered here
By lovers of such things from far and near,
Who revel in the nearness of their art
And almost seem to be of it a part,
Creates an atmosphere like some sweet dream,
And he, the master relic, reigns supreme.

—Eugenia Bragg Smith

LIFE

We enter life's vale like the rising sun,
With the bloom of youth life's battle begun;
We are carefree and happy, give little heed
To the troublesome world and its wonderful need.

We laugh and play, labor and sing,
And learn great lessons from sage and king.
The mind of man, God's greatest treasure,
Reaches out to grasp the world's full measure.

At last we find the task begun
Is far too great to finish at set of sun;
So our hands grow tired, we sit and dream,
And think like this as we drift downstream;

Life is a battle in a narrow span
And yet too short for mortal man;
When finished we silently close the gate
And cross the Bar and yield to fate.

—*Mrs. F. S. Smith*

TO MOTHER

Oh soul so sweet! around Thy tomb
    Green grasses grow, red roses bloom.
And Thou did'st love all nature new:
    The morning star—the evening dew,
Majestic mountains, towering high,
    The fleecy clouds across the sky;
With each coming season Thou wert in tune.
    Each flower, each bird was to Thee a boon.

But Thou art gone! oh heart of gold,
    Leaving us stricken, heartache untold.
Still I can hear, o'er that far, weary way,
    Thy loving voice, as Thou would'st say,
"Be brave, have faith, and always be true;
    Remember, my dear, I'm watching o'er you."

—*Geraldine Smith*

IRONY OF FATE

When I would soar on wings of song
    Or write some rhythmic rhymes,
My husband wants a patch sewed on,
    My children ask for dimes.

It's hard to go from clouds to earth,
    Yet makes me want to grin
To have my husband ask again,
    "Is that new patch sewed in?"

—*Grace Jervis Smith*

I LOVE A STORM

I love a storm, yes, I, who all my life
Have courted harmony, sought quietude;
Who cringe at every cruel word and rude,
Avoid unpleasantness, hate brawl and strife
And all harsh scenes with noise and discord rife.
Yet awed, I unafraid, exultant stand
And view with ecstasy the storm-god's hand
That devastates and spills with ruthless knife.
Some primal impulse answers to the storm;
My spirit welcomes in the threatening air
The conquering force it lacks but fain would share.
In elemental strength it sees the form
Of God, who glories in the conqueror's song
And bids faint hearts have courage and be strong.

—*Grace Turner Smith*

MEMORIES

Only just to be at home once more,
Just to ease the longing from our hearts,
To live again the years that are gone forever;
In sadness, one remains and one departs.

We see again the dear familiar step-stone;
In one's fancy is the brook that brightly gleams.
But should we still this longing of our memory,
We should have to burn our golden bridge of dreams.

The glorious sunset sweeps the distant meadows,
The wailing notes of the dear old whippoorwill;
As years roll on those memories come more often,
Sweet memories that never can be still.

—*Jean Smith*

GOOD FRIDAY

Come we unto an altar, kneel, and pray,
Oft do we try to pierce life's somb'rous way;
Come we to claim the heritage of years,
Calm aching grief, extenuate our fears.

O God, Who sees and knows our every need,
Come now to our Gethsemane, we plead.
We who have passed within the garden's gate,
Know each must bear a burden soon or late;
Lift Thou our thought, our hopes beyond Earth's skies
Give dreams of Thy immortal Paradise.
                                                    —*Lucy H. King Smith*

THE RHYTHM OF THE HILLS

Blown leaves—a toss of spinning gold and fire,
The drowsy trickle of the freezing spills,
A wedge of honking geese, the sun a pyre
Of flame to crown the rhythm of the hills.
                                            —*Mrs. L. Worthington Smith*

FATHER OF OUR COUNTRY

George Washington, a name to love and revere.
He lived a life immune to fear.
Unselfish service makes his name to all so dear,
On history's pages, our most honored seer.

His constant loyalty to mother, wife, and home
Made him trusted and loved where'er he'd roam.
His unerring faith in God
Made his life for others a measuring rod.

Towards bitt'rest enemy he'd never take revenge.
On the rights of dearest friend he'd not infringe.
So loyal, so faithful, so selfless, so true!
Founder of Old Glory, the Red, White, and Blue.
                                            —*Mrs. Madrid H. Smith*

MISSOURI

I cannot sleep when sunrise comes to wake
My blue Missouri hills, for there I see
Each day the beauty of eternity.
Light runs too fast for me to overtake,
But I will trail its footsteps while I wake.

Sometimes I hear the beat
Of early settlers' feet
Along forgotten roads;
And where two rivers meet,
The "voyageurs" slip by
With sudden warning cry;
With glad and gallant song,
The "voyageurs" slip by.

I live and grow beneath Missouri trees.
They draw me closer to the heart of earth;
They make me one with every seedling's birth,
With those remote, those age-old mysteries
That dwell within the bark of living trees.

Sometimes I hear them pass
Across the meadow grass,
Between the old oak trees.
I see our grandsires pass—
Missourians who sought
By word and deed and thought
To mold a splendid State;
For this they fought.
Missouri gave them rest,
They lie within her breast,
Their children's children tread
The paths their feet have pressed.

When night comes down to dim the sunset skies
And those bright lands beyond the evening star,
My heart turns back from visions, vast and far;
My homing heart turns back where evening lies
On these dark hills beneath Missouri skies.

—Floriaa Watts Smyth

A PRAYER

Keeper of my soul tonight,
　Teach me what is best, is right,
Make my thoughts, Lord, pure and sweet,
　Keep me humbly at thy feet.

As I go about my daily task,
   Give me wisdom, this I ask,
To be of service in thy work,
   Let me not, Lord, shun nor shirk.

And when I hear that last clear call,
   Let me feel that I've done all
That I could to help some soul
   Run the race, win life's goal.

                            —*Clyde Wood Sneed*

THREE SONGS

Of all the songs my mother sang
   I most remember three
That come across the waste of years
   And bring her voice to me.

The first about a faded rose
   Once given as a token
Of love that should live on and on
   When vows and hearts were broken.

The next a lilting lyric is
   Of wild brooks running gay
As lovers under orchard trees
   When all the world is May.

The last of one lone Stranger tells
   Who made the blind to see
And walked with pierced and bleeding feet
   The shores of Galilee.

Life's Maytime spread its blooms for me
   And all its joys paraded;
I long ago have lived to see
   Love's fairest flowers faded;

But he who walked beside the lake
   In sunny Galilee
Remains as faithful as he was
   When mother sang to me.

                         —*Mary Grace Snyder*

TO A FRIEND

More precious by far than an exquisite pearl
Is a friend—one tested and true;
Life gives nothing better to mortal below
Than a friend who will love and trust you.

A rose may be sweet, but I hold not more so
Than a friend—one who ever is near
To shield you, protect you, and ah, what a joy,
To cheer you when some days are drear.

The sky may be dark—the sun may not shine,
My frail barque may be tossed, it is true;
But I shall not be troubled, I shall not repine,
For, my wonderful friend, I have you.

—*Mrs. Louis Solem*

RECOMPENSE

It is autumn in my heart.
But if that means the garnered glory of the many happy years
Behind this autumn day,
Then 'tis not all of sadness that should brim
Within my heart.

But if 'tis black despair,
And treasured 'membrance of unhappy things,
And present desolation and welling loneliness
Alone dwell there,
Then 'tis indeed a chill and dark autumnal day,
And all the light has gone from my poor heart.

Ah no, for as a crystal chalice held on high,
My heart holds memories as bravely bright and gold,
In spite of autumn day,
As all the garnered wealth of Ind,
And says to sad repining, "Peace, be still,
God lives and all is well;
Once more shall Summer come into thine heart."

—*Anna M. Spencer*

THE SUN—A PRODIGAL

The Sun was prodigal tonight,
With gold he decked the stream;
He opened wide his treasure chest,
Flung out the gems that he loved best;
On every blade of grass they rest,
And every leaf's agleam
With rubies, emeralds, diamonds bright,—
The Sun was prodigal tonight.
                              —*Jessie Florence Springer*

HEAVEN

Heaven is not in some far-distant space,
An Eden out of reach beyond the blue.
'Tis not a vagrant longed-for mystic place,
Glowing with latent treasures, strange and new;
But here, deep in a spotted foxglove's throat,
Or twined around a lily's golden heart;
Or where the wood thrush sings his silvery note
In forest's leafy aisles, a place apart;
A sun-drenched web ablaze with sparkling dew,
Or when a rainbow 'gainst the sky is cast.
And when the noble tasks of day are through,
The peak of Heaven's bliss is reached at last
As sunset colors streak the distant west,
When baby's curly head lies on my breast.
                              —*Nina Dudley Staples*

BEAUTIFUL YOSEMITE

Dauntless Captain of his corps,
Bravely standing in the fore;
On the left the mighty fall,
Over on the other wall
Floats that misty veil of tulle,
White, mysterious, and cool.
Beautiful Yosemite,
Fair as Paradise to be.

Lying there with walls of grey,
Beautiful by night and day;
Murmuring the Merced goes,
Whispering the breeze now blows;
Mirrored grandeur, lovely scenes
Painted azure, greys, and greens;
Beautiful Yosemite,
Fair as Paradise to be.

When the stars shine in the sky,
Fire comes falling from on high;
When the moon sheds silvery beams,
Haloed there the Captain seems;
Will you turn away from this
Vision of the realm of bliss?
Beautiful Yosemite,
Fair as Paradise to be.

—Viva I. Stark

MY GARDEN

My garden is a plot of painted poems,
Each struggling plant a thought divinely born,
And God is here to wake the words to music
When wooing winds come whispering in the morn.

—Margaret Ann Stevens

THE LURE OF THE BUTTERCUP

"Why do you hang your head like that?"
Said a buttercup to a violet:
"You turn your pretty face away
And hide beneath your bonnet gay—
Your bonnet so blue with a bow on the crown
And a long green ribbon hanging down.
You're such a modest little flower
As you nestle down in your leafy bower.
Won't you look up at the sunny sky?
Do you never watch the clouds go by?"

The violet tossed her dainty head
And to the buttercup she said:
"I love in the earth's embrace to rest,
She folds me close on her tender breast.
I love the shadows under the trees,
The gentle rain and cooling breeze.
I grow aweary of the sun,
And so I keep my bonnet on.
Do you not find his rays too bright,
And await with joy the caress of night?"

To this the buttercup made reply:
"'Tis the sun's great task to glorify
And to make glad this world of ours
As he runs his course and tells the hours.
He turns bleak winter into spring,
The hills and valleys bloom and sing.
His gracious bounty he'll not withhold,
He fills to the brim my cup of gold.
But yours is a beauty of richer hue
For love was given the heart of you."

The little violet thus beguiled
Looked up at the buttercup and smiled.
And the buttercup, with winsome grace,
Bent down and kissed the lovely face.

—*Eleanor Stimmel*

SPRING IN THE WOODS

Away to the woods!
Where the shadows lie deep;
The flowers have awakened
From winter's long sleep,
The air's richly laden
With perfume so sweet,
A violet carpet
Is laid for our feet,
A green leafy arbor
O'erhead stretches high;
Hear the song of the birds!
See the blue of the sky!

Here's jack-in-the-pulpit,
With gay coat of green;
Here's a buttercup maiden,
The fairest I've seen;
Here are pure white lilies
And adder tongues gold;
What wonderful treasures
A spring day can hold.
Here are fine green umbrellas,
Should a sudden shower fall;
Here's a toadstool to rest on,
And here's a puffball.

So we wander and gather
The flowers at will;
The springtime is ours,
Our hearts with joy thrill.
We gather in handfuls,
How eager the quest;
Flowers seen in the distance
Seem brightest and best;
On and still onward
To a yet fairer land,
Those picked first are withered
By the warmth of the hand;
So in life's search for pleasure
Those beyond seem so sweet,
In our mad rush to pluck them
We miss those at our feet.

—*Nina Gail Stong*

THE HOUSEWIFE'S LAMENT

From morning till night and all through the day
    I work and I worry without any pay.
There's washing and ironing and scrubbing to do—
    O dear! it seems I'll never get through.
There's sweeping and dusting and beds to be made,
    And never a soul to lend any aid.
The cake and the pies and the bread to bake,
    Leave me no time for some pleasure to take.

The socks must be darned, the chickens be fed,
    The dishes be washed ere I go to my bed,
And when I would drown all my troubles in sleep
    There's naught I can do but lie there and weep—
And think of the things I would like to do
    But never get time and never get through.
For the wonderful books and the magazines, too,
    The moments for reading are all too few.
Methinks I would leave all the dust and the grime—
    On a journey I'd go to a far distant clime—
Where I'd have nothing to do but just live at ease
    And bask in the sun and the cool ocean breeze,
Forgetting the toils of a weary housewife—
    The worry and work of everyday life.
It may be the tasks I seem so to hate
    Would then appear not nearly so great;
And I would hasten to begin over once more
    The homely duties just as before.
For we only need a little more time
    To brush the cobwebs off our mind.
It matters not what we eat or wear,
    Just so long as there is love to share.
And I opine that the homey things
    A greater joy and more pleasure bring.
So whether we work or whether we play,
    We must meet each duty day by day.
And the small, still voice that speaks to all
    Is heard in service, whether great or small.

—Eloise Story

GEMS ON TENDRILS

Strewn upon the tendrils (the years),
I have an array of gems of sparkling hue:
Pearls are laughter; diamonds, tears;
And bits of song, both old and new.

Upon each fledgling tender limb
Hangs a dream no time can mar,
Age nor weather their brilliance dim,
For each twig holds a wishing star.

Into the silken roots within my breast
A molten stream of gold flows free,
A crown of coral is my crest—
Each year is a tendril, and I'm the tree.
—*Lucy Stout*

DEDICATED TO MRS. E. R. JONES

Now Mrs. Jones, she say to me,
"Did you ever write poetry?"
And I say to her I sez, sez I,
"No, I never did, but I can have a try."

So that very evening, just after tea,
I settled myself on the old settee,
By a bright wood fire, with pencil and pad;
My heart was happy, and my heart was glad.

And I sez to myself, "Why, any dub
Can write a poem for that Woman's Club."
I thought and I thought, but I thought in vain,
But who ever heard of a poet with the name of Strain?

I met her next day and I sez, sez I,
"Well, I gave it a thought and I gave it a try,
But I wasn't cut out for a bard, you see,
So get Fay Butler to write your poetry."
—*L. Lillian Strain*

CIRCUMSTANCE

It is not place, nor time, nor grace
    That makes the great of earth,
It is not chance, but circumstance
    That proves what man is worth.

It is not the kind of paper,
    Nor the place we sit to write,
Or the finely written manuscript
    So pleasant to the sight;

For dungeon walls responded
  To Bunyan's noble thought;
And Lincoln's hasty, scribbled speech
  Can never be forgot.

From mud the fairest lilies
  In purest beauty rise;
There is no depth so dark but there's
  An outlet to the skies;

Gethsemane, a battlefield;
  The tomb, a door to light;
With wings of faith we can surmount
  Each circumstance in life.

It is not place, nor time, nor grace
  That makes the great of earth,
It is not chance, but circumstance
  That proves what man is worth.
                                    —*Maggie Woody Stratton*

FLAME

At midnight I awoke from tranquil sleeping,
Discordant voices roused the somnolent air;
Grotesque and crooked forms were sprawling, creeping—
Over the room, the windows, everywhere;
While stars and moon by scarlet Flame were hidden—
A monster who devoured my treasure and home—
An ogre, hated, feared, always unbidden,
Whispered, "Nothing is left to you but loam!"

"Monster—the best you can never consume,
Though roof and walls are charred and timber crashes;
Up from blackened soil the flowers can bloom,
And hope will rise from gray and crumbling ashes."
Should my spirit mourn or with longing yearn
When Beauty, Love, and Life can never burn?
                                    —*Elizabeth Greene Streater*

TO AN OLD BLUE BOWL

The ghosts of long-dead women bend with me
Above you, frail blue bit of beauty we've all loved,—
She whose long hands set you on teakwood tenderly
In a Manchu's garden,—she who wore
The simple grays of Salem,—she who rode
Through wildernesses to the great jade sea
Of Michigan,—she whose thin hands showed
Work-scarred against your blue translucency;
Glowing, and dustless, through twice a hundred years
We've kept the quaint perfection of your loveliness. And when
I too shall stand, a wraith in their dim circle, and the living one
    appears
Who finds you answer to her dreams of worlds beyond her ken,—
Dark gardens, strange seas, fragrances that haunt her sleep,
Walled cities, crumbling towers, far lands where she would be;
Remembering, I'll call to her across the mysterious deep,
And bind myself to life as these dead women now are bound
    to me!

—Frances E. Street

JUST SMILE

If your heart is "kinda" blue,
    Just smile;
If the day seems dark to you,
    Just smile;
It will drive the blues away,
Bring to you a happy day;
You will find that it will pay
    If you smile.

When you start the day anew,
    Just smile;
Happiness will come to you,
    If you smile;
All your troubles fly away,
You'll be happy and be gay,
And you'll have a gladsome day
    When you smile.

—Mrs. Zell Struthers

VACATION

I love to lie beside a babbling brook,
Where spreads a canopy of leafy boughs,
And listen to the twittering goldfinch gay—
The while I browse the pages of a book,
Or dream perchance of love and you afar,
Or watch the coming of the evening star.

Such leisure brings both rest and rich content—
My face uplifted to the vast unknown—
My thoughts go drifting on in rhythmic mood—
Refreshing breezes bring a woodsy scent;
Lying alone, head pillowed on green sod,
I realize the presence of my God.
                                    —*Mrs. A. J. Stukenberg*

THE NEW YORK CLUBWOMAN MEDITATES ON HAMLET

To be on time, or not to be; that is the question.
Whether 'tis nobler on the feet to suffer
The crowds and violence of outrageous Subways,
Or to take arms against a sea of pushers
And in a Bus avoid them? To sit, to doze;
No jam; and, with a seat, to say we end
The footache, and the thousand maddening jabs
That Subway flesh is heir to, 'tis a mode of travel
Devoutly to be wished. To sit, to crawl;
To crawl, perchance be late; ay, there's the rub;
For that by being late, we reap the scowls
Of fellow members who arrived on time,
Must give us pause. There's the sad thought
That makes calamity of so slow going;
For who of us would bear the quibs and scorn of crowds,
The closing door, the guard's strong push,
The pangs of despised shoves, the sudden lurch,
The insolence of elbows, and the stares
Of men upon whose outstretched feet we tread,
When she herself might her way make
To a calm Bus. Who of us would bear
To grunt and sway under a swinging strap,

But that the dread of something in those eyes,
The undisguised hostility from whose glare
No late-comer escapes, freezes the will,
And makes us rather bear those Subway ills
Than crawl in seated comfort to our Clubroom, late?
Thus Conscience does make cowards of us all.

—Olive Tait Sutherland

THE VAMPIRE

Once on an early May-day morn
With Heaven's warm sunshine glistening on the dew,
Wandering o'er wooded hills, sweet love was born;
For I met you.

Red were your lips, ah, red!
And full of promise and of mad desire.
You kissed me; Life was ecstasy, my heart
A flaming fire.

Too swiftly sped the day,
Which foolishly I dreamed would last forever.
Our world a paradise through which to stray,
Nor death could sever.

How could I know the selfish love of power,
The mockery of your eyes, the vain deceit?
Your glowing beauty, mine for one brief hour,
Then love, a broken thing beneath your feet.

—Dolores Swart

NEGLECT

June . . .
Has forgotten my garden.
It is full of little lost hopes
And dried rose leaves,
Memories of a time when June—
Remembered . . .

—Annette Mason Swift

IN MONMOUTH

In Monmouth, in Monmouth
    I heard the cuckoo call—
'Twas in the greying twilight
    When night begins to fall;
He called aloud in passing,
    I stood beneath the yew
And caught his wing-tossed greeting—
    "Cuckoo, cuckoo."

I'm far away from Monmouth,
    Yet every Spring of year,
If I but listen closely,
    I fancy I can hear
Beyond the rippling breezes
    The murmur of the yew,
And just above an echo—
    "Cuckoo, cuckoo."

                                    —*Eve Gilbert Swift*

ECHOES

Standing by the gateway
In the evening glow,
Listening to the footfalls
Of the long ago.

Not so long in days and years
If you count it so;
Count the time in heart throbs,
Then you come to know.

Mother's little toddlers
Walked at just a year.
Bounding steps of schoolboys—
Listen! do you hear?

Romping home at close of day
No other sound so dear,
Gallant lads so trim and tall
Stepping quite the beau.

Merry, laughing, teasing ways,
Mother loves them so;
Life is calling from afar—
Eagerly they go.

Now they walk in places far
Firmly without fear,
Leading busy earnest lives.—
Very quiet here,
Listening to the echoes
Of the vanished years.

—*Mary Ellen Tanner*

SPINNERS

Spider—spinning up and down,—
Busy creature—round and round;
House of silv'ry, gauzy thread,
Through the swaying branches spread.

Happy little Laddie Boy,—
With a shining brand-new toy;
See it spinning on the ground—
With its merry humming sound.

Mother—rising with the sun,—
Daily spinning to be done
For some money to buy bread;
Hungry children must be fed.

Grandpa—'neath a shady tree
With his comrades—two or three,—
Spinning old-time, salt-spiced tales,
When he weathered ocean gales.

—*Ovie Pedigo Tanner*

BONFIRES

You ask me why so sad a look is mine?
I can't explain; you wouldn't understand
The smoldering fires that lie within my heart.
Once they flamed high, like bonfires fed with leaves;
They flamed—and ever reached for more and more;

But, like the bonfire, finally burned down,
When negligence, like wet leaves, blanket it;
Yet did not die; ah, no,—and hence the pain.
Some day peace, like the gentle rain from Heav'n,
Will calm the fires forever in my soul.
                                        —*Edith Haskell Tappan*

MY LITTLE HOUSE

I love my little house with its broad gallery,
Where dewy breezes flit, soft, caressingly.
The high-ceilinged rooms, so virginal white,
Bathed in warm benediction of morn's rosy light.

And when night's purple shadows embrace, instead,
Like a tired happy child, it goes sleepy to bed.
For all the day long such sweet secrets it tells
That I am greatly bewitched, and live under its spell.

As a Rock of Gibraltar in the scheme of my life,
It holds me securely 'gainst outer-world strife;
A dear little house brimming over with cheer.
Unpretentious? Perhaps—but Love lives here!
                                        —*Zephyr Ware Tarver*

KEEP CLIMBING

Oh, Life is a ladder
    To climb day by day,
And will you keep climbing?
    Or will you just stay
At the foot of the ladder
    While others pass by?
For you may reach the top
    If you will only try.
                                        —*Elizabeth Cushing Taylor*

THE STAFF THAT SUSTAINS

To be contented is to choose the staff
Of brave restraint to ever lean upon;
It is to know the time to laugh, to sing,
Or greet with smiling face noon, night, or dawn.

It is to feel that somewhere beauty flowers
Into a perfect bloom, even though men know
Its mirrored loveliness alone is ours,
Its shining, shattered petals pale as snow;
For only those who daily lean for aid
Upon restraint may find that by and by,
Within the heart a firm foundation's laid
To hold Love's house and find it satisfy.
Oh, rugged staff, be mine as on I wend,
That I may know your peace until life's end.

—Elkanah East Taylor

FRIENDS IN NEED

I came to you with troubled heart,
      I knew not what;
Evil, fear, imagination had played their part.

Your tender care—your quiet thought
      Renewed the strength,
Courage, hope, and faith I sought.

But when you bared your heart to me,
      Mountains of Love
Arose—to help you crown a victory.

'Twas then my troubles melted as the brightening sun
      Swallows the darkness;
With unfaltering step—renewed life was begun.

And now I know it was to be;
      Time tempers all—
I needed you—you needed me.

—Estelle Taylor

THE GREATEST GIFT

The woman of this age, the present hour,
Is gaining in leadership and noted power.
In art, drama, philosophy, ode, and song
She has the plaudits of a famous throng.
In science "a bit of radium illumes the way."
The world accepts her gifts today,
But the greatest gift is "a human life."

This gift will live through aeons of years,
Through the annals of history, through smiles and tears.
Kinship with the divine, eternity will not efface;
Abiding joy will at last reward the race.
When your contributions are placed at the Master's feet,
The one gift that will weld the universe and make complete,
Will be the cosmic gift of "a human life."

Hours spent in training your girl, your boy,
Have their recompense in love free from alloy.
Ideals of service, a forum built on human love,
Lend strength that comes as grace from above.
The lullaby may be a prayer in the purple glow
When the shadows are dim and the lights are low.
Accept my gift—"a human life."

                                        —*Dr. Annie J. Teem*

PERSIAN INTERLUDE

As I was looking at my Persian Shawl,
    My beautiful Persian Shawl,
A little flower fell at my feet
    In a scalloped dress of magenta deep;
From a silver vase on a mantel high,
    Winging through air, I heard it sigh
And whisper softly in its downward fall
    To the unseen Lady of the Persian Shawl.

The fringe of the shawl, in quivering delight,
    Caressed the flower in its aerial flight,
Like a Chopin Lady in silken gown
    With a quaint curtsey to the flower she had found.
"Dearest Lady," I heard it say,
    "Do you remember that far day,
When you walked in a garden by a lonely sea?

"There were Sharon roses everywhere,
    And the shawl you wore was always there,
Brought by the Prince or your maidens fair,
    To protect your beauty from the salt sea air.

"You always passed the stately flowers
  With their colors that seemed to burn,
And came to the pool, the silent pool,
  Dipping your fingers so white and cool.
You seemed to me divinely tall,
  With sandaled feet so slender and small.
The passion I felt, wind-swept on the wall,
  Was for you, sweet lady in your Persian Shawl.

"You turned to the Prince and your maidens fair
  With pale hands pressed o'er your bosom there.
'Bury me here, when I am dead,
  Where Magenta Petunias may bloom o'er my head.'

"But now we are transplanted to a different place,
  You cover gay melodies with crimson face,
While I am left dying in a tall silver vase.
  You see, dear lady, I have always been true.
I am off to a land of cerulean blue,
  Where I may bloom once again for you,
With Magenta Petunias all sparkling with dew."

So the little flower sleeps on the polished floor,
  Its iris-rimmed eye is hidden from sight,
It looks so peacefully still in its blight.
  I am sure the angels are smiling tonight
With the Magenta Petunia on the cold sea wall,
  And the beauteous lady of the Persian Shawl.

—Rose B. Tharp

RAIN IN A GARDEN

I love to watch God's charwoman
Patter around all day
Washing the hangings of the trees,
Brushing the webs away;

Carrying off the grime and dirt
The winds brought from the road;
Dusting a birdling's littered nest,
Joking a friendly toad;

Mopping the threadbare sun-stained sod,
Sweeping the tangled walk;
Chiding an errant wet-winged bee
Shivering on a stalk;

Wiping the faces of the flowers,
Scrubbing their dusty feet;
Smoothing the creases of their beds
With fingers deft and fleet;

Toiling throughout the long, gray day—
Doing the tasks with skill—
Leaving my garden at nightfall
Star-lighted, clean, and still.
                              —*Alice Winchell Thayer*

EN MASQUE

Behind each mask there is a story;
It tells of thwarted things,
Of hopes deferred, of dreams defiled,
Of hurting outward stings.
Sometimes a smile, a mirthless laugh
Conceal a broken heart;
Behind the grotesque face and painted lips
A jester plays his part.
Disguised, the bandit shoots and threatens,
Plundering for his treasure;
'Neath the domino of satin black
The dancer seeks his pleasure.
Behind each mask there is a story;
Ah! these sad and funny faces,
The smile, the shrug, the cynic's pose,
But tattered pride replaces.
                              —*Io Sloan Therme*

LIGHT

Give us light,
More light, O God!
Or else
More understanding
To use the light we have.

We grope drunkenly,
Poking with pointed finger
A drop of water
Glistening at our feet,
Thinking it a diamond;
And then, disillusioned,
We turn away
Belittling its inherent beauty.

—*Aimée Paul Thomas*

MY GARDEN

My garden seemed an endless toil
To rake the leaves, to lift the soil—
The sunshine beamed, the showers fell,
My garden now—A Magic Spell!

Sometimes life seems a ceaseless grind
To purge the soul—to feed the mind.
Bright joys shine out—dark sorrows roll,
And life at last—A Blended Whole.

—*Eleanor Smith Thomas*

WHIM

I am a mountain stream
Pregnant with motion,
Seeking a distant dream,
Be thou my ocean!

Let me be lost in thee
As the swift stream
Merged with the mighty sea,
Be thou my dream!

—*Beryl V. Thompson*

GOD'S GIFT TO MAN

Death is not all there is to life,
Glorious victories follow strife,
Darkest nights are turned to day
With the sun's first morning ray.

The mighty oak would cease to be
The strong and sturdy stalwart tree,
If death ruled this world supreme
Without one hope or future dream.

Life is God's gift to man.
To destroy it nothing can;
Ever present 'twill always be
Through days, years, eternity.
Let not death mar your plan,
When Life is God's gift to man.

—*Elizabeth B. Thompson*

TWO SONNETS

CHRYSALIS

She wore a gown of latest mode, soft blue
That matched her eyes and made her golden hair
A shining halo around her brow so fair.
Her jewels, those she loved the best, were few,—
Two rings, one plain, the other jade's clear hue,
Adorned her perfect hands; a necklace rare,
Of dainty hand-wrought silver dared compare
Its beauty with her throat. But ah! I knew,
(And held my heart lest it should burst with pain!)
That stilled were all those joyous notes that fell
So blithely from her lips each day; in vain
To her calm ears would I my fond hopes tell,
For ne'er would ope those azure eyes again:—
God had her soul, and I,—the lovely shell.

ALPHA AND OMEGA

She whispered low, "I cannot understand!"
And then she died. How strange that she, whose years
Were only seventeen, untouched by tears,
Just meeting Life with eager, outstretched hand,
Should go, and leave behind that weary band
Of pilgrims, worn with struggle, pain, and fears,
Who've pondered long on Death, and gazed like seers
Out to the Great Unknown,—All-Knowledge Land!

Who shall say why? Perchance her pure young soul
Was like some crystal stream, swift flowing down
From snows eternal to a rocky bowl,
Only to be drawn back to summit's crown
E'er dust or dross of world hath marred its whole.
God said, "Have faith! I take back but mine own."
　　　　　　　　　　　—Kathryn Bruchholz Thomson

TO THE VILLAGE CLUB

Under the sunny Eastern skies
This club of ours stands;
Governed by good officers,
The best in many lands.
The presidents could not be beat—
Have wills like iron bands.

We started many years ago
(I might say in September).
The dues were only fifty cents,
And I, a charter member.
We struggle on through thick and thin
To do whate'er we can—
We look the whole world in the face
For we owe not any man.

Month in, month out, most any day
You can hear this—if you choose,
"Please bear in mind the meeting,
And don't forget your dues,"
Like a sexton ringing the village bell
To spread some welcome news.

We visited counsel many times
To help clean up the town.
And helped at many other things—
Were never yet turned down.
We tried to banish cigarettes
And, also, all the soaks,
But finally gave up in despair
'Cause everybody smokes.

And people coming from other clubs
Look in at our open door.
They marvel at the work we've done,
Go out and spread it o'er,
And catch the sparks of good that fly
Like chaff from a threshing floor.

We come on Tuesday to this room
And sit among our friends,
And hear the president *preach* and talk;
(We only say Amens).
We think we hear our daughter's voice
Singing in the Junior meeting;
It surely makes our hearts rejoice
And send to them a greeting.

We often think of the Juniors,
And know when we've finished the race,
They will be ready and willing
To step in and take our place.

Toiling, rejoicing, chattering—
Onward through years we go.
Each month we see some task begun
Even if it goes very slow.
Something attempted, something done;
We have earned a little dough.

Thanks, thanks, to thee, Our Women's Club,
For the lessons thou hast taught.
Thus at the flaming forge of life
Our fortunes must be wrought.
And as we pass off, one by one,
To the other land,
May we leave clean records,every one,
And a "Memorial," as we planned.
                                    —*Mrs. Boyd Thorn*

MARCH WIND

Here I come shrieking across the plain
And over and over and over again
I fling myself with a mad delight
On the trees and shake them with all my might.

And some will bend and some will break,
And on I rush and leave in my wake
Disaster sometimes,—sometimes maybe
A hint of the Spring who is following me.

I sweep the clouds that leaden lie
Beneath a dull grey bowl of sky
And send them scudding as souls set free
To the chant of my pagan ecstasy.

I lash the waves to an angry roar,
And high in the air the white gulls soar;
I seize the puny craft of man
And strew its wreck as far as I can.

Long have I waited in silence grim
In the Cave of the Wind's recesses dim
For this—the hour when Earth shall be
Naught but a playground made for me.

—Hazel Partridge Thorne

MEMORY'S PAGEANT

In memory of James Whitcomb Riley

Mystical melody in the air,
Unheard whisperings everywhere;
Soft, swift rustle of angels' wings,
A song of sadness the lone wind sings;
Perfume of beautiful flowers unseen,
Pale light of even in silvery sheen;
Troops of fond memories floating by
In billowy clouds of the evening sky:
    A pageant of sorrow they meet,
    In little Lockerbie Street.

A myriad host as in days of yore
Is greeting a friend at the open door;
Still, muffled footsteps are passing now,
To rhythmic music as heads low bow;
Countless numbers in memories' train
Breathe in sad cadence a sweet refrain
Of love and homage,—a tender lay
To the children's poet and friend today:
    Whose presence in spirit they greet,
    In little Lockerbie Street.

                                        —*Eva D. Thrasher*

THOUGHTS

Is love in vain? It cannot be—
The God of Love looks down—to see.
Our griefs—torn hearts—our tear-dimmed eyes,
Tokens of Love's great sacrifice.

This God of Love—who made the sea,
The mountain's lofty majesty—
The glory of the harvest moon! the stars!
And then the mother's croon.
In lullabys—and loving plan—
Could He do more for lowly man?

Our breaking hearts, our hopes, our tears—
Are love-strewn paths to higher spheres.
Where life goes on—in love supreme—
Through endless aeons—and the dream—
Of hopes and longings far above
This life—is found in realms of love.

                                        —*Lillian Hastings Tomey*

NOVEMBER 11, 1918

I start awake and stare into the dark
Through my chamber windows opened wide,
And lie and listen to the quiet room
And soft rustlings of the poplar tree
The house beside.

Then by the lift and change
In that clear atmosphere,
I feel through the dark
That dawn draws near,
Although but a joy anticipated.

Then suddenly the dawn awakes!
And down the street
Are rushings as of many feet.
Glad bells peal out and whistles scream;
From a thousand throats a mighty shout;
And then the blare of horns again,
And every freak of sound.
Above and beyond, the siren's shriek
Beats and falls and rises
Against my chamber walls.
Still I lie and listen,
Tense with the great portent.

Like bubbles coming to the surface
From the surging depths below,
My thoughts keep rising, bursting,
Tossing to and fro:
Of the long, long years;
Labor's fevered stress and strain;
Of the sunken ships, the wounded,
And the departing train;
Of smiling mothers
Growing old before our eyes;
Of the trenches red, of the sacrifice.

That rigid self-control is broken
Of the need but to be brave,
As joy unspeakable keeps mounting
Wave on wave;
Until my pounding heart
Would burst its confines
Under that mighty surge of thought.

Then through the Pandemonium sound,
Like balm upon a wound,
The thought goes singing through my heart,
"Our loved ones will return."
For all along the battle line
The dark night is done,
And smiling Peace, a tear on her cheek,
Is hushing every gun.

But he lies asleep upon the field of France,
Nor wakes to heed the happy circumstance;
And that great company, The Silent,
From life and laughter hurled,
Come and wait before the throne
Where God looks forth with brooding eyes
Upon an outraged world.

O God, shall the Nations forget?
Nor heed Thy word?
"Neither shall they learn war any more."
May The Blind be made to see,
And the Deaf be made to hear.

—*Mary Shepard Towler*

TO CREATIVE ART

Little I know what room you will grace,
    Or can I tell in whose heart a place
You will find or a need you will fill.
    I only perceive, "Be still
And know that I am God," the pattern will free;
    The wherefore is not meant for me.

—*Edith Loomis Traver*

IN MEMORY

"My work is finished that
Thou gavest me to do."
She has lived her life of beauty,
Now her tasks on earth are through.

She is gone. How we shall miss her!
How we find our lives bereft!
'Tis not she that we would grieve for
But the empty place she left.

She is gone; but she's still with us.
In our hearts we hold her dear,
Our lives are fuller, gentler, nobler
For her presence here.

—Pearl C. Trimble

WASHINGTON AT HOME

Today I fain would walk or ride
With my fair Martha by my side;
What more could mortal man desire,
A chair, a book, a pleasant fire,
Perchance a visit from a friend;
Thus I would spend life to the end.

I love to plant a tree or vine,
To watch them grow, the joy is mine.
Mount Vernon lures as ne'er before,
Life's failing strength she will restore;
To leave her portals ask me not,
Here I would toil and cast my lot.

—Jennie Triplett

OLD HOUSE

This old house on a busy street
    Where traffic rushes by,
Does not reflect our new-gained wealth
    Or our standing signify.

But it holds the richest memories
    Of life's challenge bravely met,
A steady flame on a sacred hearth
    With sacrifice beset.

It befits our tempo of living,
   Styled of another year,
A shrine to us of Unity,
   Of Faith and Warmth and Cheer.

I'll have no house of spacious rooms
   Built on the Avenue,
But only the accustomed things
   I've used since Love was new.

                      —*Bess Truitt*

NEW HAMPSHIRE LILACS

The hills are sweet with lilacs now,
   All freshened by the rain,
And on the distant mountainsides
   Love's hues are warm again.
Swift through my heart resurgent sweep
   The tides of many Junes,
And life and love are oft renewed
   In our cool sweet northern noons.

I see the wine-like shadows fall,
   And the hyacinthine glooms,
While the cloud-fleets roll on their silver way
   O'er the tossing lilac plumes.
Now the flaming lights of sunset pour
   Among the apple fleece,
And through my heart steals love, steals life,
   As the evening bell-notes cease.

                      —*Sylvia Tryon*

LOVE AGLOW

Just we alone are in the world tonight,
Here on the peaceful summit of a hill.
Let us not think of else beside our love—
Tomorrow is a day beyond our will.

Enveloped in the radiance of night
And love, I would that we, forgetting, might
Be by the world forgot, ecstatically
To dwell in Arcady by day and night.

And then! . . . Life is so short! The Great Beyond
So wrapped in mystery . . . How can we know?
To tear apart a rose and see its heart
Is life's short span, as moments go.
                                        —Blanche Chalfant Tucker

TO A ROSE

Oh lovely rose,
As you unfold your petals
Full of fragrance rich and rare,
I count the many blessings
Of my heav'nly Father's care,
And find them
Full as fragrant, sweet—
As your lovely blossoms fair.
                                        —Mrs. O. O. Tucker

WHY FEDERATE?

In pondering o'er the question
Why Clubs should federate,
I'll answer it by telling—
Of our club at Pleasant Lake.

Ten years ago we organized,
A band of women true,
Intent on self-improvement,
And civic work to do.

We've studied art and music,
History, ancient and new,
We've planted trees in April
And sponsored lectures too.

And while we all were trying
To do our little bit,
We knew that other women
Were showing the same grit.

Women from Howe, Whitley,
From Fremont and Auburn too,
From Ft. Wayne, our sister city,
In numbers not a few.

We wanted to know these women,
To clasp them by the hand,
To unite in bigger projects
And thus our work expand.

And so we joined the District,
The County, and the State;
We hope to join the General soon,
And then be up-to-date.

And when up here in Old Steuben
We plant a rambler rose
To beautify the highway,
We know the prospect grows.

And when we buy our linen
From our dear friends, the blind,
And send our girls to college
Through student loan, we find—

That we have added to the sum
Of joy and happiness,
Of usefulness and knowledge,
Which comes the Earth to bless.

We've always felt that women
In politics should share,
That they to be good citizens—
Should try with unremitting care.

We believe we owe a duty
To folks of every clime,
And our International Relations
Will be settled right some time.

"God Bless Our Home" is our motto,
But this we know full well,
That He needs some assistance
From women trained to tell

Sore throat and croup from measles,
The worth of spinach, too,
And how to train the children
To be square and kind and true.

And we believe our Juniors,
The women of forty-three,
Will be better wives and mothers
Than we can hope to be.

But should our children, like the flea,
Go to the dogs, why then
Our committee on Social Morals
Will set them right again.

Now all of these departments
Are placed at our command,
When we unite with other women
In the Federation Band.

We'll work for Club Extension,
With pleasure we will give
The story of club benefits,
And by giving we shall live.

And when in our "Club Woman,"
Of others' deeds we read,
We vow that we will imitate
And maybe excel their speed.

We always like to follow
A leader who leads on
To success in each endeavor,
And Mrs. Canine is that one.

So for inspiration,
For programs, and for plans,
She and her fine helpers
Can supply all our demands.

True we can't all go to College
And earn a coveted degree,
But we may have its equivalent
In club work, don't you see?

Since we've joined the Federation,
We're as busy as can be,
We haven't time for gossip—
Or frivolity.

So here's to the Federation,
May it grow and grow and grow,
Till we've done everything there is to do,
Learned everything there is to know.

                                        —*Mrs. Carl Tuttle*

THE OPENING OF THE LILIES

In the still cool of the morning
The dewdrops gleam on the grass.
The atmosphere's pine-scented,
And flying birds swift pass.

In this, man's first cathedral,
The lofty arches ring,
As before a mountain altar
The birds sweet anthems sing.

Between the choir and altar
A lake and its lilies lie,
Their buds green-sheathed uprising
Beneath a carnelian sky.

Across the dark, still water
In my canoe I glide,
And among those cloistered lilies
I open a pathway wide.

Then in a burst of music,
I see the Sun-god rise
Over that lofty altar,
And before him the shadow flies.

He touches with his fingers
Those sheathed buds, one by one,
And as he them caresses,
They open to the sun.

Oh, slowly, slowly open,
Till on the lake they lie
White chalices of fragrance,
Gold centers to the sky.

—*Grace Robertson Tuttle*

WAITING

Earth wore the beauty of promise
When the woodland paths we trod,
The fairies played
In the sylvan shade,—
The roses and lilies were God.

The budding rose,—
Then the rose full-blown,—
The petals have fallen all,
And the lily bells
In the sylvan dells
Are no longer stately and tall.

My heart—like the broken lily,—
My life—like the faded rose;
Do the fairies still play
At the close of day?
I wait for what—God knows.

—*Inez Sheldon Tyler*

LOCOMOTIVES

Like wounded giants whom time and age have stripped
Of splendid strength, these locomotives stand,—
Forgetting for a while how they have slipped
On wingèd feet across the steel-tracked land.
Here, waiting for man's cunning, sentinels;
And motionless they rest beneath skies gray
Or blue; their heartbeats still, their noisy bells
Silent through all the hours of night and day.

But soon, by love and labor, each iron toy
Will know the healing touch, regain their youth,
And men will honor them,—and with great joy
Let them go forth. O simile of truth:
That life must age, but in some far-off land,
Man, too, grows young, touched by his Maker's hand.
                                        —*Mary Pollard Tynes*

THE DEEP BLUE SEA

Oh restless sea! confide in me,
Say why your ceaseless moaning?
You seem distressed, no time for rest,
Your waters ever foaming.

Oh wondrous sea! of mystery,
I stand and gaze and wonder,
While billows roar and lash the shore
Like distant winds and thunder.

Oh deep blue sea! all will agree
Your colors so artistic,
A tinted hue of green and blue,
Present a scene most mystic.

Oh stormy sea! you've heard the plea
Of seamen drifting, drowning;
Beneath your waves are countless graves,
A cause for groans and frowning.

Oh trackless sea! no land or tree
The traveler can discover,
No mile post show, the way to go,
While sea birds near us hover.

Oh rolling sea, make known to me
The mysteries of ages,
In your distress and heaviness
A conflict ever rages.

When the tide comes in with rush and din,
No message comes to me;
When the tide goes out, still left in doubt,
Roll on, thou deep blue sea.
                                        Mrs. Thomas B. Upchurch

MOTHER DEAR

"Mother, what makes the sky so blue?
And the clouds all fleecy and white?
What holds the sun 'way up in the sky?
And where does he go at night?
Would I be happy to be with God—
Like my Sunday-school teacher said?
But won't I ever see Him at all—
Exceptin' when I am dead?"

Mother

"Why—God, my dear,—
Well—He's right here
In the good that we do or say.
You see Him in me—
In the flower—and bee—and—
But run now—my dear—and play."

Child

"Mother,—I saw the teeniest bird
Just kicking out of his shell.
How did he get there—anyway?
The storybooks never tell.
Did—He put the bird inside the shell?
And paint the sky so blue?
I think I could love Him, mother dear,
If He were at all like you."

Mother

"Listen, my dear!
And you will hear—
His voice in the robin's note.
In the babblings gay
Of the streamlet's lay—
—But don't you want to run now, and play?"

Child

"Mother, I b'lieve God talked to me—
Yesterday, under the apple tree.
'Cause I didn't want to do what you said—
'Bout pulling the weeds from the flower bed.

But the smell of the blossoms and robin's note
Made a great big lump come right in my throat,
And I got all over the mad like you said,
And was just all happy inside, instead."

Mother

"Ah, darling boy,
Would I could hear
His voice, as clear as thou,
Feel His presence near—
In the falling tear,—
My dear.
Teach me to hear! teach me to hear!"
                                                    —*Lettie Earley Van Hoesen*

THE WISE YOUNG LAWYER SPEAKS

I answered Him discreetly—that I know—
    As one well learned in all the Holy Writ,
And He Himself did quietly say so,
    And seemed to praise me greatly, saying it.

"Thou art not far"—now mark His very talk—
    "Not far from out God's Kingdom," then He said.
In thankfulness I stooped upon the walk
    And kissed His vesture's fold that from His head

Reached almost to His feet without a seam.
    But now as I sit here before the Law,
His face forever comes as in a dream;
    His eyes have lost that happy light I saw,

And sadness covers them, as clouds the sun
    Across fair Judah's blue and light-kissed skies;
I see no cheering smiles across them run—
    Why were there tears within His deep brown eyes?

"Thou art not far," He said to me, "*not far!*"
    My pride is gone and now my soul is fraught
With dreadful fear, for I have felt the bar
    Across the praise, a deeper meaning caught.

They call Him Rabbi, Holy Teacher, Friend,
  But all are sure He is a prophet too,
A seer of the things that have no end,
  Who knows the future as no others do;

Perhaps Elias once again on earth,
  Or just a lesser prophet of the age,
Who comes to Israel, from lowly birth,
  To mock me now of Abram's heritage.

I have no pleasure in the parchment scroll,
  I cannot gloat over the Gentiles' sin;
I hear those saddened tones in thunder roll—
  Could He have meant *I should not enter in?*
                —*Millicent H. Velhagen*

POINSETTIA

Great, crimson-petaled flower,
Glowing in the dark,
I think you are the radiant star
That lighted up the Holy night
In Bethlehem afar.

I think you fell from out the sky
To hide the cruel wound
In piercèd side;
And now you bloom in flaming red
At Christmastide!
                —*Florence J. Vordenberg*

LIFE'S PAGEANT

Through panic, grief, and grim chaotic times,
  Who gets the most and who the least in life?
One man will fight, another embrace crime,
  Each, all, are moving down the paths of time.

On crowded streets or on the lonely paths
  Searching to find, a self-appointed task,
Watching the humblest, the man of wrath,
  To see the soul of man behind the mask.

I love to sense the movements of the world,
   The action of the wheels of throbbing time,
How thoughts of men and women free speech hurl,
   May mold themselves in love of all mankind.

Temples of queer distorted man-made creeds;
   Spirits of evil dancing now to jazz.
A still small voice, not hushed by brutal deeds;
   His word and truth still stands, and ever has.

I love to watch life's pageant forward move,
   Through bewitched dark and artificial bright.
Man's ego brain can create endless grooves.
    Where I was frightened, now behold the Light!
                      —*Mary Hawley Vreeland*

SACRIFICIAL FIRES

Across the sunlit hills of Dawn,
As chill winds scurry by,
Blaze Autumn's sacrificial fires
Beneath a cloudless sky.

The golden torch of cottonwoods,
Red sumac's scarlet flail,
The flaming plumes of maple trees
Adown a woodland trail.

The hollows where green shadows hid
The glory of the sun
Till Autumn calls to colors
Her brave recruits—one by one.

The great procession marches on,
Night breezes' trumpets blow,
The silver starlight overhead,
And Autumn's fires burn low.
                    —*Neva McFarland Wadhams*

EXILED

There's a country that I love, far away,
Where my thoughts in vagrant fancy play,
  O'er that rolling prairie land
  Where the gorgeous maples stand,
With autumn leaves uptossing, far away.

Oh, the evergreens in winter, far away,
When snow has fallen softly through the day,
  They are lovely statues white
  In the starlit, glittering night.
They cast a hint of magic, far away.

By an ivy-covered farmhouse, far away,
Where my aged loved ones ever stay,
  In a flower-shadowed yard
  Where the hollyhocks stand guard,
There's a green-grown tiny mound, far away.
                                    —*Myra Wadsworth*

HOPE

Have you wished for summer sun
In the Winter's bitter reign?
Don't forget when day is done,
One as vital comes again.

Keep in mind when joys are few
And fresh disappointments rise,
Each day something born, or new,
Takes the place of that which dies.
                                    —*Hortense Drucker Wagar*

TO MY JACOBUS STAINER

Oh silent Violin,
Whose strings once sounded the immortal music
Of souls now gone,
Give to mine ears again the magic
Of thy sobbing songs of sweetness,

And blend thy harmonies with the strains
No mortal hand hath wrought
Or ear received—but whose fair chimes
Awake an echo of dear sadness
As breaks the heart!

Oh give again, as once thou gavest,
Love's fairest songs of longing,
And let a hand that loves thee
Caress thy strings—or sting them into life
That throbbing prays, and praying fades away,
As fades the beauty of an autumn day.

                                        —*Edith Flint von Wald*

THE SILENT MARTYR

We've honored Martha Washington
In story and in song;
She's been enshrined in ev'ry mind
As wholesome, sweet, and strong;
A lady of an ancient day,
Of poise and queenly grace,
Some trait Divine in ev'ry line
Upon her saintly face.

We've honored, too, with tongue or pen,
A man we all revere,
An iron heart, a soul apart
From selfishness or fear;
A fighting man who laughed to scorn
The armies of a king,
Yet mindful of the slightest wound
A little child could bring.

But, after all,—allow his strength
Of soul and mind and heart;
Allow to her a woman's love,—
Who gave the greater part?
His was to serve the cause of men
Throughout that trying span,
And hers—the silent, patient task
Of serving *just one man*.

                                        —*Bertha V. Walker*

THOUGHTS AT CHRISTMAS

What do I get out of Christmas?
Thoughts that last the whole year through!
The star, the song of an angel,
Joseph, Mary, and the Christ child too,
The Shepherds watching by their flocks,
Three wise men from a country far,
The patient waiting for a King,
The quiet of a lonely hour,

The spire of a country church
Towering upward to the skies,
The chiming of the Christmas bells,
Cheer and laughter, dreams and sighs,
The inner searching for a faith,
Longing for a cleaner heart,
The silent passing of a friend;
All, of Christmas, are a part.

Memories of a Christmastide,
Faces in the firelight's glow,
Throngs of people, looking forward,
Happy, weary as they go.
So I have the thought of Christmas
In my heart throughout the year,
Home and loved ones, truer friendships
Are God's gifts I hold most dear.

—Grace Mathews Walker

A SNOWY MORN

The storm king came to earth last night,
This morn the world's a fairy sight.
The roofs of houses take strange shapes,
They're frosted just like wedding cakes,
And every twig and bush and tree
Is outlined in white tracery.

Across the roadway down below
Our minister is shoveling snow.
The soft light stuff is just as white
As gospel truth he preached last night.

With desperate haste he clears away
For feet that might be led astray,
Straight to the church, a broad white track;
No turning there, nor looking back.
He wields the shovel like the Word
With earnestness, and not deterred
By anything. His coat is black
As sin. It's boundless white
That makes that spot stand out so bright.

The doctor's lawn, next to the manse,
Is buried 'neath the white expanse.
Its master fusses here and there
With anxious eye and busy care
As if he shoveled up in pills
An antidote for human ills.
Though carefully he cleans the walk,
At the least chance he stops to talk,
And sends across a grouch barrage
Which we all know is camouflage.
"He doesn't like this kind of work!
The minister is sure a shirk
Who hasn't shoveled to the line!"
Ah, we are thinking all the time
Of who it was that just last year
To that same minister brought cheer,
Spaded his garden, cut the grass,
Nor let one deed of kindness pass
Within a neighbor's thought or care
When sickness lay so heavy there.
A heart more soft I do not know,
He never turns deaf ear to woe;
With sympathy he mixes pills
To ease both mind and body ills.

The minister, his task all done,
Shoulders his shovel like a gun,
In boyish fun turns toward his friend
With kind intent a hand to lend.
His cheery voice rings on the air,
"Need any help now over there?"

Mary D. Wallace

MY LITTLE DAY

A tiny bit of endless time is mine!
How best can I, a mortal, use this power
Placed in my hand? May there be one short hour
That stands above its fellows, to combine
The worth of all my actions in a sign
Of something great! Or, maybe, only dower
Of trifling days, that stands at last a tower
Built up of hopes to be but simply fine.

Whatever life shall give for me to choose,
Let me not fill the hour so full of dust
That sense of sky dimension I may lose;
Yet I must see the devastating rust
To keep the shine on little ways, and use
The golden thread of time to hold my trust.
                              —*Christine Hamilton Watson*

AFTERGLOW

Great-grandma sat in her hickory chair
    In the dusk of the long ago;
On her knee was spread an old scrapbook,
    And she read in the dim afterglow:
"I am not old, I cannot be old,
    Though threescore years and ten
Have waved away, like a tale that is told,
    The lives of many men."

Grandmother sat in the same old chair
    When her hair was white as the snow;
Turning pages of the same old book,
    She read in a voice, soft and low:
"I am not old, I cannot be old,
    Though tottering, wrinkled, and gray;
Though my eyes be dim, and my marrow cold,
    Call me not old today!"

Then mother sat in that hickory chair
  In a faraway western land;
As the years sped past, she too would read,
  As she held the book in her hand:
"A dream, a dream,—it is all a dream!
  A strange, sad dream, good sooth;
For old as I am, and old as I seem,
  My heart is full of youth."

The same chair stands beside my fireplace;—
  It is sturdy, though black with age;
And on it I keep the old scrapbook
  And I read from a yellowed page:
"Forever young—though Life's old age
  Hath every nerve unstrung;
The heart, the heart is the heritage
  That keeps us forever young."

—Dona Wayland

LIFE

This, then, is life . . . of such our dreams are made,
Eternal reaching out toward some strange land,
To seize the fragile joys with eager hand—
The brief, elusive joys that had betrayed
Our questing mind. Through dawnings unafraid,
We seek the power that makes a grain of sand,
Or whirls a star in space at its command,
And find no answer, but are undismayed.

We follow silhouettes: a shadow blur
Upon a cloud; the quiet stabbed by thunder;
A rainbow bridging space and lovelier
Than any man-made citadel of wonder.
And while we travel onward, bit by bit,
Our dreams are vain, no doubt, but exquisite.

—Tessa Sweazy Webb

WITHHELD

At night an artist coated all the trees,
Till far across the wide expanse one sees
   What waits but inspiration from the sun
   To gild in crystaled beauty work begun
Upon a mighty frost king's wondrous home,
'Neath fretted twigs of nature's silent dome.

Impatient, too, the king awaits the light—
That royal touch of fire and glorious bright—
   And chafes at all the cold gray overspread,
   Perhaps in fear of some annoying dread
     O'er what's withheld.

But, unseen king of regions cold,
Pray stay those wishes to behold
   The thing that glitters silver dew,
   In heightened splendor tinged anew.

Remember, what's withheld is often best,
And that in time develops, blessed;
   For so it is in acts and deeds withheld,
   Or with anticipations sadly felled,
The burst of glory through the door
Is vastly better than before—
   Because withheld.

—Florence Gray Webster

THE CURRENT

Life's adorings, life's outpourings,
Life's strange needs and life's rewards,
Life's unseeming, life's redeeming,
Life's divisions, life's accords
Are the pulse-beats marking, marking
Ceaseless steps toward the goal,
Endless growing of the spirit,
Full perfection of the soul.

Knowing naught of lost endeavor,
Rhythmic, constant, undeterred,
Beating, lashing, all compelling,
Driving, forcing, groans unheard,
Grows the unseen life within man
To a power undreamed, unsaid,
Fixed beyond all human changing,
By a master workman led.
—*Alice C. Weitz*

I LIKA DA PEOPLES TO SPEECK

I lika da peoples to speeck dat I meet
Each day as I go to my work up da street.
An' I lika da smile an' wave of da han'
W'en dey pass my banan' an' peanutta stan';
Eet maka me so happy to hear dem say,
"Good morna, Alfio, how ees you today?"
    Yeh, I lika da peoples to speeck.
—*Anne Acton Welborn*

TO MY DAUGHTER

It seems but yesterday your baby feet
    Wove slow uncertain patterns on the floor,
Your little fumbling fingers at the door
    And dimpled smile made home-comings so sweet.
And now you stand before me, woman grown,
    Clear-eyed, courageous, rich in heart and mind,
Facing the future, be it harsh or kind,
    Knowing the years will bring you to your own.

When all too soon our paths lie far apart,
    And lonely days cause hidden tears to start,
The many happy hours that we have shared,
    The little bed-time talks when hearts were bared,
The words of tenderness you never spared,—
    Are treasures I can hold against my heart!
—*Frieda S. Whalen*

COLOR IN NOVEMBER

The leafless trees their bony structure show
And pencil a gaunt loveliness below
The hill. Only one in palest amber
Keeps a delicate reminder
Of leaves that were; while on the hawthorn near
Red berries glow like rubies. Their jewels clear
Might have a name as precious, dear,
As Badakhshan or Burma if they would!

In late November's trembling wood,
When colors are so rare and Autumn's hood
Has lost its green, a solitary jay
Upon a tree may seem a sapphire gay,
And these few amber leaves and berries red,
As precious as things upon a mummy's head,
Carefully unwrapped by those who see the dead
King's glory in his ornaments.
                                            —*Larah F. Wheaton*

HOLIDAY

One day I chose to be Queen of the May,
My leaden world turned golden and gay.
I loosed the bond that held me tight,
I danced with unalloyed delight.
With trembling hands I seized the cup of bliss
And drained its dregs with one long rapturous kiss.
I can't recall one single word I said;
I know not where my buoyant feet were led.
But if I yielded to this lure,
The path was straight, the kiss was pure.

No scar remains from this glad day in May,
For to each child God gives one holiday.
                                            —*Gertrude Lee Wheeler*

LINES INSPIRED BY THE MUSKRAT'S HOUSE

When Adam from the garden fled,
  Up to the mountains high he sped;
There with Eve he made his bed.
  But as the winds blew cold, he said,

"My gentle Eve, what shall we do?
  These airs, they chill me through and through.
I am so cold I can't say Boo,
  The housing problem's up to you."

Now Eve she had a seeing eye;
  The muskrat's dome was rearing nigh,
So unto Adam she did cry,
  "What they have done—let's you and I."

The pliant willow soon they bent,
  Then crisscross the small branches went.
At set of sun, their strength well spent,
  Their house to them looked Heaven-sent.

Whene'er you see St. Peter's dome
  Beside the Tiber's stream at Rome,
Think of the lowly muskrat's home;
  They wrought it first—the perfect Dome.
                   —*Grace E. Wheeler*

COMPENSATION

Lord, I am glad that I must needs
To live an humble life,
Else many lovely things
I might have missed.
The timid blushing of early dawn;
The helping my small children off to school;
The preparation of their daily bread
With mine own hands;
The sweet, washed smell of clothing
From the line;
The miracle of planting tiny seeds
To harvest gorgeous blooms;

And then at end of day to sit at peace,
Tired and worn, perhaps not overneat,
With those I love around the fireside,
And rest and think and read.
Lord, I am glad that I must needs
To live an humble life,
Else many lovely things
I might have missed.

—*Emma Boge Whisenand*

SPRING IN THE ARIZONA DESERT

A tempest of rain
Has wakened the heart of the desert.
The giant Sahuaro is crowned
With white flowers;
It has filled its arms with them.
Pastels of dawn
Glide from the mountains
And the grey Cholla is a tree of pink coral.
While the slender stems of the Ocotillo
Kindle into small flames.
The Great Spirit smiles
On the desert.

—*Grace Hoffman White*

SONNET TO WINTER

For every sorrow, every faded thing,
Exultant joy will ride again this way;
Full soon will come the softly shaded spring,
(Grim winter always dreams a dream of May!)
Though robes of icy sleet enfold the earth,
Yet . . . inwardly the heart may still rejoice,
Forgetting sullen days, heart-broken dearth,
Hearing in dreams the sound of summer's voice.
Courage abides in happy hearts held high,
As fireflies lift their little lamps at night . . .
The steadfast stars gleam in the somber sky,
Transmuting paths of dusk to silver bright.
I thank Thee, that beyond the cold and pain,
I scent the honeysuckle in the lane.

—*Stella Muse Whitehead*

GRATITUDE DOWN SOUTH

I'se des a little cullud boy,
An' I knows dat it ain't right
To allus be a-wishin'
Dat God had made me white.

I ax His pardon for my sin,
Though Mammy says some-day
Dat God will tell me why it was
He made me dis-er-way.

Now don't misunderstan' me—
There's times I'se glad I'se black;
Like when I been er-fishin',
An' when I'se comin' back

An' pass erlong de Jem'son farm
An see—mos' in de road,
A great big watermelon,
Jes' lookin' like it growed

Right in my very footsteps.
Den somethin' down inside
Says, "Boy, *you'se jest er nigger;*
Let yo' *co'science* be yo' *guide*."
                                    —*Edwina Wood Whiteside*

THE TELEPHONE POLE

A mighty pine tree on a hill
Invited the winds with upflung arms
And wove them into harmonies,
Sometimes a sighing, murmuring song,
Again a thousand elfin bugles,
Music the druids loved.

Came pygmies with sharp biting steel
And laid the pine tree low.
Now far away it stands,
Shorn and dumb, and listens
To the chatter of pygmies.
                                    —*Myrtle Martin Wickey*

CLOUDS

Come with me to wonderland, and in the azure sky
Let your fancy have free reign as the clouds drift by.
How slowly they move on a warm summer day;
Like feathery billows they toss and they sway.
They are constantly changing in shape and design,
Now mountains are forming, now flowerets fine.
A huge throne whose monarch is wearing a crown
Is scarcely built up till it comes tumbling down.
And now in a meadow we see flocks of sheep,
And off in the distance, mountains rugged and steep.
Another time nature is boisterous and gay,
And lowering storm clouds rush on their way.
They are threatening and dark and fill us with fear,
But storms always scatter and soon disappear.
How like the clouds our lives are each day,
Sometimes thoughtful and solemn—sometimes happy and gay.
Each cloud in the sky has its own silver lining,
And back of life's clouds the sun is still shining.

—Beulah Will

THINGS TO LOVE

There are so many things to love,
　　Like prayers and trees and skies,
And sorrows that have slipped away,
　　And memories and sighs.

An old house filled with beauties' store,
　　A garden with old flowers,
A day that is long remembered,
　　Its gladsome, sunny hours.

We love the tintings on a tree,
　　The ocean white and blue,
A heaven full of singing stars,
　　And then, my love, there's *You.*

—Ethel Scott Williams

THE ORPHAN CHILD

Just lend me an ear and I'll tell you
What's the saddest thing in the world,
And I'm sure that you will agree too
That it's the orphan boy or girl.

Sometimes they are given a comfortable Home,
But seldom a parent's love.
Most all of the time they feel so alone,
Often given a downward shove.

If you are not an orphan child,
You can never understand
The heartaches and the longing
For a mother's loving hand,

For a father's kind protection,
For someone to call you their own.
Oh, if you have never been an orphan,
Their sorrows you've never known.

So I beg of you to always be kind
To the orphan child that you know;
I'm certain that you will always find,
"We reap just what we sow."
                                                    —*Grace Wagner Williams*

THE RARE BOOK

'Twas just a little while ago—or so, to me, it seems—
He stood beside my rocking chair and told me of his dreams.
"Mother, I'll make a pretty book like one I saw last night;
It was full of pretty flowers, and birds, and dogs that would not
    bite."
So with paste and shears and magazines, down on the floor he sat
To cut out flowers, a boy, a dog, or maybe a woolly cat.
Oh, no, it has not been so long; I see him through the years,
How hard his little fingers strove to work the heavy shears!

O little book so precious! Not because of beauty rare,
But because his small hand fashioned it with eager, loving care.
Now bitter tears, beyond control, fall as my vision lingers
Long upon the cherished pages marked by baby fingers.
—*Edna Scruggs Williamson*

WEEPING WILLOW TREES

Weeping willow trees
Are peaceful trees,
Like old men with long beards
Dreaming in the sun;
Old men at rest
With all their labor done;
Men who held life close
And found it good,
Who have not only dreamed
But practised brotherhood;
Men who have met sorrow
And accepted loss,
Yet garnered from the year
More of its laughter
Than its tears;
Whose hearts have held no room
For bitterness;
Weavers who have never let
The thread of gold
Slip from the loom.

They sway,
These weeping willow trees,
In graceful acquiescence
To the breeze,
And through their curtained coolness
Birds come and go
Upon their singing way,
And sheep have made
A rendezvous with drowsiness
Within their mottled shade.

There is no sadness
In weeping willow trees—
Only a quiet gladness.
They stand so tranquil
In the sun,
Like kindly old men
With all their labor done—
My father—he is one of these.
Weeping-willow trees
Are peaceful trees.

—Nell Griffith Wilson

THE SOVIET

They say the State is all,
That all mankind unto the State must bow;
His labors for its future all be bent;
His gains must go its coffers to endow.

Their womenfolk equality have won—
The right to earn their bread by sweaty brow;
No hampering ties of motherhood and home
To hold her in its slavish thralldom now.
And when her portion 'tis a child to bear,
No tender ties are hers, no soft caress;
Forthwith she turns him o'er, the State to rear—
No hampering sentimental tenderness—
Her freedom has begun.

There is no God; all power lies in mankind.
'Tis weakness to believe in any God;
Religion must not hamper any mind;
No hope of future life beyond the sod.
And churches built to God, once so ornate
With painting and with sculpture, now must go
To build great clubs, where workers congregate
That they of their new idol more may know,
And bow to worship her.

No faith in God must bind;
No sentimental love of child enthrall;
No home life there to claim man's heart and mind;
The State, their all in all.

—Louise Windsor

IN A HOSPITAL CORRIDOR

She was an alien. Her large sloe-black eyes
Melted with unshed tears of deep distress.
Hers the dumb herded look such women wear.
Azure and golden skies of Italy
Had lately bent above that olive brow.
She leaned, abject, against a tight-closed door,
As if the pungent ether-drifted air
Had halfway deadened her most poignant pain.
Bewildered, she could only understand
That in the room some grim and hideous thing
Was being done to one she loved—her Man!
The few words that I knew of her own tongue
Would not avail to quiet or allay
The wildly beating terror of her heart.
Since lately I had known such grief as this
And felt with her the sisterhood of pain,
I pressed her hand, that she might feel not quite
So lonely in that hour of awful dread.—
And then the shawl-wrapped bundle at our feet,
A great cocoon, of gay and motley hue,
Began to wriggle, and split open wide!
Out thrust a small dark head, and then a fist
Waved weakly in the air, adventuring.
"Ah, a bambino!" and I stooped to let
Those wee exploring fingers curl round mine.
Looking at her, "He's such a lovely one!"
And though she could not understand my words,
We had a universal language now.
Forgetting all her agony—she smiled!
—*Anne-Elise Roane Winter*

AT THE GATE

I stood at the gate one evening,
     And watched the sunset glow
In colors of gold and crimson
     O'er the dark'ning world below.

I gazed in awe at the picture,
   So wild, so joyous, so free,
And thought with a thrill of rapture
   God painted that picture for me.

We may not all be travelers
   And visit in places fair,
And see the wonderful paintings
   That fingers of men placed there.

But here, in our own Indiana,
   We can stand in the evening and see
The wonderful glow of the sunset,
   The picture God painted for me.
                    —*Mae Clover Winters*

THE INDOOR WOMAN

Her busy days are filled with tasks, no time has she for roaming;
But she can see the tracery of branches, just at gloaming,
Thrown in a fretwork, intricate, against the sunset's glow,
Where massive columns, iron gray, rise upward from the snow;
     (The little furry folk below;
     And overhead the wingèd crow).

And when, in iridescent sheen, Spring veils the naked trees,
And from the distant swamps are heard batrachian symphonies,
Phlox and spring beauty spread the banks in lavender and rose;
The busy bees are rioting where maple blossom glows;
     (Brown snakes on willow boughs are sunning,
     On green hillsides young lambs are running).

So, amid glistening summer leaves, the pageant passes by;
October's trees climb regally to meet an azure sky;
And even when the waning year, rich in its browns and grays,
Draws to an end, she feels no sense of sameness in her days—
     When gorgeous pheasant stalks from cover,
     And wild geese thrillingly pass over.

No masterpiece upon the wall of gallery known to fame
Equals the ever-changing scene her shabby windows frame;
No irksome task, however drear, can hold her quite apart,
Who loves all nature with God's gift,—the understanding heart.
                    —*Margaret Winters*

THE QUEST OF MOTHERHOOD

I am going down in the valley,
Where the tall, pale lilies grow,
Lilies whose breath is the breath of death
But whose blooms are as white as snow.

I will to go to the valley,
For a gift awaits me there,
A gift so dear that it mocks at fear
And sheds its wonder afar and near,
And my heart is bold to dare.

One holds my hand at the valley's gate,
But with me he cannot go;
Though his heart would fain, in the path of pain,
Which leads to the gift that I would gain,
Go on to the end, I know.

So he waits my return at the valley's gate,
And he bows his head in prayer;
But my soul mounts up and I smile to go,
Though the end of the way I cannot know,
For my gift awaits me there.

Down through the twilight, shadow-cast,
Down through the voiceless space
Where the tall, white lilies sway and part,
And the heavy perfume hurts my heart;
And the chill is on my face

Till I come again from the valley's gloom,
From the shadows, mist and dim,
To the one who must wait at the valley's gate,
Bringing my gift to him.

—Wilna Wintringham

A LAMENT

It's hard to be a turnip,
When you'd want to be a rose;
It's hard to dress in homespun,
When you'd love to wear fine clothes.

It's hard to be a pauper
And watch the passing show,
When you'd rather be a millionaire
And pass around the dough.

It's hard to have opinions
And air them just for fun,
When you'd rather be a Pollyanna
And agree with everyone.

It's hard to be an honest man
And on your honor dote,
When you'd rather be a politican
And gather in the vote.

It's hard to be a diplomat
And watch the faker do his stuff,
When you'd rather be a thoroughbred
And call his measly bluff.

It's hard to be a dumbbell
And take life's slights and jeers,
When you'd rather be a wise man
And dwell with kings and seers.

It's hard to be a poet
And paint life's joys and woes,
When you'd rather be prosaic
And think in common prose.

                                      —Mrs. A. J. Wirtz

THE MILLENNIUM

The armaments and power of kings,
Desire for wealth and pride,
Have torn the world before and since
The time our Saviour died.
Greece, Rome, and Carthage, not alone,
For Babylon came before;
Assyria and a host beside
Were empires built with gore.

Napoleon and Charlemagne,
Striving for earthly power,
Like Alexander built with arms,
And had but a brief hour.
Wilhelm and Nicholas in our time
Have learned the lesson too
That peoples cry aloud to God
As czars and kaisers do.

Peace! Peace! Descend and reign on earth!
How long will you delay?
Until the time when Jesus comes
And wipes our tears away?
God! Give us peace a thousand years
When men in love may dwell,
And cast grim war with Satan's hosts
In chains in deepest hell!

—Ida Teeple Wittenberger

MY DOGWOOD TREE

I wish that you could see
My flow'ring dogwood tree.
It stands so straight and tall
Quite near my garden wall,
With Spanish mosses twined
Which flutter in the wind,
Like mantles old and gray
That lightly swing and sway.
When blossoms first appear,
You'd think Snow had been here
Scatt'ring her flakes of white
All through the silent night.

—Ethel Davidson Wood

A TREASURE HUNT

I seek
The baby breath of dawn hour,
    Soft tintings of changing sky,
The sportive "tag" of raindrop
    As she and the breeze dance by;

The cautious look of wood folk,
    Tiptoe, half minded to flee,
The smiling shy of wild blooms,
    Young leaves' tender melody;

The ringing call of songster
    Who senses and hails me friend,
The arching proud of rainbow,
    Its golden lure at the end.
                                        —*Ida May Wood*

PRAYER FOR DISARMAMENT

Again they make a pilgrimage for peace—
Those who have known and felt the pangs of strife—
Hoping to outlaw Mars, war plans to cease,
And place a worth-while price on human life.

As Wise Men came two thousand years before
To see the Christ Child laid in Bethlehem's stall,
And angel's voice turned them from Herod's door,
Making all nations know, "Good Will To All";

So now, we pray that selfsame voice to guide
These men, that ancient joy be known again.
For God lives on, is ever by our side,
And whispers: "Peace on Earth, Good Will to Men."
                                        —*Nettie Blanche Wood*

RESURRECTION

O, I have learned how Beauty, lingering, sings
Long after Song is dead and vibrant strings
Are stilled.
I have felt hyacinth and mignonette
Stir in my nostrils after storms beset
And killed
Their bloom. I can close covers on a cherished book
And feast upon it endlessly; or look
Into the sky
When midday challenges Belief to sight
The stars that wait on darkness for their light.

And I—
Pressing to heart these vows from God to me,
That Death is tempered with Eternity,
Reverence the worth
Of men who, singing, join the wept-for dead,
Valiantly, forward-looking, laying head
Upon the earth.

—Harriet Anna Wratten

CATHEDRAL WOODS

On Sunday morning I leave town;
Away from tired people
I go where woods are green and brown,
Each pine a spired steeple.
My street-worn feet soft aisles can tread
Toward shrines in white-birch dells;
In treetops high the wind o'erhead
Chimes faintly like church bells.

The slanted rays of sunlight fall
In stained-glass patterns rare;
The holy quiet over all,
The incense in the air,
Are like a benediction thrown
O'er sermon from the sod.
Who will may kneel in church of stone,
I pray in church of God.

—Augusta Wray

CANDLE LIGHTS

When my windows blaze with light
        and warmth and cheer,
No one knows that shadows dark
        may linger near.
But when darkness spreads a pall
        and lights go out,
I light my unseen candles
        my fears to rout.

Yellow ones bring courage back;
      Their steady glow
Restores my fast-failing faith
      and cheers me so.
Candles white are prayers to me;
      When burning bright
They seem to bring me peace and hope
      through darkest night.

When I'm humbled and my pride
      goes trailing low,
Many candles red and tall
      give cheery glow.
When loneliness besets me,
      small candles blue
Light for me the lonely hour
      I'm living through.

I go about my lighted rooms
      where candles burn,
And feel my courage rise again
      and hope return.
Colorful candles flaming
      unseen may be,
But peace and joy and gladness
      they bring to me.

                  —Edna Allen Wright

HER OWN

Faded not, nor fading, pictures bright
In a realm unseen by common sight;
Countless children live, and move, and prove
All the constancy of mother love.

Though the years dim mother's mortal view,
Memory's eye remains forever true,
Giving to her soul the power to see
All her children as they used to be.

Though her ear be soundless, she can hear
Laughing voices ringing sweet and clear,
As her mind repeats their words and songs
E'en amid the din of outward throngs.

Seeing, hearing, feeling, all may go;
Death-claimed be her person. Even so,
Still in some fair place, all dimness clear,
Angel arms can draw her children near.

—*Mayme C. Wyant*

THE DREAM

I had a dream the other night,
And in the distance, framed in light,
A lowly stable did I see
Where castle of royalty should be;
And a tiny baby snuggled warm
In the loving curve of a mother's arm,
And near by, adoring, there knelt three men;
So I knew the babe was the Christ Child then.

The scene changed, and outlined 'gainst the sky
I saw three crosses raised on high;
Two held representatives of Life's bitter dross,
With the Hope of the world on the middle cross;
And 'bove Him who hung in second place,
With unspeakable anguish on His face,
And crown of thorns to mock and bruise,
I read the inscription "The King of the Jews."

That scene faded, and in its place
A tomb's outline did I then trace;
And as my eyes pierced the misty air
I noticed that the tomb was bare.
A man appeared robed in dazzling white,
Triumphant and holy in the dawning light;
Forgotten Golgotha, the anguish, and scorn,
I knew 'twas my Saviour on Easter Morn.

I awoke, and as I opened my eyes
Over the hill stole the pink sunrise,
And my thoughts lingered on the strange dream,
As I vaguely wondered what did it mean.
Christ's birth must mean joy, the Crucifixion, pain;
The Resurrection, triumph o'er death we attain;
And I breathed a prayer of thanksgiving and praise
For the lowly Nazarene of ancient days.

—Mrs. Ross Yocom

MY GARDEN

Once it was but barren land,
Just a bit of clay and sand;
So with spade we planted trees,
Flowering shrubs for birds and bees,
Planted grass and bulbs and seeds,
Spaded, hoed, and pulled out weeds;
And where once 'twas brown and bare
We now have a garden there.

Larkspur, blue beside the wall,
Hollyhocks so straight and tall,
Columbine and poppies bright
Glow beside the daisies white;
Here and there the bluebells nod,
And above, the goldenrod;
All my garden blooms so fair
Where 'twas once so brown and bare.

O'er a trellis hangs a vine,
From a pool the lilies shine,
In the trees the robins sing
Songs and melodies of spring;
Everywhere is music gay
Chasing every cloud away;
Blue and clear the sky above,
All my garden whispers love.

—Mary Ramthun Young

LULL

The frightened night
Cowers under the watchful eye
Of the menacing storm,
Crouched like a black cat waiting.

—Rhea B. Zehr

THE OLD MILL GARDEN

Trickling water
Musically falls,
Turning the wheels of the mill;

Beyond, our Lake,
Where the sea gull calls—
People are strangely still.

The hush of the garden
Offers peace
In the hectic rush of the day;

In November its motion
And growth will cease,
But its memory will stay!

—Margaret Yost Zethmayr

A TRIBUTE TO THE FEDERATION

Let us consider some of the things
That Federated club work brings!
Method and system and precision,
A wider outlook, a clearer vision;
Exactitude and care for details,
Impartial Judgment that rarely fails.
A broader outlook upon life,
Co-operation without strife;
Inspiration and atmosphere,
Self-expression without fear;
   The urge to create,
   To discuss, to debate;
   Tolerance and sympathy,
   Broad-mindedness and Charity.

A tendency to nourish
And help all talent to flourish;
The will to encourage expression,
To combat and discourage repression,
To be ourselves, without fear or favor;
When we've made a decision, not to waver.
To rise above petty differences,
For once and for all, to be free of these;
This is the campaign that we plan,
This is our duty to God and Man;
To live in an atmosphere rarefied
  Purified and clarified,
  Where thought reigns King,
  And blossoming,
Brings forth, as from a cocoon,
Fruit that is worthy of the loom.
Other and varied activities,
All on the same high plane as these,
The State and General Federation
Are fostering throughout the nation.

                    —*Mrs. D. H. Zimmerman*

FLIGHT

I wonder if a bird on wing can thrill,
  When darting through the air he streaks his flight,
As I, now speeding faster at my will
  Into a fragrant, star-hung, dewy night.

Swift gusts of rushing air beat on my brow,
  Then woo me with a soft seductive breeze.
I sweep beyond great cities lying low.
  What seems so insignificant as these?

Nor lights nor sights seem worth a fleeting glance,
  Nor people dwarfed by horizon or sky.
Beneath my hand the singing engines dance.
  Only the thrill of flight can satisfy.

                    —*Florence Glenn Zipf*

INDEX BY AUTHORS

INDEX BY AUTHORS

ACKERMAN, Zella . . . . . . Indiana . . . . *The Lincoln Home* . . 5
ADAMS, Alice Gardner . . . . Ohio . . . . . . *Surcease* 6
ADAMS, Loyce . . . . Texas . . . . . . *Noontide* 7
ADAMS, Marguerite Janvrin . . New York . . . *Ancestress* 7
AGATE, Grace Bordelon . . . Louisiana . . . . *Shirk or Work?* . . . 7
AGNE, Mrs. Mary . . . . . . Idaho . . . . . . *Eventide* 8
AGNEW, Jean Cameron . . . . Alabama . . . . *Most Any Bit of
                                                Landscape* 8
AKEN, Hannah K. . . . . . Illinois . . . . . *Together* 9
AKERS, Mrs. Maud . . . . . Oregon . . . . . *My Prayer for Today* . 9
ALFORD, Dorothy Moore . . . Mississippi . . . *Recompense* 10
ALLEN, Anna M. . . . . . . New York . . *Our Juniors* 10
ALLEN, Gwendolen . . . . . Indiana . . . . *My Little Garden* . . 11
ALLEN, Irene Cooper . . . . Illinois . . . . . *Negro Girl* 11
ALLEN, Jessie M. Ball . . . Illinois . . . . . *Recompense* 12
ANDERSON, Julia S. . . . . Mississippi . . . *The Rose I Grew* . . 12
ANDERSON, Mrs. Ruth . . . Minnesota . . . . *O Glorious Snow* . . . 13
ANDREWS, Adelaide A. . . . Pennsylvania . *May Day* 14
ANDREWS, Florence R. . . . Connecticut . . *My Mother* 15
ANGLESBURG, Eva K. . . . North Dakota . *Pioneer Woman* . . . 15
ANNETT, Laura B. . . . . . Illinois . . . . . *The Dunes* 16
ANTHONY, Rebecca . . . . . Illinois . . . . . *Vision* 17
ARMSTRONG, Mary J. . . . . Illinois . . . . . *Peace Guaranteed* . . 18
ASHCRAFT, J. Margaret Crute . Oregon . . . . . *Happiness through
                                                the Year* 19
ASHER, Mrs. Mary Otto . . . Iowa . . . . . . *Memory's Door* . . . 19
ATCHERSON, Lillian . . . . . Minnesota . . . *A Legend of Minnesota* 20
ATKINS, Laura L. . . . . . . Tennessee . . . *Your Smile* 21
AUSTIN, Grace Jewett . . . . Illinois . . . . . *Old Saugatuck Mill* . 22

BAILEY, Clarissa M. . . . . . New York . . . *Why Did You Depart
                                                at Dusk?* 22
BAKER, Josephine Turck . . . Illinois . . . . . *The Triumph of Art* . 23
BALDWIN, Kathrine . . . . . Hawaii . . . . . *I Am Here* 23
BALLARD, Frances M. . . . . Kansas . . . . . *From an Office
                                                Window* 24
BANTA, Mildred Dosch . . . New York . . . *The Beachcomber* . . 24
BARBER, Carolyn M. . . . . . Indiana . . . *Maiden's Choice* . . . 25
BARBER, Hope S. . . . . . . Maryland . . . . *A Song of the
                                                Western Eden* 26
BARCLAY, Rhoda S. . . . . . Pennsylvania . *Wild Roses* 27
BARCLAY, Sylvia Dillavou . . Illinois . . . . . *Our Club* 27

BARLOW, Amanda Luella . . Indiana . . . . *Memory* 28
BARNES, Elizabeth I. . . . . Michigan . . . . *Peace Pictures* . . . 29
BARNETT, Josephine . . . . Illinois . . . . . *Song of an Atom* . . 30
BARNEY, Augusta M. . . . . . Iowa . . . . . . *Sunset across the
                                            Lake* 30
BARRY, Mamie Collins . . . Colorado . . . . *A Thought for
                                            Mother's Day* 31
BARTH, Ella . . . . Nebraska . . . . *Open Season* 32
BASSETT, Helen D. . . . . . Connecticut . . . *And Then?* 32
BAY, Helen Iffla . . . . . New Jersey . . . *On Return from the
                                            Shore* 32
BEAL, Alice Colburn . . . . Illinois . . . . . *Old Sarum* 33
BECK, Clara . . . . Kansas . . . . . *The Washington
                                            Bicentennial* . . . 34
BECKER, Easter Rohrer . . . Ohio . . . . *The Magnolia Tree* . 35
BEEBE, Cora Blakeslee . . . Wisconsin . . . . *Wisconsin* 36
BELL, Besse Burnett . . . . New York . . . *My Jewel Case* . . 37
BELL, Laura . . . . Pennsylvania . . *The Taj Mahal* . . 38
BELL, Mrs. Wilbur . . . . Indiana . . . . *Dickey* 38
BENNETT, Gertrude Ryder . . New York . . . *Harvest* 39
BEST, Susie M. . . . . Ohio . . . . . . *Child of Mary's
                                            Soul* 39
BICKLEY, Beulah Vick . . . Iowa . . . . . . *My Mother* . . . 40
BIGHAM, Margaret Estella. . . Illinois . . . . . *The Day* 40
BINGHAM, Alma C. . . . . . Idaho . . . . . *The End of the
                                            Sunset Trail* 41
BIXBY, Laura Rew . . . . . California . . . *George Washington* . . 42
BLACK, Mrs. Ralph . . . . Indiana . . . . *An Invitation* 43
BLATCHLEY, B. M. . . . . . Indiana . . . . *Faith* 43
BLOSS, Pearl B. . . . . . . Colorado . . . . *Autumn Leaves* . . 44
BOARD, Maude Philips . . . Illinois . . . . . *March's Daughter* . 44
BONDI, Eva Marbell . . . . California . . . *As Lovely as they* . . 44
BOONE, Adele Shaw . . . . New York . . . *Music to Me* . . 46
BOSS, Berenice K. . . . . . Minnesota . . . *Small Things* . . . 46
BOSTON, Nancy S. . . . . . Georgia . . . *An Easter Offering* . . 46
BOWERS, Emma . . . . . New York . . . *The Eternal Triangle* . 47
BOWMAN, Hazel McGee . . . Indiana . . . *The Seekers* 48
BOYD, Anna Tillman . . . Arkansas . . . *The Indian Dancer* . 49
BRADLEY, Helena Grace . . . Nevada . . . *Nevada* 49
BRADLEY, Routh Pickett . . . Idaho . . . . *Moonrise in the
                                            Rockies* 50
BRADSHAW, Margaret . . . Oregon . . . . *Oswego Lake* . . . 50
BRENEMAN, Mildred Sutton . . Pennsylvania . . *Searchlights* . . . 50
BRINSON, Hazel Cannon . . . Mississippi. . . . *Recompense* 51
BRISTOW, Nellie . . . . . South Carolina . . *Spring's Wooing* . . 52

BROADHEAD, Grace Lowe. . . New York . . . *The Hills We Love* . . 53
BROOKINGS, Merta M. . . . . Vermont . . . . *Snowless Winter* . . . 53
BROUGH, Helen M. . . . . . Illinois . . . . . *I Would I Could Dance* 53
BROWN, Flora Warren . . . . Pennsylvania . . *Pity* 54
BROWN, Julia Field . . . . . Colorado . . . . *Novice* 54
BROWN, Margaret Marchand . Colorado . . . . *Pottery Maker* 55
BROWNE, Mrs. Virgil . . . . Oklahoma . . . . *Hospital Flowers* . . . 55
BRUMFIELD, Julia E. . . . . . Mississippi . . . . *The Thud of the Clods* 56
BRUTON, Iva Purdum . . . . Tennessee . . . . *Winds Are the Watchmen* 57
BRYAN, Mildred Hatton . . . Wisconsin . . . . *Victorian Ladies* . . . 57
BRYAN, Mildred Southworth . Georgia . . . . *Twilight Time* . . . 58
BRYANT, Blanche Brown . . . Vermont . . . . *Queen Mountain* . . . 58
BUAMBLETT, Agnes Cochran . Georgia . . . . *To the Daughter of a Nymph* 59
BUCK, Anna Shaw . . . . . Maine . . . . . *Beauty Crucified* . . . 60
BURRINGTON, Carrie . . . . Iowa . . . . . . *If I Were You* . . . 61
BURTON, Mabel M. . . . . . Pennsylvania . . *Youth Speaks* 61
BUTLER, Fay H. . . . . . . Colorado . . . . *My Lad* 62
BUTLER, Maud McKinsey . . Indiana . . . . *Symbol of Our Country* 62
BYERS, Anna Mikesell . . . . Pennsylvania . . *My Mother's Hands* . 63

CAIN, Mary D. . . . . Mississippi . . . . *On Happy Women* . . 64
CAIN, Maud Ludington . . . Iowa . . . . . . *Ravine Path* 64
CAMDEN, Harriet Parker . . . California . . . . *God's Answer to a Grieving Mother* . . . 65
CAMPBELL, May Lackey . . . Arkansas . . . . *A Song of the Hills* . 66
CAPP, Daisie le Reu S. . . . Pennsylvania . . *An Autumn Day* . . 66
CAPPLEMAN, Josie Frazee . . Arkansas . . . . *From a Car Window* . 67
CARLETON, Mrs. W. N. . . . Colorado . . . . *The Voice of Human Labor* 68
CARRAHER, Anna C. . . . . Nebraska . . . . *Love's Evening* . . . 69
CARSTENSEN, Catharine . . . Iowa . . . . . . *Mother* 69
CASEY, Pearle R. . . . . . . Colorado . . . . *New Vision* 70
CASTELLO, Almeda M. . . . . New York . . . *The Meteorite* . . . 70
CAVE, Claire . . . . Nevada . . . . *Longing* 70
CAVENDER, Catherine Key . . Mississippi . . . *Mothers* 71
CHAMBERLAIN, Mary Ingersoll. Michigan . . . . *We're Homeward Bound* 72
CHAMBERLIN, Lily Pearl . . . Texas . . . . . . *A Dream of Peace* . . 73
CHAMBERS, Ann . . . . . . Kentucky . . . . *Summer—The Nun* . 74
CHANDLER, Blanche Edens . . Mississippi . . . . *A New Year's Message* 75

CHARLES, Mabel Munns . . . Iowa . . . . . . *Stones* 75
CHARMLEY, Beulah . . . . . Wisconsin . . . . *To a Silver Birch* . . 75
CHATHAM, Agnes M. . . . . . Ohio . . . . . . *Morning* 76
CHURCHWARD, Daisie Dell . . New Jersey . . . *Autumn* 77
CLARK, Ada Neill . . . . . . Mississippi . . . . *Debts* 77
CLARK, Calista Barker . . . . Wisconsin . . . . *Glad Youth* 77
CLARK, Dorothy A. . . . . . Iowa . . . . . . *Home* 78
CLARK, Rose Gould . . . . . Minnesota . . . . *Unconquered* 78
CLARKE, Marianne . . . . . Minnesota . . . *The Favorite Flower* . 79
CLAUSEN, Eleanor B. . . . . . Wisconsin . . . . *New Year's Greeting* . 79
CLAYTON, Cyrinthia J. . . . . Indiana . . . . *Longing* 80
CLEAVER, Ethelyn Hardesty . New York . . . *Illusion* 81
CLEVENGER, Glenna Morris . Ohio . . . . . . *First Wife to the
                                                  Second* 82
CLOOS, Oleta Fox . . . . . . Pennsylvania . . *My Childhood Home* . 83
CLYMER, Grayce Cole . . . . Indiana . . . . *Vagabond's Verse* . . 84
COALSON, Alla . . . . Texas . . . . . . *Texas* 84
COATES, Ethel Gates . . . . Pennsylvania . . *The Happy Voyage* . 85
CODDINGTON, Elizabeth Roosa . New York . . . *Life* 85
COLBERT, Nelle J. . . . . . . Iowa . . . . . . *The Old Pathway* . . 85
COLLOW, Nelle . . . . Ohio . . . . . . *Mary* 86
COLONY, Sylvia T. . . . . . Wisconsin . . . . *"The Peace of God,
                                                  which Passeth All
                                                  Understanding"* . . 87
COLVIN, Mary Miles . . . . . Ohio . . . . . . *Beauty of Life* . . . 87
CONOVER, Nettie McCarver . . Tennessee . . . . *Flowers* 88
CONVERSE, Caroline . . . . . California . . . . *Good-By Summer* . . 89
COOK, Effie Truex . . . . . Indiana . . . . *A Supplication* . . . 89
COOPER, Elizabeth M. . . . . Ohio . . . . . . *Remembrance* 90
CORBIN, Inez Culver . . . . . Michigan . . . . *Pine Woods in
                                                  Winter* 91
CORNELL, Annette Patton . . Kentucky . . . . *On the Program* . . . 91
COTTRILLE, Audra Powell . . Michigan . . . . *Life's Morning, Noon,
                                                  and Evening* 92
CRAIG, Flossie Deane . . . . Georgia . . . . *The Brown Beaver* . . 92
CROKER, Maria Briscoe . . . Maryland . . . . *On Catoctin* 93
CROMER, Mary . . . . Iowa . . . . . . *The Old Brass Clock* . 93
CROOKS, Pearl . . . . Illinois . . . . . *When Winter Comes* . 94
CULVER, Elsie Thomas . . . Illinois . . . . . *To One Who Never
                                                  Knew I Cared* . . . 94
CUTRIGHT, Lucy . . . . . . Maryland . . . . *Christ Writes in the
                                                  Sand* 95

DAGUE, Irene T. . . . . . . Iowa . . . . . . *A Dream* 96
DARBYSHIRE, Martha Brindley . California . . . . *Moments* 96

Davis, Bert	Mississippi	*Shadows*	97
Davis, Eliza Timberlake	Virginia	*Life's Secrets*	97
Davis, Harriet Winton	Maryland	*Ashes to Ashes*	98
Davis, Helen H.	Texas	*Unrecompensed*	99
Davison, Sarah Field	New York	*Abigail*	99
DeLong, Ann Hawley	Indiana	*The Forest*	100
DeLong, Edith Curtis	Ohio	*Recompense*	100
DeLong, Juanita	Indiana	*Regret*	101
DeMary, Elizabeth	Idaho	*Pioneer Woman*	101
DeMotte, Lucia Stevens	Illinois	*The Return*	101
Devitt, Pauline Lewelling	Iowa	*Another Tomorrow*	102
Dill, Julia Hadley	Indiana	*Youth*	103
Dillard, Susie B.	Oregon	*Home on the Columbia*	103
Dodge, Mildred Gavitt	Idaho	*My Mountain Neighbors*	104
Donelson, Mrs. L. M.	Washington	*"This Contract Stuff"*	105
Doria, Floria	Connecticut	*Memorial Day*	106
Dougan, Vera Wardner	Wisconsin	*Realism*	106
Downey, Nettie A.	Indiana	*Wealth*	107
Draper, Innice M.	Colorado	*A Tribute to Mother*	107
Dunkerly, Helen Ritterskamp	Indiana	*"The Club Woman"*	108
Dunlap, Kathryn Roeser	Missouri	*A Golden Dream*	109
Dunn, Bessie Cary	Pennsylvania	*Home Is where the Heart Is*	109
Dunn, Maude Huston	Indiana	*Kindo' Different*	110
Dunn, Minnie C.	New Mexico	*Shadows*	111
Dupuis, Ethel Pechin	Ohio	*Remembrance*	112
Durkee, Caroline Cain	Kansas	*Courage*	112
Early, Pige	Oklahoma	*Autumn Leaves*	112
Easterday, Katheryn Sweet	Iowa	*What Gold Cannot Buy*	113
Edge, Maude Brannen	Maryland	*A Passing Thought*	114
Edmison, Lillian M.	South Dakota	*Possessions*	114
Edwards, Clara	New York	*Americanization*	115
Edwards, Zoe Brainerd	Illinois	*What Makes a Woman's Club*	116
Eish, Lois M.	Ohio	*Lest We Forget*	116
Ellis, Maryann Weeks	Vermont	*George Washington*	117
Emery, Mrs. Jennie	Illinois	*From Dawning till Dawning*	118
Entrekin, Clara P.	Illinois	*The Wild Canaries*	118
Epperson, Clara Cox	Tennessee	*When God Speaks*	119

ERDMANN, Myrtle Hill . . . . Ohio . . . . . . *Nostalgia* 119
ETZ, Pearl Potter . . . . . . Maryland . . . . *Frosty Shadows* . . . 119

FAHRINGER, Estella Shields . . Pennsylvania . . *Even Weeds* 120
FARGO, Ruth Scofield . . . . Oregon . . . . . *The Fable of the
                                              Finches* 120
FARNSWORTH, Maude Arney . Pennsylvania . . *Life Was all about
                                              Him* 121
FARR, Hilda Butler . . . . . Illinois . . . . . *Liebestraum* 122
FELDWISCH, Zoe H. . . . . . Indiana . . . . *Misplaced Sympathy* . 122
FERGUSON, Margaret Cotter . . Illinois . . . . . *January* 123
FERGUSON, Tilla . . . . . . Idaho . . . . . *Just Words* 123
FERNANDEZ, Helen Wilson . . Louisiana . . . . *'Tis Spring* 124
FETTER, Margherita Gardner . Florida . . . . . *An Illusion* 125
FIELD, Iduna Bertel . . . . . Iowa . . . . . . *Evening* 125
FINCH, Maud Brockett . . . . Illinois . . . . . *Sunset Clouds* . . . 126
FINNEY, Emma O.. . . . . . Illinois . . . . . *To Nature* 126
FISH, Lisbeth . . . . Colorado . . . . *Earth-Bound* 127
FITZSIMMONS, Caroline Darr . New York . . . *Spring and Mother* . . 127
FLACK, Margaret Paxson . . . Pennsylvania . . *America's Flower Song* 128
FLEMING, Elizabeth Poate . . Illinois . . . . . *Motherhood* 128
FLETCHER, Lillian R. . . . . New Hampshire . *Ode to Washington* . . 129
FOGLE, Rhoda Hartman . . . Tennessee . . . . *Christmas Morn—Then
                                              and Now* 129
FOLSOM, Ida M. . . . . . . Maine . . . . . *Love Speaks* 130
FORREST, Ida M. . . . . . . Pennsylvania . . *Youth* 131
FORTSON, Nannie Laura . . . Kentucky . . . . *Rainy Nights* 131
FOSTER, Mrs. Dorothy Talbott Kentucky . . . . *Sunset* 132
FRALICK, Mrs. Ovie . . . . . Kansas . . . . . *We Know* 133
FRANCIS, Martha Jeannette . . Pennsylvania . . *A Prayer* 134
FREAR, Elizabeth . . . . . . Pennsylvania . . *Alone* 134
FREAR, Mary Dillingham . . . Hawaii . . . . . *To Her* 135
FRINK, Grace Brown . . . . Connecticut . . . *Do You Know?* . . . 136
FRY, Susie Whitmarsh . . . . Illinois . . . . . *Loneliness* 137
FULLAM, May Bryant . . . . Vermont . . . . *Heritage* 137
FULLMER, Merle . . . . . . Minnesota . . . *The Ruin* 137
FURNISH, Mary Wanzer . . . Kentucky . . . . *A Mother's Love* . . 138

GABELL, Katharine Gordon . Pennsylvania . . *A Little Bit of Heaven* . 138
GAGE, Roberta . . . . Mississippi . . . *My Garden Guests* . . 139
GALE, MARION PERHAM . . . Massachusetts . . *Desire Minter* . . . 140
GANNER, Mrs. Cora Young . . Connecticut . . . *Heavenly Faces* . . . 141
GARRETT, Uarda Rosamund . Arkansas . . . . *Immaculate* 142
GARVIN, Margaret Root . . . New York . . . *Echoes* 142

GEIGER, Frances Moore . . . Ohio . . . . . . *Fulfillment* 142
GEMMER, Edith M. . . . . . Indiana . . . . *A Mother's Prayer* . . 143
GERRY, Marie D'Autremont . Minnesota . . . *Arcturus Lends his Light* 144
GETTY, Sara Roberta . . . . Maryland . . . . *House of Cards* . . . 144
GEWIN, Mrs. Louise . . . . . Mississippi . . . *My Prayer* 145
GHENT, Kate Downing . . . Florida . . . . . *The Thoroughbred* . . 145
GIANELLA, Marguerite . . . . New York . . . *Empty Air Castles* . . 146
GIBBONS, Bertha L. . . . . . Ohio . . . . . . *Prayers I Saw Ascend* . 147
GIFFORD, Ethel Annette . . . Illinois . . . . *My Garden* 147
GILBERT, Demmon . . . . . Mississippi . . . *My Pine Tree* . . . 148
GILLESPIE, Elise Brice . . . Minnesota . . . *Wings* 148
GILLESPIE, Mary White . . . Mississippi . . . *Heart Balm* 148
GILLILAND, Elizabeth Cox . . Indiana . . . . *The Whippoorwill's Song* 149
GILMORE, Irene R. . . . . . Mississippi . . . *A Memory* 149
GOODFELLOW, Gladys F. . . . Pennsylvania . . *A Sonnet* 150
GOODRICH, Minnie Rowan . . Connecticut . . . *This House of Mine* . 151
GORDON, Ruth Winslow . . . Ohio . . . . . . *Ulysses Grant* 151
GRADICK, Laura M. . . . . . Florida . . . . . *Nostalgia* 152
GRANNISS, Ida Myrtle . . . . Connecticut . . . *Sublimity* 153
GRAVES, Ada . . . . Illinois . . . . . *Trees* 153
GREENE, Marjory Titus . . . Indiana . . . . *The Song American* . 154
GREENLEE, Gaileen . . . . . Colorado . . . . *Nightfall* 154
GREENWOOD, Helen D. . . . Pennsylvania . . *Glory* 154
GRIERSON, Mrs. Flora D. . . . Michigan . . . . *Cathedral of St. John the Divine* 155
GRIFFITHS, Jessie Stearns . . . Massachusetts . . *The Passing of a Friend* 156
GRIMES, Emma E. . . . . . Minnesota . . . *Thermopylae* 157
GRISSOM, Irene Welch . . . . Idaho . . . . . *A Pioneer Woman* . . 158
GROSSE, Garnet Davy . . . . Arizona . . . . *Alice Winter* 159
GUILD, Eva T. . . . . Maine . . . . . *To My Chickadee* . . 159
GUNDERSON, Gertrude B. . . . South Dakota . . *If We Could See* . . 160

HAHN, Eleonore F. . . . . . New York . . . *Some Mothers and Some Others* 160
HAINES, Minna D. . . . . . Illinois . . . . . *Nature* 162
HALL, Albertine O. . . . . . Mississippi . . . *My Mother's Hands* . 163
HALL, Corinne S. . . . . . . Missouri . . . . *Fancies* 164
HALSTEAD, Mrs. R. B. . . . . Indiana . . . . *The Story Retold* . . 164
HAMBLY, Nancy Winifred . . Massachusetts . . *Calvin Coolidge* . . . 165
HAMILTON, Florence . . . . . New York . . . *Elegy* 166
HAMILTON, Maude Slinkard . Indiana . . . . *Ladies, We Greet Thee* 166
HAMMER, Mabel . . . . . . Kansas . . . . . *A New Day* 167

HAMMOND, Hala Jean . . . . Oklahoma . . . *Origins* 167
HARDY, Adelia Fraser . . . . Pennsylvania . . *Wild Crab-Apple Tree* 168
HARLAN, Fern M. . . . . . . Indiana . . . . *A Lean Lament* . . . 169
HARMON, Joy Williams . . . . Indiana . . . . *October's Heart of Gold* 170
HARTT, Dorothy Goldsmith . New Jersey . . . *A Song of Stratford* . . 171
HARVEY, Ethel Meers . . . . Illinois . . . . . *Ode for Women's Clubs* 172
HARVEY, Lina . . . . Ohio . . . . . . *Contemplation* 174
HARVEY, Vera Andrew . . . West Virginia . . *To a Dead Babe* . . . 174
HARVEY, Victoria Adelaide . . Missouri . . . . *Orange* 175
HASSON, Ethel M. . . . . . . Ohio . . . . . . *The Redbird in Winter* 175
HASTINGS, Mildred . . . . Pennsylvania . *Morning* 176
HATCHER, Lucy Louise . . Mississippi . . . *Traveled* 176
HATTON, Lula Ensley . . . . Alabama . . . . *Authors, We Greet Thee* 177
HAWKINS, Clarissa Hill . . Pennsylvania . . *Too Late* 178
HEALY, Catharine R. . . . . Pennsylvania . . *A Mission Fulfilled* . 179
HELFRICH, Elsa F. . . . . . Illinois . . . . . *Dialogue* 180
HEMBLING, Nina . . . . . Kansas . . . . . *Lilac* 180
HENLEY, Bessie S. . . . . . Michigan . . . *Gold for Gold* . . . 181
HENLEY, Lucy Hall . . . . Virginia . . . *Growing Old* . . . 181
HENLINE, Mae Baker . . . Pennsylvania . *A Prayer for Great Men of the Nations* . . 181
HERGET, Mary C. . . . . . Louisiana . . . *Mammy Sue* 182
HERRICK, Benita Adams . . California . . . *Midway* 183
HERZOG, Rose L. . . . . . Pennsylvania . . *George Washington* . 183
HICKERSON, Daisy Faulkner . Tennessee . . . *Rain Pool* 185
HICKMAN, Maude Hicks . . Iowa . . . . . *The Censor* 186
HIEBERT, Mrs. Lillian . . . Minnesota . . *Ring on, Love Bells* . 187
HILL, Charlotte T. . . . . . Maine . . . . *To Woman* 187
HILL, Ethel Osborn . . . . Texas . . . . . *A Heart's Protest* . 188
HILL, Margaret Frater . . . New York . . . *Universal Peace* . . 188
HINER, Fannie Hoffman . . Ohio . . . . . *I Love It, Don't You?* 189
HODGSON, Hattie Josephine . Minnesota . . *Memories* 189
HOISINGTON, May Folwell . New York . . *Reason and Song* . . 190
HOLLAND, Lillie Edson . . Michigan . . *Time* 190
HOLY, Edna M. . . . . . Illinois . . . *Redbird* 191
HONN, Olive . . . . Illinois . . . *Faith* 191
HOOKE, Florence Harris . . New Jersey . . *They Tell Me of a Place* 4
HOPWOOD, Elsie K. . . . . Pennsylvania . *Mrs. Frick's Anecdote* . 191
HOWARD, Mrs. L. J., Jr. . . Mississippi . *God's Own* . . . 192
HOWARD, Marion . . . . . Iowa . . . . . *Hands* 192
HOWARD, Myrtle H. M. . . Washington, D.C. *The Jazz Girl* . . . 193

HOWELL, Inez Baker . . . . Texas . . . . *Unanswered* 193

HOWES, Hannah Cushman . . New York . . . *Song to Aviators* . . . 193

HUDSON, Edith Folwell . . . Georgia . . . . *Verbum Indictum* . . 194

HUFFMAN, Nora E. . . . . . Iowa . . . . . *Mountains* 194

HUMPHREYS, Vira K. . . . . Florida . . . . *Calendars* 194

HUNN, Flora Louise . . . . . Connecticut . . . *Flood Tide* 195

HUNOLDSTEIN, Mrs. Charles . Mississippi . . . *Lights and Shadows* . . 196

HUNT, May M. . . . . Iowa . . . . . *Ioway to Iowa* . . . 196

HUNTER, Lillian Crane . . . Ohio . . . . . . *He Who Waits at
Twilight* 198

HURLOCK, Mrs. Frances Boyd . Oklahoma . . . *My Sweetheart* . . . 198

HUTCHCRAFT, Helen . . . . . Kentucky . . . . *Armistice Day* . . . 199

INSCHO, Doris W. . . . . . . Indiana . . . . *Lovers' Lane* 200

INT-HOUT, Gladys Melville . . Illinois . . . . *The Gazing Ball* . . 200

IRELAND, Irma Thompson . . Louisiana . . . . *Ecstasy* 200

IVES, Mabel Lorenz . . . . . New Jersey . . . *Songs to an
Unbeliever* 201

JACOBS, Josephine Grider . . . Arkansas . . . . *Moon Daughter* . . . 201

JAHNKE, Mrs. F. C. . . . . . Iowa . . . . . *The Great American
Home* 202

JEFFERSON, Laura D. . . . . Maryland . . . *Recompense* 203

JEFFRESS, Mamie Cread . . . Mississippi . . . *My Bungalow* . . . 204

JENNER, Nadine Newbill . . . Illinois . . . . *Mud Puddles* 205

JENNINGS, Louise B. Olmstead . Connecticut . . . *October in Connecticut* . 205

JENSEN, Ellen Marie . . . . New York . . . *In an Apartment* . . . 206

JOHNSON, Gertrude M. . . . . Minnesota . . . *Moonlight at Sea* . . . 206

JOHNSON, Marian Phillips . . North Dakota . . *The Poet* 207

JOHNSON, Marvea . . . . . Iowa . . . . . *Life* 207

JOHNSON, Ruth M. . . . . . Kansas . . . . *Resignation* 208

JOHNSTON, Ella Colter . . . . Ohio . . . . . . *A Voice from Flanders
Fields* 209

JONES, Mrs. Lucille Brock . . Alabama . . . . *An Acrostic to Sorosis
Club Members* . . . 210

JORDAN, Katharine W. . . . . Kentucky . . . . *Little Love Song* . . 210

JUDD, Alice . . . . Ohio . . . . . *On Being Asked to
Write an Original
Poem* 211

KATTERHENRY, Rose Carolyn . Indiana . . . . *Life Is Like a Golden
Lyre* 212

KEAHY, Nancy E. . . . . . . Texas . . . . *Returning Bluebirds* . 212

KELL, Rowena Millar . . . . Pennsylvania . . *Childless Christmas* . 213

KELLEY, Mrs. W. O. . . . . Alabama . . . *Clubs* 214

KELLY, Candace Hurst . . . Pennsylvania . . *Devotion* 214
KIMBERLY, E. Grace . . . . Florida . . . . . *Song of a Vine and Nest* 215
KINDER, Caroline M. . . . . Colorado . . . . *Easter Dawn* 216
KIRK, Edna Fuller . . . . . Minnesota . . . *My Airship* 216
KIRK, Mary Wallace . . . . Alabama . . . . *Gone* 217
KIRK, Mrs. Victor . . . . . Kansas . . . . . *A Man* 217
KIRKENDALL, Alice Pilcher . . Ohio . . . . . . *Two Birds* 218
KLOPFENSTEIN, Frances R. . . Iowa . . . . . . *Depression without the "Die" in It* . . . 219
KNAUER, Kate Robertson . . Ohio . . . . . . *An Epitome* 219
KNOBLOCK, Jessee Inwood . . Louisiana . . . . *"Little Mother of the Navy"* 220
KUHL, Fannie M. . . . . . . Pennsylvania . . *Longing* 220

LADLEY, Laura M. . . . . . Pennsylvania . . *Unwritten Music* . . 221
LAIDLAW, Louise Burton . . . New York . . . *Friendship* 223
LAIRD, Helen C. . . . . . . Wisconsin . . . . *Ad Interim* 223
LANE, Sara F. . . . . Massachusetts . . *The Wreath on the Door* 224
LARKIN-COOK, Mary . . . . Indiana . . . . *Morning in the Hills* . 224
LASERTE, Georgette Grenier . Massachusetts . . *Crisis* 225
LAWSON, Roberta Campbell . Washington, D.C. *Flowers* 226
LEDBETTER, Mrs. Shep . . . Mississippi . . . *Mississippi Federation* . 226
LEE, Laura . . . . Illinois . . . . . *House versus Home* . . 229
LEE, Mildred Bentley . . . . Minnesota . . . *Faith* 229
LE FLORE, Mrs. Marion . . . Oklahoma . . . *Our Club Creed* . . . 230
LEGGETT, Grace Patchen . . . Connecticut . . . *The Storm King Trail* 230
LEHMER, Verona Watson . . . Puerto Rico . . . *Puerto Rico* 231
LEICHLITER, Retta Irwin . . . Pennsylvania . . *Two Thoughts on Youth* 232
LEIGHTON, Louise . . . . . Minnesota . . . *Minnesota Landscape* . 232
LEISER, Adeline Evans . . . . New York . . . *Art* 233
LELAND, Marian . . . . . . Florida . . . . . *Christmas in Florida* . 233
LEMMON, Mrs. Maud . . . . Indiana . . . . *Reverie* 234
LESLIE, Lutie Price . . . . . Missouri . . . . *Prayer* 234
LEWIS, Adia James . . . . . Kentucky . . . . *The Brook* 235
LIDDELL, Nell Tillotson . . . Mississippi . . . *Morning* 235
LIDE, Virginia Hart . . . . . Mississippi . . . *Absent* 236
LINDSEY, Alice . . . . Texas . . . . . *Individualist* 236
LINKHART, Pearl . . . . . . Oklahoma . . . *The Land of "Might Have Been"* 237
LIPPINCOTT, Grace Miner . . Connecticut . . . *Calm* 238
LITTLE, Martha W. . . . . . California . . . . *California Color* . . . 238
LLOYD, Grace R. . . . . . . Connecticut . . . *A Winter Sea* 239

LOCKHART, Aileene . . . . . Texas . . . . . *Rivalry* 239
LOCKWOOD, Anna Patten . . . Indiana . . . . *Visiting* 240
LOCKWOOD, Hazel Funk . . . Minnesota . . . *Spring* 241
LOMON, Grace Johnson . . . Texas . . . . . *My Lady of the Roses* . 242
LORRAINE, Lilith . . . . . . Texas . . . . . *Why Should I Wait?* . 3
LOVELL, Elva N. . . . . . . Oklahoma . . . *Our Lovely Pioneer* . . 242
LOVELL, Frances Stockwell . . Vermont . . . . *Eternity* 243
LOVELL, Mabel Brackett . . . New Jersey . . . *Brotherhood* 243
LOVELL, Phebe Beach . . . . Louisiana . . . . *Glamour* 244
LOWN, R. Geraldine . . . . . Iowa . . . . . . *Tableau* 245
LOWRY, Lillian . . . . Kentucky . . . . *Peace* 245
LUEBKE, Pearl H. . . . . . . Kansas . . . . . *To a Mockingbird* . . 246
LUKE, Lou Mallory . . . . . Iowa . . . . . . *Hill and Sea* . . . 246
LUKER, Florence O. . . . . . Iowa . . . . . . *Gems of Today* . . . 246
LUMPKIN, Elizabeth Welton . . Connecticut . . . *The Library Speaks* . 247
LUTGEN, Grace Welsh . . . . Nebraska . . . . *A Prairie Miracle* . . 249
LYON, Carrie Ward . . . . . New Jersey . . . *Homespun* 250
LYON, Mabel . . . . New York . . . *Crystallization* . . . 250

MAAK, Emme . . . . New York . . . *Your Accounting* . . . 251
MAAS, Hallie Davis . . . . . Illinois . . . . . *Beauty Marks an Urge* 251
MACCASTLINE, Mae Wallace . Maryland . . . . *At Slumber Time* . . 252
MACKAY, Mirza French . . . Illinois . . . . . *Pixy Heart* 253
MAHON, Nora Hefley . . . Texas . . . . . *Candlelight* 253
MALARKY, Marcella Drennan . Kentucky . . . . *My Mother's Rocking Chair* 254
MALCOLM, Bertha Osler . . . Colorado . . . . *Time* 254
MAPLETHORPE, Iowa Marshall Iowa . . . . . . *At the End of the Day* 255
MARSH, Susan R. . . . . . . Indiana . . . . *The Long Journey* . . 256
MARSHALL, Pearl M. . . . . Mississippi . . . *The Grandchild* . . . 256
MARSTON, Mabel Standley . . Iowa . . . . . . *What Mother Said* . . 256
MARTIN, Clara Tull . . . . . Missouri . . . . *My Road Leads to You* . 257
MARTIN, Eleanor Beckman . . Illinois . . . . . *Sonnet to Monadnock* . 257
MARTIN, Eva Jones . . . . . Mississippi . . . *Her Poem* 258
MARTIN, Leona Bolt . . . . . Indiana . . . . *From a Car Window* . 258
MASON, Ella . . . . Massachusetts . . *A Woman's Wish* . . 259
MAYES, Malvina Yerger . . . Mississippi . . . *Resignation* 259
MCBROOM, Dora Dickson . Iowa . . . . . . *Fallen Leaves* 260
MCCOWN, Minnie Parker . . Kansas . . . . . *George Washington—A Portrait* 261
MCCRACKEN, Marta S. . . . Illinois . . . . . *A Lover* 261
MCELROY, Mrs. John . . . . Massachusetts . . *John and I* 261
MCELVEEN, Vera . . . . . . Georgia . . . . *Nature's Song of Georgia* 262

McGaw, Blanche Baldwin . . California . . . . *Pause ere Life Has*
                                              Spent Its Course . . . 263
McGiffert, Gertrude Yates . Minnesota . . . *Night's Beauties* . . . 264
McGill, Nelle Graves . . . . Mississippi . . . *Mute* 264
McLaughlin, Mrs. R. E. . . Iowa . . . . . . *Memories* 264
McQuaid, Mabel Ward . . . Vermont . . . . *Adolescence* 265
Merriam, Ida Carothers . . . Illinois . . . . . *Phoenix* 265
Merriman, Mary Royce . . . Wisconsin . . . . *In Summertime* . . . 266
Merritt, Maud Woodward . New Jersey . . . *Courier* 267
Meyer, Maude R. . . . . . Mississippi . . . *Thoughts in a Beauty*
                                              Shop 267
Milchrist, Cora Holbrook . . Iowa . . . . . . *Phoenix* 267
Miller, Blanche Powell . . . Iowa . . . . . . *Lone Little House on*
                                              the Desert 268
Miller, Estelle Wiepking . . New Jersey . . . *Consecration* 269
Miller, Helen Janet . . . . Michigan . . . . *Old Street* 269
Miner, Jessie S. . . . . Kentucky . . . . *Wings* 270
Mitchell, Lulu W. . . . . . California . . . *The Happy Pilgrim* . 270
Montgomery, Nancy Red . . Texas. . . . . . *Afterwards* 271
Monyhan, Elizabeth . . . . Indiana . . . . *To a Modern Poet* . . 271
Moody, Minnie Hite . . . . Georgia . . . . *Prairie Stars* 272
Morgan, Angela . . . . . . New York . . . *Wild Prophecy* . . . 272
Morgan, Beulah Russel . . . Missouri . . . . *My Cup Is Nearly*
                                              Empty 273
Morlan, Mrs. Elsie . . . . . Colorado . . . . *I Thank Thee.* . . . 274
Morrissey, Clara Whittaker . New Jersey . . . *Twilight* 274
Morse, Mrs. Helen S. . . . . Florida . . . . . *Read a Book a Week* . 275
Morton, Rebecca Emery . . Colorado . . . . *To the Blue, High*
                                              Mountain 276
Moseley, Rebecca L. . . . . Wisconsin . . . . *A Clubwoman's Prayer* 276
Moses, Ruby M. . . . . . . North Dakota . . *Mother Love* 277
Movius, Anne Murry . . . . North Dakota . . *Garden Dreams* . . . 277
Mullen, Eva W. . . . . . . Indiana . . . . *My Western Home* . . 278
Munson, Ida Norton . . . . Connecticut . . . *As a Little Child* . . 278
Murphy, Olive Lavena . . . Indiana . . . . *The Teakettle Song*. . 279
Muterspaugh Amanda . . . Indiana . . . . *Keeping Store* 279
Muzzy, Florence E. D. . . . New York . . . *Love Sang from over*
                                              Yonder 280

Nance, Berta Hart . . . . . Arizona . . . . *Desert Mother* . . . 281
Nelson, Irma Jeffers . . . . Iowa . . . . . . *A House that's*
                                              a Home 281
Nevin, Lillias C. . . . . . . Pennsylvania . . *The Lonesome Hill* . 283
Newman, Mabel . . . . . . Indiana . . . . *Old Lover* 283
Newsom, Martha . . . . . . Illinois . . . . . *Repose*. 284

NICHOLAS, Bertha E. . . . . Illinois . . . . . *Christmas Secrets*. . . 284
NICHOLS, Gertrude Florence . Colorado . . . . *Colorado* 285
NOLEN, Kathleen Moody . . Alabama . . . . *My Six Little Boys* . 286
NORMAN, Jeannette Hazelton . Minnesota . . . *Another Day* 287
NORRIS, Emma Penrod . . . Indiana . . . . *Comfort* 288

O'BRIEN, Florence . . . . . Illinois . . . . . *Sails* 289
O'DONNELL, Kathleen . . . . Arizona . . . . *That Desert Waste* . 289
Ogle, Nedra Vance . . . . . Nebraska . . . . *Silver and Gold* . . . 290
O'Meara, Madge Maley . . . South Dakota . . *We Thank Thee* . 290
O'Neal, Martha Fay . . . Indiana . . . *The Good Ship
"Prayer"* 291
O'NIELL, Lila Todd . . . . Texas. . . . . . *Revelation* 291
OREDSON, Mrs. Emily . . . Minnesota. . . . *Life* 292
ORR, Grace Fitzgerald . . Missouri . . . *Spring* 292
ORR, NAOMI G. . . . . . . Illinois . . . . *Faith* 292
ORTON, Virginia Keating. . . Washington . . . *Price* 293
OSMUN, Florence Tucker . . . New Jersey . . . *Peace* 293

PAGE, Virginia Weigel . . . Kansas . . . . . *Queen Creek Canyon* . 293
PALMER, Mabel Ethleen . . . California. . . . *A Shower* 294
PANTER, Ellen Daniels . . . Kansas . . . . . *Milking* 294
PARK, Ada Cora . . . . . Iowa . . . . . . *We'll Mother the Town
With Mother* 295
PARKER, Julia Edna . . . . New York . . *The Master Hand* . 295
PARSONS, Helen M. . . . . New York . . *Modern Babel* . . . 296
PEARCE, Ruby Bransford . . . Louisiana . . . . *Her Garden* 297
PEPOON, Florence A. . . . . Illinois . . . . *Resurrection*. 298
PERKINS, Mrs. Edgar A. Sr. . Indiana . . . *Two Paths* 298
PETTUS, Martha Elvira . . New York . . . *A Blackbird Singing
at Dawn* 300
PHILLIPS, Beulah Wyatt . . . Ohio . . . . . . *Life* 300
PHILLIPS, Gertie Stewart . . . West Virginia . . *The Reaches of a Song.* 301
PHILLIPS, Harriet Duff . . . . Pennsylvania . . *My Garden* 302
PHILLIPS, Marie Tello . . . . Pennsylvania . . *The Starry Heights* . 302
PIERCE, Elsie K. . . . . . . Indiana . . . . *Carefree Way* 303
PIERCE, Enid Crawford . . . Vermont . . . *Wall Street Wail* . 303
PINCKNEY, Claudia A. . . . . South Carolina . *The Mystery* 304
PINKNEY, Agnes Stowell . . . North Dakota . . *Scraps* 304
PINKSTON, Mamie Gray . . . Mississippi. . . . *In a Garden* 305
PIPPEN, Sally Macon Garland Alabama . . . *Triumph.* 306
PLOUGHE, Mary Wimborough Indiana . . . . *Recompense* 307
POLLOCK, Lillian Irvine . . . Colorado . . . . *Gardens of the Mind* . 308
POSEGATE, Mabel . . . . . . Ohio . . . . . . *Prayer for Peace* . . . 308

POTTER, M. Eugenia . . . . . New York . . . *The Snowflake's Farewell* 309
POWELL, Diana Kearny . . . Washington, D. C. *Mothers' Eyes* . . . 309
PRICE, Winnie Lita . . . . . Washington, D. C. *Purpose* 309
PRUDDEN, Helen Danforth . . New Jersey . . . *Atelier* 310
PRUESER, Sara V. . . . . . . Ohio . . . . . . *The Bobolink's Song* . 310
PRUETT, Jessie Hubbard . . . Minnesota . . . *Hope* 311
PURCELL, Martha Grassham . Kentucky . . . . *The Old Rail Fence* . 311
PURYEAR, Edna Eades . . . . Kentucky . . . . *Gifts and Sins* . . . 312
PUTNAM, Anna Hawks . . . . New York . . . *Air Mail* 313
PUTNAM, Grace Brown . . . . North Dakota . . *Atavism* 313

QUIER, Bess Munson . . . . Colorado . . . . *The Universal Rhythm.* 314
QUINN, Melicent Athleen . . Kentucky . . . . *Sunset* 314

RAE, Jess Campbell . . . . . Oregon . . . . . *Hummingbird* 315
RAFFETTO, Bertha . . . . . Nevada . . . *March* 316
RAMSEY, Blanche Banta . . . Indiana . . . . *A Mother's Prayer* . . 316
RANDLE, Bessie Clark . . . . Colorado . . . . *Dorcas* 317
RAY, Marguerite . . . . . . Washington . . . *Blind Toilers* . . . 317
RAY, Monna Merle . . . . . Ohio . . . . . . *Homeland* 318
RAY, Reba . . . . Pennsylvania . . *Touch* 4
REDDING, Stella B. . . . . . Oklahoma . . . . *Oklahoma* 318
REDDY, Marie E. . . . . . . Georgia . . . . *Hunter's Moon* . . . 319
REED, Gertrude . . . . . . Pennsylvania . . *A Thought* 320
REGEN, Rosalie . . . . . . New York . . . *Forest Pool* . . . 321
REID, F. Isabelle Goodwin . . Ohio . . . . . . *An Appeal* 322
REILEY, Louise Loflin . . . . Pennsylvania . . *I Open my Windows to the Morn* 323
REYNOLDS, Kate Hassell . . . North Carolina . *Awakening* 324
RICHARDS, Elizabeth Davis . . West Virginia . . *Pine-Clad Hills* . . 324
RICHARDSON, Isla Paschal . . Tennessee . . . . *Leaving Harbor* . . 325
RICKARD, Clara Lynn . . . . New York . . . *Earn a Dollar* . . . 325
RIENOW, Leona Train . . . . New York . . . *Aux Étoiles* 326
RILEY, Mrs. Caddie J. . . . . Colorado . . . . *In Commemoration of Son's Twenty-First Birthday* 326
RINGHOFER, Mrs. George . . Minnesota . . . *Babyhood* 328
ROADS, Helen Pursell . . . . Ohio . . . . . . *Procession* 328
ROBB, Elizabeth B. . . . . . Pennsylvania . . *Poetry Week* . . . 329
ROBINSON, Mrs. Marcella . . Indiana . . . . *Welcome, Husbands* . 329
ROCKETT, Winnie Lynch . . . Alabama . . . . *A Mother before a Military Monument* . . 330
ROSENBERG, Flora C. . . . . Washington . . . *Your Lamp of Friendship* 330

Ross, Delle Oglesbee . . . . Illinois . . . . . *A Pastel* 331
Ross, Margaret Wheeler . . . Arizona . . . . *Catechism for the Clubwoman* . . . 331
Rowe, Bessie Maas . . . . Illinois . . . . . *Beggars* 332
Royer, Laureame M. . . . . Pennsylvania . . *Good Night* 332
Rumell, Lynn K. . . . . . Indiana . . . . . *The Garden of Life* . 332
Rushmer, Margaret . . . . . Ohio . . . . . . *My Mother's Quilt* . 333
Russell, Lillis L. . . . . . . Nebraska . . . . *Our Yesterdays* . . . 333

Saltsgiver, Mrs. Oliver J. . . Iowa . . . . . *Hollyhock Time* . . . 334
Sample, Sarah Steele . . . Pennsylvania . . *Lancaster* 334
Sanders, Bertha Capper . . . Illinois . . . . *Redbud Time* . . . 335
Sargent, Elizabeth Rial . . Pennsylvania . . *A Heart Song* . . . 335
Sauer, Lora Evans . . . . Kansas . . . . . *Recompense* 336
Saxe, Helen A. . . . . . . New York . . . *Destiny* 337
Sayre, Louise Wilt . . . . Pennsylvania . . *Ode to Housecleaning* . 337
Schinzel, Adelaide Foerch . . Connecticut . . . *Prayer* 338
Schmidt, Lois Ethleen . . . Iowa . . . . . . *Blind Spots* 338
Schmitz, Jennie . . . . . Minnesota . . . *The Blessed Rain* . . 339
Schwartz, Mrs. Emma M. . Minnesota. . . . *A Simile* 339
Schwartz, Mary Elizabeth . Ohio . . . . . . *Waiting* 340
Scott, Flo Hampton . . . . Mississippi. . . . *Our Family Doctor* . 340
Scott, Geneva Harris . . . . Indiana . . . *When John Turns on the Radio* 341
Scott, Rose M. . . . . . Illinois . . . . *Returned* 342
Seager, Mary Chisholm . . . Massachusetts . . *The Garden* . . . 342
Seagrave, Sadie Fuller . . Iowa . . . . . *Song for a Year* . . 343
Seaman, Alice Marston . . . Massachusetts . . *Ships at Anchor* . . 343
Segerstrom, Carrie I. . . . . California . . . . *The School* 344
Seibert, Leafa Dorne . . . . North Carolina . *Grandma's Bible* . 344
Sercombe, Marie . . . . . Pennsylvania . . *Bedside Flowers* . . 345
Shades, Maggie . . . . . Oklahoma. . . . *A Wise Counselor* . 346
Shaffer, Gertrude Kurzenknabe . . . . . Illinois . . . . *Lying Awake* . . . 347
Shaffer, Ines V. . . . . . New York . . . *On the Heights* . . 347
Shank, Edith H. . . . . . Maryland . . . *The First Frost* . . 348
Sheetz, Wealthy . . . . . Michigan . . . *Love's Song* . . . 349
Sherman, Daisy. . . . . . West Virginia . . *The Call of the Wild* . 349
Sherwood, Ada Simpson . . Kentucky . . . *Things* 349
Shoaff, Emma Reed . . . Illinois . . . . *Fire* 350
Shurtleff, Isabel Brown . . New Jersey . . *I Have Known Beauty* 351
Sidley, Florence L. . . . . Ohio . . . . . *Farewell, Old Year* . 351
Siegert, Katharine R. . . . Pennsylvania . . *The Fountain in the Rain* 352

SKAER, Georgia Blaney	Kansas	*Reverse Pity*	353
SMELTZER, Ruth	Colorado	*Adversity*	354
SMITH, Alma	North Dakota	*Plus or Minus*	354
SMITH, Edith M.	Wisconsin	*Give Me Gay Courage*	354
SMITH, Eugenia Bragg	Alabama	*Relics*	355
SMITH, Mrs. F. S.	Iowa	*Life*	355
SMITH, Geraldine	Montana	*To Mother*	356
SMITH, Grace Jervis	New York	*Irony of Fate*	356
SMITH, Grace Turner	Wisconsin	*I Love a Storm*	357
SMITH, Jean	Iowa	*Memories*	357
SMITH, Lucy H. King	Tennessee	*Good Friday*	357
SMITH, Mrs. L. Worthington	Iowa	*The Rhythm of the Hills*	358
SMITH, Mrs. Madrid H.	Mississippi	*Father of Our Country.*	358
SMYTH, Florida Watts	Missouri	*Missouri*	358
SNEED, Clyde Wood	Mississippi	*A Prayer*	359
SNYDER, Mary Grace	Indiana	*Three Songs*	360
SOLEM, Mrs. Louis	Minnesota	*To a Friend*	361
SPENCER, Anna M.	Minnesota	*Recompense*	361
SPRINGER, Jessie Florence	New York	*The Sun—A Prodigal*	362
STAPLES, Nina Dudley	Vermont	*Heaven*	362
STARK, Viva I.	Kansas	*Beautiful Yosemite*	362
STEVENS, Margaret Ann	Minnesota	*My Garden*	363
STIMMEL, Eleanor	Ohio	*The Lure of the Buttercup*	363
STONG, Nina Gail	Ohio	*Spring in the Woods*	364
STORY, Eloise	Iowa	*The Housewife's Lament*	365
STOUT, Lucy	New York	*Gems on Tendrils*	366
STRAIN, L. Lillian	Colorado	*Dedicated to Mrs. E. R. Jones*	367
STRATTON, Maggie Woody	Ohio	*Circumstance*	367
STREATER, Elizabeth Greene	Louisiana	*Flame*	368
STREET, Frances E.	Indiana	*To an old Blue Bowl*	369
STRUTHERS, Mrs. Zell	Oregon	*Just Smile*	369
STUKENBERG, Mrs. A. J.	Illinois	*Vacation*	370
SUTHERLAND, Olive Tait	New York	*The New York Clubwoman Meditates on Hamlet*	370
SWART, Dolores	Colorado	*The Vampire*	371
SWIFT, Annette Mason	New Jersey	*Neglect*	371
SWIFT, Eve Gilbert	New York	*In Monmouth*	372

TANNER, Mary Ellen . . . . Illinois . . . . . *Echoes* 372
TANNER, Ovie Pedigo . . . . Kansas . . . . . *Spinners* 373
TAPPAN, Edith Haskell . . . New Hampshire . *Bonfires* 373
TARVER, Zephyr Ware . . . Louisiana . . . . *My Little House* . . 374
TAYLOR, Elizabeth Cushing . . Massachusetts . . *Keep Climbing* . . . 374
TAYLOR, Elkanah East . . . Virginia . . . . . *The Staff That
Sustains* 374
TAYLOR, Estelle . . . . . . Illinois . . . . . *Friends in Need* . . 375
TEEM, Dr. Annie J. . . . . . Arkansas . . . *The Greatest Gift* . . 375
THARP, Rose B. . . . . . . Indiana . . . *Persian Interlude* . . 376
THAYER, Alice Winchell . . . Minnesota . . . *Rain in a Garden* . . 377
THERME, Io Sloan . . . . . Iowa . . . . . . *En Masque* 378
THOMAS, Aimée Paul . . . . Pennsylvania . . *Light* 378
THOMAS, Eleanor Smith . . . Mississippi . . . . *My Garden* 379
THOMPSON, Beryl V. . . . . . Iowa . . . . . . *Whim* 379
THOMPSON, Elizabeth B. . . . Indiana . . . *God's Gift to Man* . . 379
THOMSON, Kathryn Bruchholz . Iowa . . . . . . *Two Sonnets* 380
THORN, Mrs. Boyd . . . . . Pennsylvania . . *To the Village Club* . 381
THORNE, Hazel Partridge . . . Ohio . . . . . . *March Wind* 383
THRASHER, Eva D. . . . . . Indiana . . . *Memory's Pageant* . . 383
TOMEY, Lillian Hastings . . . Indiana . . . *Thoughts* 384
TOWLER, Mary Shepard . . . Minnesota . . . *November 11, 1918* . 384
TRAVER, Edith Loomis . . . New Jersey . . . *To Creative Art* . . 386
TRIMBLE, Pearl C. . . . . . Colorado . . . *In Memory* 386
TRIPLETT, Jennie . . . . . . Illinois . . . . *Washington at Home* . 387
TRUITT, Bess . . . . Oklahoma . . . . *Old House* 387
TRYON, Sylvia . . . . . . Massachusetts . . *New Hampshire Lilacs* 388
TUCKER, Blanche Chalfant . . New Jersey . . . *Love Aglow* 388
TUCKER, Mrs. O. O. . . . Wisconsin . . . *To a Rose* 389
TUTTLE, Mrs. Carl . . . . Indiana . . . *Why Federate?* . . . 389
TUTTLE, Grace Robertson . . Pennsylvania . . *The Opening of the
Lilies* 392
TYLER, Inez Sheldon . . . . Washington, D. C. *Waiting* 393
TYNES, Mary Pollard . . . . Alabama . . . . *Locomotives* 393

UPCHURCH, M   Thomas B. . North Carolina . *The Deep Blue Sea* . 394

VAN HOESEN, I   ie Earley . California . . . *Mother Dear* . . . 395
VELHAGEN, Mil   ent H. . . . Colorado . . . . *The Wise Young
Lawyer Speaks* . . 396
VORDENBERG, Florence J. . . Ohio . . . . . . *Poinsettia* 397
VREELAND, Mary Hawley . . New Jersey . . . *Life's Pageant* . . . 397

WADHAMS, Neva McFarland . Iowa . . . . . . *Sacrificial Fires* . . . 398
WADSWORTH, Myra . . . . . Colorado . . . . *Exiled* 399
WAGAR, Hortense Drucker . . Pennsylvania . . *Hope* 399
WALD, Edith Flint von . . . . Wisconsin . . . . *To My Jacobus
                                                Stainer* 399
WALKER, Bertha V. . . . . . Missouri . . . . *The Silent Martyr* . . 400
WALKER, Grace Mathews . . . Minnesota . . . . *Thoughts at Christmas.* 401
WALLACE, Mary D. . . . . . Iowa . . . . . . *A Snowy Morn* . . . 401
WARLOW, Halle W. . . . . . Florida . . . . . *And after All* 3
WATSON, Christine Hamilton . New York . . . *My Little Day* . . . 403
WAYLAND, Dona . . . . . . Idaho . . . . . *Afterglow* 403
WEBB, Tessa Sweazy . . . . Ohio . . . . . . *Life* 404
WEBSTER, Florence Gray . . . Pennsylvania . . *Withheld* 405
WEITZ, Alice C. . . . . . . Iowa . . . . . . *The Current* 405
WELBORN, Anne Acton . . . Indiana . . . . *I Lika Da Peoples to
                                                Speeck* 406
WHALEN, Frieda S. . . . . . Illinois . . . . . *To My Daughter* . . 406
WHEATON, Larah F. . . . . . Massachusetts . . *Color in November* . 407
WHEELER, Gertrude Lee . . . Minnesota . . . . *Holiday* 407
WHEELER, Grace E. . . . . . Vermont . . . . *Lines Inspired by the
                                                Muskrat's House* . 408
WHISENAND, Emma Boge . . Nebraska . . . . *Compensation* 408
WHITE, Grace Hoffman . . . New York . . . *Spring in the Arizona
                                                Desert* 409
WHITEHEAD, Stella Muse . . . New York . . . *Sonnet to Winter* . . 409
WHITESIDE, Edwina Wood . Alabama . . . . *Gratitude down South* . 410
WICKEY, Myrtle Martin . . . Iowa . . . . . *The Telephone Pole* . 410
WILL, Beulah . . . . Pennsylvania . . *Clouds* 411
WILLIAMS, B. Y. . . . . . . Ohio . . . . . . *Participation* 5
WILLIAMS, Ethel Scott . . . Iowa . . . . . *Things to Love* . . . 411
WILLIAMS, Grace Wagner . Arkansas . . . . *The Orphan Child* . 412
WILLIAMSON, Edna Scruggs . Alabama . . . . *The Rare Book* . . . 412
WILSON, Nell Griffith . . . California . . . . *Weeping Willow
                                                Trees* 413
WINDSOR, Louise . . . . . Illinois . . . . *The Soviet* 414
WINTER, Anne-Elise Roane . . Mississippi . . . *In a Hospital
                                                Corridor* 415
WINTERS, Mae Clover . . . Indiana . . . . *At the Gate* 415
WINTERS, Margaret . . . . . Ohio . . . . . *The Indoor Woman* . 416
WINTRINGHAM, Wilna . . . Ohio . . . . . *The Quest of
                                                Motherhood* . . . 417
WIRTZ, Mrs. A. J. . . . . . North Dakota . . *A Lament* 417
WITTENBERGER, Ida Teeple . Illinois . . . . *The Millennium* . . 418
WOOD, Ethel Davidson . . . . North Carolina . *My Dogwood Tree* . . 419

WOOD, Ida May . . . . . . Alabama . . . . *A Treasure Hunt* . . 419
WOOD, Nettie Blanche . . . . Arkansas . . . . *Prayer for*
                                               Disarmament 420
WRATTEN, Harriet Anna . . . Wisconsin . . . . *Resurrection* 420
WRAY, Augusta . . . . . . North Carolina . *Cathedral Woods* . . 421
WRIGHT, Edna Allen . . . . . Ohio . . . . . . *Candle Lights* . . 421
WYANT, Mayme C. . . . . . Iowa . . . . . . *Her Own* 422

YOCOM, Mrs. Ross . . . . . Indiana . . . . *The Dream* 423
YOUNG, Mary Ramthun . . . Illinois . . . . . *My Garden* . . . 424

ZEHR, Rhea B. . . . . Indiana . . . . *Lull* 425
ZETHMAYR, Margaret Yost . . Illinois . . . . . *The Old Mill*
                                               Garden 425
ZIMMERMAN, Mrs. D. H. . . . Ohio . . . . . . *A Tribute to the*
                                               Federation 425
ZIPF, Florence Glenn . . . . Pennsylvania . . *Flight* 426